COMPETITION IN HEALTH CARE

Reforming the NHS

ECONOMIC ISSUES IN HEALTH CARE

General editors

Professor Gavin Mooney
Institute of Social Medicine
University of Copenhagen
2200 Copenhagen N, Denmark

Dr Alistair McGuire
Centre for Socio-Legal Studies
and Pembroke College
University of Oxford
Oxford OX2 6UD, England

COMPETITION IN HEALTH CARE

Reforming the NHS

Edited by

A.J. Culyer
Professor of Economics
University of York, UK

Alan Maynard
Director, Centre for Health Economics
University of York, UK

and

John Posnett
Senior Lecturer in Health Economics
University of York, UK

MACMILLAN

First published 1990 by
THE MACMILLAN PRESS LTD
Houndmills, Basingstoke, Hampshire RG21 2XS
and London
Companies and representatives
throughout the world

ISBN 0–333–55168–0 hardcover
ISBN 0–333–55169–9 paperback

A catalogue record for this book is available
from the British Library.

Printed in Hong Kong

Reprinted 1992, 1993

Contents

Acknowledgements

Thanks for financial support are due to the Department of Health (Chapters 1 and 8) and the Economic and Social Research Council, funded under project WB04250012 (Chapters 3 and 5). The editors heartily thank Lorna Foster for her editorial contributions and the extraordinary patience and forbearance she has shown despite constant revisions by contributors. Thanks also go to the secretarial staff of the Centre for Health Economics, University of York, under the capable direction of Sal McNeil.

Notes on the Contributors

John Brazier is a Lecturer in Health Economics in the Medical Care Research Unit, Department of Community Medicine, University of Sheffield, formerly Research Fellow in the York Health Economics Consortium.

Roy Carr-Hill is a Senior Research Fellow in the Centre for Health Economics at the University of York.

A.J. Culyer is Professor of Economics and Head of the Department of Economics and Related Studies at the University of York.

John Hutton is a Senior Research Fellow in the Centre for Health Economics at the University of York.

Richard Jeavons is Director of Research Management at the Northern General Hospital, Sheffield, formerly Deputy Director of the York Health Economics Consortium.

Alan Maynard is Professor of Economics and Director of the Centre for Health Economics at the University of York.

David Mayston is Professor of Public Sector Economics, Finance and Accountancy at the University of York.

John Posnett is a Senior Lecturer in Health Economics and Director of the Graduate Programme in Health Economics at the University of York.

Carol Propper is a Lecturer in Economics, University of Bristol and formerly Research Fellow, Centre for Health Economics, University of York.

Peter Smith is a Lecturer in Economics, Finance and Accountancy at the University of York.

Alan Williams is Professor of Economics in the Department of Economics and the Centre for Health Economics at the University of York.

Ken Wright is a Senior Research Fellow and Deputy Director of the Centre for Health Economics at the University of York.

Reforming Health Care: an Introduction to the Economic Issues

A.J. Culyer, Alan Maynard, John Posnett

1. INTRODUCTION

The purpose of this book is to explore the strengths and weaknesses of the most radical reform of the National Health Service since 1948. This reform has been influenced considerably by the work of economists who have long advocated that care should be allocated on the basis of need and that the efficiency of resource use be improved by the explicit measurement of costs and outcomes. Inevitably, when such advocacy is translated by the political process into the reform of the health care system it may be less than complete and consistent. It is on the apparent shortcomings of the changes which the authors focus in this book. Given the emphasis on change in this series of books on Economic Issues in Health Care, a book on the reform of the British National Health Service sits well in this series.

2. THE REFORM OF THE NATIONAL HEALTH SERVICE

The reforms introduced in 1989 are made up of three interlocking packages of change: for the hospital service, for general practice, and for community care. The principle which permeates all these changes is the separation of the purchaser and provider functions and the creation thereby of greater 'transparency' in trading so that the prices, volumes and quality of services are explicit and providers can be made more accountable. Underlying this is another principle: to create a situation in which need is better assessed at the community level with the delivery of care responding to this expressed need more efficiently.

2.1   The reform of the hospital service

The means by which the objectives embodied in the reforms are to be achieved is the creation of a competitive market on the supply side where providers, public and private, compete for the budgets of publicly financed purchasers. The White Paper *Working for Patients* (Department of Health, 1989a) proposed the creation of two types of budget holders.

The first type of budget holders are general practitioners working in practices of more than 11,000 patients (subsequently reduced to 9,000 patients). Such GPs can elect to become budget holders for diagnostic services and cold elective surgery. They would thus hold cash limited budgets, originally proposed to be £700,000 for a 11,000 person practice, with which they would purchase, from competing public and private providers, such items of care as X-rays, pathology tests, hernia repairs and varicose veins treatment.

The second type of budget holder is the District General Manager (DGM) who is resourced to fund the care not met by general practitioners. These purchasers will hold the majority of funds now available in the hospital sector (Hospital and Community Health Services (HCHS)) and will buy care from the most efficient provider, public or private and within or without the District so 'money follows the patient' to wherever the best care can be acquired most efficiently.

Each of these budget holders is required to assess needs, determine the cost-effective means of meeting such needs and prioritise the pattern of health care delivery by determining how much will be spent on each service, diagnostic and therapeutic. Their budgets will be cash limited and determined, now that the RAWP formula has been abolished, by a population formula weighted by need (which could be regarded as a new RAWP formula!) but with specific preferential funding for the London regions.

The budget holders will seek out providers, comparing prices and quality, and enter into contracts (known as 'agreements') with purchasers. These contracts will be for specific time periods and may take a variety of forms but they will not be enforceable at law and disputes will be resolved by 'pendulum' arbitration (which favours only one party and does not permit compromise) with appeal to the Secretary of State.

Working for Patients creates a new public provider, the self-governing Hospital Trust, which will have a greater degree of freedom in the management of its affairs than 'directly managed' NHS hospitals. The proposals advocate the rigorous adoption of medical audit, including consideration of costs, to which the Presidents of the Royal Colleges have agreed with varying degrees of speed and specificity, and the creation of 100 new consultant posts annually for three years. These facets of the reforms are significant in themselves and will have considerable influence on the performance of the market in a few years if they are developed imaginatively and flexibly.

However there are a series of potential problems in the reforms. The legislation has created two budget holders with overlapping roles and no indication of who is *primus inter pares*. DGMs who have GP budget holders in their Districts may set priorities that are different from those of GPs and the only mechanism for reconciliation is informal negotiation. DGMs will have little power to control the referral practices of GPs. The freedom to refer wherever GPs deem appropriate is part of their 'clinical freedom'. However, if GPs send patients outside their District and the DGM's contracts are let either in the 'home' District, or elsewhere other than the referral site, this may create financial embarrassment if insufficient reserves are not kept back. However if such reserves are high, 'home' contract letting may be below local capacity levels and will raise questions about what can be done about excess capacity.

For a competitive market to operate in the short term there needs to be excess capacity in the public and private sectors, and/or an ability for existing providers to expand capacity quickly, and/or an ability for existing providers to switch resources from one use to another. In the long run, when new capital investment can create new capacity and new entrants come into the market, greater flexibility will be evident. However the capacity of the system to change its patterns of resource use in the next few years may be limited. Although excess plant (for example, hospitals and wards) may be closed, subject to electoral pressures, the removal or reform of inefficient or excessive numbers of doctors in particular specialties is less easy. Hospital consultants have 'jobs for life'. Their activities will in future be more explicit and subject to auditing but their priorities may remain difficult to change and, in extreme circumstances, it may prove necessary to dismiss them. The effects of this inflexibility may be significant for hospital costs and providers' ability to provide the services preferred by purchasers.

The contracts which regulate the relationships between purchasers and providers in the naive paradigm of market relationships may be the means by which opposing forces compete vigorously to maximise their interests, that is, least costs or maximum profits. In fact the contract frequently seen in the market place is a long term relationship which permits the purchaser to acquire economies of scale and influence of service quality (see for example Deming, 1982), and American experience indicates that these considerations influence health care contracts (Enthoven, 1989). The obvious UK examples are the practices of Sainsburys and Marks and Spencers who use clearly defined long term contracts to regulate relationships between themselves and their suppliers. By entering into such contracts they establish trust and recognise that mutual inter-dependence and a sense of duty may be a more important force in regulating human conduct than the self interest and greed of the first year economics text books (Maynard, 1989). This was clearly recognised by Adam Smith (1790) and has been elaborated elsewhere: as Sen put it, 'the simple pursuit of self interest is not the great redeemer' (Sen, 1987, p.25).

> 'Those general rules of conduct when they have been fixed in our mind by habitual reflection, are of great use in correcting the misrepresentations of self-love concerning what is fit and proper to be done in our particular situation ... The regard of those general rules of conduct, is what is properly called a sense of duty, a principle of greatest consequence in human life, and the only principle by which the bulk of mankind are capable of directing their actions'.
>
> Smith (1790), chapter IV, para. 12,
> chapter V, para. 1, pages 160–162.

A problem with contracting is the potential for monopolists and monopsonists to distort market processes and produce inefficiency. The risk of local monopolies using their market power has led to a political decision to regulate price setting so that profits are constrained. As a consequence prices in health care markets may not be efficient signals to purchasers and providers. In a less regulated market if prices rise this constrains purchasers' demands and encourages market entry and increased output from providers. If prices fall in such a market purchasers increase their demand and marginal providers are driven out of business. These forces lead to prices equilibrating supply and demand but if price movements are constrained by Government fiat price signals will not produce a market equilibrium.

If prices are constrained the returns to investment may be at levels other than those produced by competitive markets, that is the returns will be poor indicators of investment productivity. As a consequence the results of investment appraisal will be biased and a poor basis for allocating capital resources. The regulators may try to 'correct' these price signals and develop shadow prices to inform investment choices. Without such regulation it is unclear how capital resources will be allocated and such a planning vacuum may lead to disputes between the Department and the Regions as to who controls such allocations.

Another uncertainty about the hospital reforms arises from the problem that, in the absence of measures of the quality of outcomes, the system may be cost driven. Cost data are poor but will improve quickly using available measurement techniques and the products of the investment in information technology. Managers will use these data to inform decisions but quantifiable financial criteria may lead to the neglect of the quality of care, an attribute which is more difficult to measure.

The desirability of measuring hospital outcomes has been recognised for many centuries. Nearly 130 years ago Florence Nightingale proposed to measure three outcome attributes: dead, relieved and unrelieved, and went on to note:

> 'I am fain to sum up with an urgent appeal for adopting this or some uniform : ystem of publishing the statistical records of hospitals. There is a growing conviction that in all hospitals, even in those which are best conducted, there is a great and unnecessary waste of life. In attempting to arrive at the truth, I have applied everywhere for information, but in

scarcely an instance have I been able to obtain hospital records fit for any purpose of comparison. If they could be obtained, they would enable us to decide many other questions besides the ones alluded to. They would show subscribers how their money was being spent, what amount of good was really being done with it, or whether the money was doing mischief rather than good.'

Florence Nightingale (1863)

NHS hospitals in 1990 measure inpatient mortality but have traditionally not used these data for management or audit purposes (Kind, 1988) despite the insights such analysis provides (Kind, 1990). The use of quality adjusted survival data (for example well-years or quality adjusted life years (QALYs)) is experimental but indicative (Williams, 1985). Both survival and QALY data are of uncertain quality and restricted availability. Yet without a major investment in such data improved outcomes, in terms of the quality of care and the quality of survival, may not be produced by the reforms (Maynard, 1989).

2.2 The reform of general practice

Whilst HCHS reforms have attracted much attention, the major source of medical opposition has arisen from general practitioners upon whom the Government imposed a new contract from 1st April 1990. The previous GP contract was exceedingly vague: to render those services generally provided by a general practitioner, that is a GP's got to do what a GP's got to do! This vagueness was compounded by a failure to measure what GPs do generally provide (let alone what they might generally provide): there are no national representative data on the services provided by GPs in the UK.

Following a White Paper (Department of Health, 1987) and a debate (Maynard *et al.*, 1986), the Government published a new contract and imposed it on a reluctant profession. This seeks to specify 'core' services which all GPs are expected to provide and relates payment to performance.

Some elements in this core are contentious (for example, whether the substantial deprivation allowances based on the Jarman index are appropriate and whether routine annual checks on the over 75 year old population are cost-effective). However, the general effect of the reform is to place much greater emphasis on the measurement of process and to encourage audit of activity and costs. The general thrust of the reformed contract is to begin the process of making GPs aware of their expenditure and in time, perhaps, budgets will be cash-limited. This development has been inhibited by the fierce opposition of the British Medical Association (BMA) to the new contract and the demonstrable ability of the profession to impose significant adverse political consequences on the Government.

Thus the significant reforms of primary care inherent in *Working for Patients* have been augmented by a limited attempt to define the GP contract, identifying core services which are to be provided, and making these GP

:e allocators more aware of the resource consequences of their
ns. Much more needs to be done to determine process treatment
protocols and to constrain behaviour by appropriate criteria if general practice
is to be shown to be as cost-effective as the practitioners assert.

2.3 The reform of community care

Separately from the reform of HCHS in *Working for Patients* and the imposition
of a new GP contract, Sir Roy Griffiths, the Prime Minister's adviser on health
care, was appointed to make recommendations about the reform of
community care for the elderly, the mentally ill and the mentally and
physically handicapped. His proposals were politically controversial because
he proposed the creation of a purchaser-provider network with the budget
being managed by local authority social services (LASS) managers. This
allocation of an important purchasing role to local government ran contrary
to the Prime Minister's wishes but Griffiths managed to convince her of its
merits and the proposals were eventually adopted (Griffiths, 1988).

The Government's proposals (*Caring for People*, 1989b) for the reform of
community care did not follow all the Griffiths' proposals. The original
proposals consisted of the allocation of the community care funds to the
LASS manager whose budget would be 'ring-fenced', that is protected from
the demands of adjacent health and social care sectors especially in the
HCHS area. However, both the authors of the Griffiths' and the Government
proposals agreed that the LASS purchaser would be responsible for assessing
clients' needs and buying an appropriate 'package' of care to meet them.

Purchasers face the difficult task of using their own and other budgets to
provide care by a coordinated response from public and private providers of
health, housing, employment, transport and social care. Although the tasks
of managers are clearly defined, their number and qualities will be sorely
taxed by this demanding task. Significant investments for training and
information are unavoidable and ought to be a high priority for central and
local government.

3. SUMMARY

The authors of the health care reforms, as set out in *Waiting for Patients*, the
reformed GP contract and the new arrangements for community care, are
seeking to establish the distinct roles of purchasers and providers and to
inform their transactions with new management information systems. These
changes will make decisions more transparent, facilitate audit and may
achieve more cost-effective use of resources.

However, the reforms will also make clearer the fact that some efficacious
treatments are not being funded and clinicians, managers and politicians
will be able to use this information to press for increased funding. Such

funding may also be needed to rectify the inevitable errors of the initial years when management data will be poor.

4. THE CONTENT OF THE BOOK

Against this background of radical change in the structure of the NHS the contributors to this book have sought to analyse a set of issues which are fundamental to the success of the reforms.

An obvious way to inform UK policy is to draw lessons from the performance of other health care systems. In Chapter 1 Tony Culyer and John Posnett critically appraise the behaviour of the United States health care system. They emphasise that hospitals tend to compete on quality, measured in terms of facilities and provision, rather than outcomes, and not price, which results in service duplication, excess capacity and cost inflation. To correct these deficiencies some purchasers (for example Medicare) have imposed fixed price payment systems (for example diagnosis-related groups (DRGs)) for hospital care, and others (for example Blue Cross and Blue Shield) have developed selective contracting to induce price competition, thereby eroding consumer influence. Such mechanisms undermine the market mechanism and may have primarily short term effects (as in the case of DRGs).

The authors argue that the implications for the UK are that regulation should take the form of contracting between purchasers and providers which is open (that is the content of contracts is available to all to scrutinise), that rules should be adopted to ensure that inefficient provider management teams can be removed by loss of franchises, and that the behaviour of monopsonist purchasers is constrained by explicit job contracts which penalise such behaviour. Obviously all these regulations have to be formulated so that due attention is paid not only to costs but also to the quality of outcomes.

An initial response to the White Paper was that it would lead to an expansion of the private sector. The implications of the NHS reforms for the private insurance (purchaser) sector are explored in Chapter 2 by Carol Propper and Alan Maynard. Although private providers will be able to compete fully for the NHS budgets of purchasers, it is possible, although the comparative data are poor, that they have little significant comparative advantage and will as a consequence have to compete vigorously to enlarge their share of the market.

The private insurance sector is highly specialised, funding cold (non-emergency) elective procedures. Over ten per cent of the population are covered by predominantly (90 per cent) non-profit insurers who have had difficulties controlling utilisation and cost inflation. The distribution of private insurance is geographically unequal with 16 per cent of elective procedures being privately financed in England but one in three such procedures being privately financed in some Thames (London) areas.

The primary change for private insurers which is introduced by the White Paper is the extension of 'tax breaks' to encourage the purchase of insurance for the over-65s. Such purchases can be made directly by pensioners or on their behalf by relatives (for example children). The likely impact of this change on private health care insurance coverage is shown in Chapter 2 to be modest. However these effects may be supplemented to an unknown extent by GP budget holders encouraging their patients to insure in order to reduce demands on the GP budget.

The impact of the reforms on labour costs is analysed by David Mayston in Chapter 3. Because the NHS is highly labour intensive it is particularly sensitive to wage cost inflation. In order to contain expenditure within cash limits and to manage with probably modest increases in expenditure in line with GNP, it will be necessary to manage capital resources effectively with the appropriate skilled labour. The creation of an internal market may improve the use of resources, both labour and capital, but the benefits may be undermined by the returns to labour being increased as monopsony power is eroded and wages are pushed to higher competitive levels.

Mayston concludes that the advantages of monopsony should not be readily given up: an annual two per cent pay increase above inflation would remove the benefits of recent annual efficiency savings. Thus regulation of the pay process may be advantageous if wage wars are to be avoided and the NHS is not to be driven into bankruptcy.

A core issue in the implementation of the reform is the rapid development of efficient information systems. Peter Smith (Chapter 4) discusses a wide range of NHS information issues. What is its cost? How much should be created? What types of information should be collected? How should it be disseminated? How is it to be used? Such questions, he says, can only be answered by well-designed trials. However, such evaluations have to confront the issue of to whom are the new information systems to be accountable? It is obvious that the consumer-patient pays a slight role in the reformed NHS and it is the purchaser guardians of the patients' interest (that is GPs and DGMs) and providers who will use information to enhance accountability.

The author emphasises that an efficient market will require better patient data record linkage so that costs and outcomes can be detected through and between episodes of care for patients. The implications for nurses, clinicians, managers and other personnel are profound and will necessitate much investment in human capital.

The White Paper proposals will lead to radical change in the management of capital. The ideal reform would create an improved system of capital accounting, better management of capital resources in the NHS involving the regional health authority (RHA) acting as banker, and the clear distinction between the RHA's cash-flow controls and the management of capital entitlements and particular products in individual Districts. Such a system would facilitate virement between current and capital allocations at District level.

However, as David Mayston argues in Chapter 5 these ideal characteristics for the reform of the NHS capital market are unlikely to be met by the reforms. No direct mechanism to improve the allocation of District capital and revenue resources over time or for optimising the capital-current mix are proposed in *Working for Patients*. However the development of asset registers will create better information for both asset replacement and its maintenance. If a capital credit system is developed between districts and their regions capital charging could be based on lease accounting between DHAs and units. The success of any system will depend on the level of NHS funding and, because of the costs of its implementation, it should have demonstrable and substantial economic and financial benefits.

Like Mayston, Alan Williams argues that the proposed reforms have much to commend them but they should not be pursued on such a wide front and in the time scale envisaged. 'To drive the NHS forward', he argues, 'into this largely uncharted territory at reckless speed is really quite irresponsible' (Chapter 6).

He also concludes that medical ethics and clinical freedom are threadbare terms misused by the medical profession. Perhaps the 'cultural revolution' inherent in the reforms will frighten the medical profession out of their complacency. Without such radical change, Williams argues, the NHS may be thrown into chaos.

The reforms have altered the basis on which NHS resources are allocated but as Roy Carr-Hill remarks (Chapter 7), the 1976 RAWP has been replaced by a new RAWP which is unlikely to enhance equality in the distribution of HCHS purchasing power between health authorities. The effects of additional growth monies for the London regions and the greater prevalence of private health insurance in the south east may augment inequalities. Furthermore, the different bases for distributing HCHS and primary care (GP budgets) is likely to create further inconsistency, particularly when other primary care and LASS funding is not distributed by a RAWP-type formula but on the basis of custom and history.

The traditions which dominate the provision of community care and have created fragmentation and inefficiency will be as difficult to remove as those which affect resource distribution. In Chapter 8 Ken Wright highlights the difficulties inherent in costing heterogeneous 'packages' of community care for the elderly, the disabled and the mentally ill and the problems of fitting these alternative packages of care to meet the dependency levels of individuals in these groups. The improvements in management, costing, and evaluation needed to improve the social care of these vulnerable groups are considerable.

In the final two chapters more general issues involved in the appraisal of the White Paper are addressed. John Brazier, John Hutton and Richard Jeavons provide a framework to classify health care systems (Chapter 9).

They then evaluate the proposals in relation to technical efficiency, cost-effectiveness, social efficiency, equity and consumer choice, after first exploring the meaning of these terms. The criticisms of the proposals are numerous and broad ranging.

Alan Williams sets out a research agenda created by the reforms in the final chapter. Using a diagram which describes the structure of the sub-discipline of health economics he explores the research priorities in relation to:

> What influences health?
> What is health and what is its value?
> The demand for health care
> The supply of health care
> Micro-economic evaluation at the treatment level
> Market equilibrium
> Evaluation of the whole system
> Planning, budgeting and monitoring mechanisms.

The scope for innovative methodological and applied research is considerable but whether this agenda is of interest to Research Council funders and the Department of Health is uncertain and as a consequence the reform process may be driven by ignorance rather than knowledge.

The complexity and importance of the reform of the NHS is reflected in the length of this book whose contents offer some insights into a limited set of issues which will challenge politicians, clinicians, other health care professionals, researchers and managers in the years to come. The reforms offer a sharp challenge not only to the management of the component parts of the NHS but also to researchers who are seeking to inform the choices of managers by producing knowledge about how the system performs in relation to costs and outcomes. The improvement of knowledge is crucial if the reforms are to achieve their objectives and the performance of the NHS is to be improved. Without improved knowledge, NHS credibility may be undermined and the principle of allocating health care on the basis of need prove impossible to implement.

References

Deming, W.E. (1982). *Quality, Productivity and Competitive Position*, Center for Advanced Engineering Study, Massachusetts Institute of Technology, Cambridge, Ma.
Department of Health (DoH) (1989a). *Working for Patients*, Cm. 555, HMSO, London
Department of Health (DoH) (1989b). *Caring for People: Community Care in the Next Decade and Beyond*, Cm. 849, HMSO, London
Department of Health and Social Security (DHSS) (1987). *Promoting Better Health*, Cmnd. 249, HMSO, London

Enthoven, A.C. (1989). *Management Intervention and Analysis for the Swedish Health Care System*, Swedish Institute of Health Economics, Lund, Sweden

Griffiths, Sir Roy (1988). *Community Care: an Agenda for Action*, HMSO, London

Kind, P. (1988). *Hospital Deaths—The Missing Link: Measuring Outcome in Hospital Activity Data*. Discussion Paper 44, Centre for Health Economics, University of York

Kind, P. (1990). Outcome measurement using hospital activity data: deaths following surgical procedures. *British Journal of Surgery* (forthcoming)

Maynard, A. (1988). *Whither the NHS?* NHS Occasional Paper 1, Centre for Health Economics, University of York

Maynard, A. (1989). *Incentive Contracts*. Paper presented to the First European Conference on Health Economics, Barcelona (to be published in the Conference Proceedings by Springer in 1990)

Maynard, A., Marinker, M. and Pereira Gray, D. (1986). The doctor, the patient and their contract: III alternative contracts are viable? *British Medical Journal*, 292, 1438–1440

Nightingale, F. (1863). *Some Notes on Nursing*, Longmans Green, London

Sen, A.K. (1987). *On Ethics and Economics*, Basil Blackwell, Oxford

Smith, A. (1790). *A Theory of Moral Sentiments*, Oxford, Clarendon Press

Williams, A. (1985). Economics of coronary artery bypass grafting. *British Medical Journal*, 291, 326–329

CHAPTER 1

Hospital Behaviour and Competition

A.J. Culyer and John Posnett

1. INTRODUCTION

This chapter provides a review of work done by economists in modelling the behaviour of hospitals under competition and draws on such empirical results as are available. It is written in a non-technical fashion and later sections draw on the literature review in order to make an assessment of the kind of constraining/regulatory environment that is likely to be suitable in a National Health Service (NHS) provider market following the implementation of the White Paper *Working for Patients* (Department of Health, 1989).

Our general conclusion is that it is indeed possible to harness competitive forces in order to promote greater hospital efficiency. We say this despite two lines of argument that seem to lead to a contrary conclusion. The first is the purely theoretical argument that, since the competitive conditions usually specified by economists for efficiency amongst producers are absent in the hospital sector, the expected result will not come about. The second is the empirical argument that in the US, where hospital competition has been most keen and where it has been most thoroughly studied (indeed, our literature trawl has found *no* satisfactory empirical work elsewhere), competition has had the *opposite* effect to that usually expected, leading to higher costs and excess capacity.

Our conclusion favourable to hospital competition is, however, conditional. In particular, it is conditional on the Government creating an environment that exploits competitive processes wherever possible and on building into that environment particular features that will counter the incentives in the US system that have tended to produce the undesired results. We have much to say about the character of this environment and about the safeguards later in the paper. We also provide a (probably incomplete) checklist of criteria to be used in evaluating the 'competitiveness' of prices in the contracting process.

Most economists have an in-trained prejudice in favour of provider competition. This derives from the economic theory of perfect competition (or, less restrictively, price-taking or, less restrictively still, contestability) in which competition for the ownership of the enterprise and in the product market, and ease of entry and exit to and from the industry, imply that:

a. firms will maximise net worth, which in turn implies that
b. output will be produced at least cost (assuming no externalities) and
c. output will be at the optimal rate in the long run (assuming that all other markets are similarly perfect).

There are manifest hazards in transferring these results to the hospital sector:

a. There is no market force promoting net worth (or profit) maximisation and it is clearly possible for non-profit organisations (even if they are still maximisers, though of something other than net worth) to pursue other objectives that may conflict with the objectives of government. What mechanism, therefore, replaces the capital market (competition for ownership) in providing systematic pressure for optimising behaviour that arises from a consistency of hospitals' missions with the objectives of government policy?
b. Even if hospital output (in practice a complex mix of services of variable quality) is the sort of output preferred by government, its production at least cost is dependent, in a competitive scheme of things, on there being sufficient demanders of service and sufficient alternative suppliers (actual or potential) for relatively high cost producers to feel sufficient pressure on them to improve their cost-effectiveness.
c. The conditions required for contestability of markets (especially under 'natural' monopoly) are often absent.
d. For the government to know whether the output is 'appropriate' or for competing health authorities or GP practices to know whether suppliers' performance is 'adequate' requires sufficient information about performance for a judgement to be reached. While this information need not be perfect (whatever 'perfection' is in this regard), it needs to be sufficient for those who represent the demand side to be able to act either to enforce contractual terms or to be reasonably confident that switching their custom to other suppliers will improve matters from their perspective.
e. The overall optimality of output rates will be highly contingent on the budget constraints imposed on purchasers. Even if the supply response is as perfectly competitive as one may wish, budgets that are too large or too small will imply output rates that are too high or too low.

At the general level, it would seem that there are three broad options confronting the government in designing a framework in which competitive hospitals may operate:

1. Design a general framework in which suppliers and demanders are free to negotiate their own contracts at agreed workloads, case-mixes, quality and prices for whatever time periods they like, with freedom to use surpluses as they see fit, subject only to the law of contract and existing policies for dealing with monopolistic and other 'unfair' commercial practice, financial probity and public accountability.
2. Design a detailed set of specific frameworks that stipulate the forms of contract that are permissible, regulate prices and profits, and that directly control a variety of dimensions of process and performance in an attempt to replicate via central planning what it is imagined a market optimum would look like.
3. Some combination of 1 and 2.

We shall have more to say on all these matters later. We shall also try to be specific about their implications for hospital competition in the UK. In the meantime, it is important to recognise that in the broader context of cost and expenditure control, increased competition between hospital providers is only one of a number of available options and one which is, to date, found almost exclusively in the United States.

2. COST AND EXPENDITURE CONTROL

A common feature of both European and North American health care systems has been the search for mechanisms of cost containment (Glaser, 1988). In the social insurance systems which characterise health finance in Western Europe, policies have been directed towards two main goals: (a) control of the level and rate of increase of per unit costs or prices, and (b) control of the level and rate of increase of total health care expenditure.

Although details differ between countries (see Table 1.1), in most cases mechanisms designed to control per unit costs have been in place since the inception of a system of social insurance, and these involve fixed rates of prospective reimbursement for hospital suppliers (originally on a per diem basis) combined with fixed fee schedules for independent physicians. In West Germany, for example, rates are negotiated locally between representatives of hospitals and physicians groups and the 1500 or so independent sickness funds which make up the social insurance system. This process of setting rates by local negotiation is typical of the systems adopted in France, Switzerland and the Netherlands.

Table 1.1: Hospital reimbursement and financing in
selected OECD countries

Country Ownership of hospitals	Basis of reimbursement for:		The role of health sector planning
	Operating costs	Capital costs	
Canada Predominantly by lay boards of trustees or by communities.	Annual prospective global budgets controlled by the provincial governments.	Separate capital budgets granted, upon specific approval of proposed investments, by the provincial government.	The hospital sector is subject to planning by the provincial government. The capacity of the system is fully determined by the provincial governments.
United Kingdom Central government's National Health Service.	Annual prospective global budgets controlled by the National Health Service (i.e. the central government).	Separate capital budgets controlled by the central government through the National Health Service.	Regional and District Health Authorities develop health plans. Because the National Health Service owns all but the few private hospitals, the Health Authorities and central government fully determine the capacity of the hospital system.
France About 70% of all hospital beds are publicly owned (mainly by local governments); the rest are privately owned.	Prior to 1984 prospective per diems and prospectively set charges for particular services. These payments were government controlled. After 1983 prospectively set global budgets.	Capital costs are recovered in part through amortization allowances in the per diems and charges. The balance of costs are financed through subsidies from the central and local governments.	The hospital sector is subject to regional and national planning. The central government, through its health plan, determines the capacity of the hospital system.
Netherlands Local communities or lay boards of trustees.	Until 1983 by negotiated per diems and charges; since 1984, by annual global budgets.	Until 1983, the per diems included amortization of capital costs. Since 1983, hospitals are reimbursed for capital costs via separately controlled line items in the budget.	Construction of facilities and acquisition of major medical equipment requires a government-issued license, which is issued on the basis of regional and national health-sector planning.
Sweden Owned and operated by local communities.	Annual budgets, controlled by the local community.	Community-financed, by means of specific appropriations voted by the community councils.	The capacity of the hospital sector is planned and controlled at the community level. There is no formal national health plan.
Finland Owned and operated by local communities.	Annual budgets, determined by a system of national health planning and ultimately controlled by the central government.	Specific appropriations; financed in part by the communities and in part by central government subsidy.	There is a system of national health planning, ultimately controlled by the central government. A system of central government subsidies effectively controls the capacity of the hospital system.
Germany Owned by local communities, by religious foundations, or by private individuals (usually physicians).	Prospective, hospital specific, all-inclusive per diems negotiated between the hospital & regional associations of sickness funds. These rates are subject to approval by the state governments.	Financed by the federal and state governments through lump sum grants (for short-lived equipment) or upon specific application (for structures or long-lived equipment).	Capital investments are approved and financed by the state governments on the basis of state-wide hospital planning. The state governments therefore control the capacity of the hospital system.

Source: Financing and delivering health care (1987). Table 6, OECD, Paris

It has always been recognised that regulation of per unit prices is only one aspect of expenditure containment, and control of capital investment in new technology and in bed-space, in order to limit the scope for expansion of patient volume, is also a common feature of European systems, as indeed it is in the US and Canada. Since the 1970s, however, significant evolution has occurred in regulatory strategy which has placed even greater emphasis on the control of total expenditure rather than on per unit costs:

a. In those countries in which rates are subject to negotiation between suppliers and payers, it has become common for negotiators to act within constraints set by national policy. In West Germany (since 1977) and in France (since 1979) fee increases have come to be linked explicitly to the expected rate of increase in GDP. In Canada, before 1977, the federal government was committed to meeting 50 per cent of provincial health expenditure. However, the extent of federal support has been increasingly restricted, initially (in 1977) by limiting the increase in federal grant to the increase in GDP, and more recently by earmarking a fixed amount of federal tax revenues to provincial governments.
b. More recently the practice of negotiating fixed per diem rates has been replaced by global budgets for hospital suppliers, and this marks a significant shift in emphasis from cost control to control of total expenditure. Global budgeting is now the norm in Italy, Canada, France (since 1983) and the Netherlands (since 1984), as well as in the UK.

A couple of important conclusions follow from this brief review. First, in contrast to the situation in the US and in Canada pre-1970, the current health systems of Canada and Europe are characterised by monopoly or near monopoly in the provision of health insurance. The expectation is that this monopoly power will strengthen the hand of payers *vis-à-vis* suppliers, and will act as a constructive force for cost control. A number of commentators have drawn attention to the (apparently) favourable impact on health care costs in Canada of the shift from mixed financing (public and private insurance, and out-of-pocket expenditure) to a universal system of social insurance in 1970 (Culyer, 1988; Evans, 1982). Secondly, the sort of cost containment policies recently 'discovered' by the Medicare scheme in the US (notably fixed-rate prospective reimbursement) have been a feature of European health systems since their inception. Two important implications follow: on the one hand it is clear that pressures for cost escalation are by no means unique to a competitive environment. But equally, and probably more important in the present context, there can be no *a priori* presumption that competition on its own is an adequate substitute for other cost containment policies. Tables 1.2 and 1.3 illustrate the fact that both the increase in total health expenditure as a proportion of GDP, and the absolute increase in nominal and real expenditures are remarkably similar for comparable OECD countries in the period 1960–84. Nonetheless, Table 1.2 also illustrates the fact that the share of GDP allocated to health expenditure in the US is significantly greater than in other countries, and we shall argue later that this is due at least partly to the perverse effects of competition (as operated in the US) on health care costs.

Table 1.2: Total health expenditures, 1960–84 (per cent of GDP)

Country	1960	1970	1980	1984
Canada	5.5	7.2	7.3	8.4
France	4.3	6.1	8.5	9.1
Germany	4.7	5.5	7.9	8.1
Italy	3.9	5.5	6.8	7.2
Japan	3.0	4.4	6.4	6.6
United Kingdom	3.9	4.5	5.6	5.9
United States	5.3	7.6	9.5	10.7
Mean	4.4	5.8	7.4	8.0
OECD mean*	4.2	5.8	7.2	7.5

* 18 OECD countries
Source: *Financing and Delivering Health Care*, OECD, Paris, 1987 (Table 18).

Table 1.3: Decomposition of health expenditure increases (compound annual growth rates, 1960–84)

Country	Nominal expenditure	GDP deflator	Health prices	Relative prices	Real expenditure
Canada	12.5	6.1	5.6	–0.5	6.5
France	15.3	7.5	6.9	–0.6	7.9
Germany	10.1	4.3	5.6	1.2	4.2
Italy	17.6	10.5	10.5	0.0	6.5
Japan	16.8	5.7	6.0	0.3	10.2
United Kingdom	13.1	8.7	8.3	–0.4	4.4
United States	11.8	5.1	6.2	1.0	5.3
Mean	13.9	6.8	7.0	0.1	6.4
OECD mean*	15.5	8.4	9.1	0.6	5.9

* 20 OECD countries
Source: *Financing and Delivering Health Care*, OECD, Paris, 1987 (Table 22).

In the remainder of this chapter attention is directed to the theoretical and empirical evidence of the likely impact of competition in general, and selective contracting in particular, on health care costs and other measures of performance.   In addressing the empirical evidence we concentrate exclusively on the relevant literature from the United States. There are two reasons for this: the United States is the only major developed economy in which health care provision is characterised by any significant degree of competition and the United States is the only economy therefore for which evidence of the impact of competition is available. In addition, the sort of reforms proposed in the UK seem counter to the trends observed in other European countries.   In particular, the move away from global hospital budgets and towards a greater emphasis on cost control through competition stands in contrast to the recent trend in both Europe and Canada towards global budgets, and cost control by means of negotiation and specialist review of hospital finances. Evidence on selective contracting and fixed-rate reimbursement within a potentially competitive supply system comes closest to providing useful insights into the likely impact of the proposed reforms, and for this evidence we must look to the US. (Although there is no comparable empirical evidence relating to European systems, descriptive reviews may be found in: Glaser, 1984; US Senate, 1976; WHO, 1981; McLachlan and Maynard, 1982.)

3.   COSTS, OUTPUTS AND COMPETITION

Our focus in this chapter is on the effects of competition and regulation on selected aspects of performance such as cost, quality, length of stay and capacity utilization.   This section is accordingly arranged around these themes. The general conclusion to which the reader is likely to come (as indeed we have ourselves) is that the typical result of competition between hospitals in the US has not been good. From this, however, it should not be concluded that competitive processes are inherently flawed in the hospital sector. It is, we believe, quite easy to pinpoint the reasons both for the lack of success in the US and for the (occasional) successes. They have more to do with the competitive environment rather than any inherent characteristic of hospitals. We therefore argue in the final section that steps can be—and should be—taken to ensure that the mistakes of the US are not replicated in the UK.

To take a familiar starting point, a profit-maximising monopolist hospital selling an undifferentiated single service will select an output rate lower and a selling price higher than a profit-maximising competitive hospital industry, though an individual monopoly hospital may be larger than a competitive hospital.   Unit cost, at whatever output rate were selected, would be minimised. However, if monopoly confers a degree of 'managerial slack', the profit may be taken in the form of X-inefficiency by converting it into types of cost that enhance the utility of influential managers (including doctors). This expenditure on inputs will still represent opportunity cost (at least as faithfully as the market for inputs permits) but it will not represent *minimum* cost per unit of output (or minimum marginal cost). An alternative to such 'on-the-job' sources of utility is to embody the rents which X-inefficiency represents in the 'take-home' form of higher remuneration (than is necessary) for selected (usually human) inputs. In this case, the expenditures will no longer correspond to opportunity cost. But with either form of X-inefficiency, examination of the hospital's accounts will afford little information as to its extent (at least, not without an exploration of the production function).

Competitive output-maximisation subject to a no-loss constraint yields the same conclusion as the profit-maximising model as regards cost: in the absence of managerial slack, there will be no X-inefficiency and cost per unit will be minimised. With freedom of entry, however, the size of each hospital will typically be smaller than in the monopoly case. If there is a degree of monopoly and some slack, costs will rise in the same way as in the previous case and X-inefficiency will result (but the hospital is now no longer maximising only output). Under both competition and monopoly, the output maximising firm will set a price equal to average cost. If expansion must be financed partly or wholly out of internal sources, modifying the constraint from no-loss to minimum surplus has no effect on the prediction about cost-minimisation at the selected output rate though there would now be a divergence between price and (operating) costs (Rice, 1966). In this connection it is worth noting that Davis' (1971) empirical finding that US hospitals tended not to practise break-even pricing but had a price-cost gap that seemed to be a function of demand is consistent with both monopoly profit-maximising and output-maximising subject to a minimum surplus.

It would be natural for those who enjoy monopoly rents via X-inefficiency to present this inflated cost as the result of enhanced quality. This poses a two-fold difficulty. First, if quality is defined in terms of the cost of inputs, then X-inefficiency may become impossible to distinguish from genuine quality-increasing activities in hospitals seeking to maximise a function with both quantity and quality as its arguments. It is difficult, however, to argue that *all* cost-increasing activity (output constant) enhances quality and one is rapidly driven to finding an independent measure of quality. The natural (and in our view proper) location of this measure is in terms of the quality of patient *health outcome* (and also patient amenities). These are both, however, notoriously difficult to measure (even in the context of carefully controlled clinical trials) and most of the literature makes either the implausible *identification* of higher expenditures with higher quality (Feldstein, 1974) or remains disconcertingly *a priori*. From the perspective of this section, however, it is to be noted that the implications of joint quantity/quality maximisation models (Newhouse, 1970) include cost-minimisation. However if the preferred quality is higher than whatever is deemed socially optimal, then cost per unit of output will, as with X-inefficiency, be higher than technical efficiency (at a lower level of quality) requires.

The major conclusion to be drawn is not surprising—though it is strengthened by being implied by all the models discussed so far. This is that cost-minimisation is not to be expected when there is 'managerial slack' conferred by local or national monopoly status or by ambiguity about the quality of the service offered. Further exploration of the nature of inter-hospital competition serves to reinforce the generality of this conclusion.

In the simplest 'textbook' comparison of monopoly and competitive profit-maximising hospitals the cost-minimising conclusion seems robust. This conclusion, however, is highly contingent on the structure of the demand side. Under health insurance (public or private) user-cost is reduced below the price charged (possibly to zero). If there is full-cost reimbursement by insurers then both profit-maximising hospitals and those with quality and/ or quantity as arguments in their objective function have, under competition, an incentive to switch from price to non-price competition. As they compete for patients directly, or indirectly through competition for physician referrals, hospitals will seek to offer higher quality of care, more convenient location, shorter waiting times and better levels of clinical and non-clinical amenity. These are all cost-raising activities and, with managerial discretion and no financial penalties for patients or referring physicians, there is no mechanism for ensuring that any of these dimensions of 'output' are optimal.

Evidence from the United States in the period up to 1982, when hospital reimbursement on a retrospective cost-plus basis was the norm, confirms the predicted relationship between hospital costs and market structure. For example, on the basis of hospital data for 1972, Robinson and Luft (1985) found that hospitals in more competitive markets recorded higher costs per day and per case than hospitals in less competitive markets. Correcting for hospital-specific characteristics (such as length of stay, bed size, ownership type), hospitals with more than ten neighbours within a 15 miles radius reported costs 20–21 per cent higher than hospitals with one competing neighbour. Correcting for differences in case-mix produced no change in the results. Hospital cost increased monotonically with the number of neighbouring hospitals. The same study also found evidence of a positive correlation between the number of inpatient admissions per year, average length of stay, and the degree of local competition.

In a more recent study covering the period 1972 to 1982 (Robinson and Luft, 1987) these earlier results were confirmed. Correcting for hospital characteristics, case-mix severity, population characteristics and wage rates, hospitals with more than ten neighbouring hospitals within a 15 mile radius reported average costs per admission 26 per cent higher (and average costs per day 15 per cent higher) than hospitals with similar characteristics in a local monopoly situation. With allowance being made for the fact that some of the control variables which directly influence costs (for example wage rates) may be endogenous to the hospital, the difference in observed cost per case widened to 35 per cent for hospitals with more than ten neighbours. Evidence on the rate of change of costs between 1972 and 1982 revealed no significant difference between hospitals according to the degree of local competition. Other empirical studies of the impact of market structure have found greater duplication of clinical services in more competitive markets (Luft *et al.*, 1986), significant differences in the efficiency of provision of specific services (Wilson and Jadlow, 1982), evidence of higher reserve margins in hospitals in more competitive markets (Joskow, 1980), higher prices (reported in Woolley, 1989) and higher quality (Joskow, 1983).

None of this evidence is particularly counter-intuitive once the importance of non-price competition is recognised, but a further question concerns the relationship between higher costs and improved quality of care. Higher levels of amenity undoubtedly increase patient satisfaction and most probably supplier satisfaction as well but the impact of competition within a fee-for-service system on clinical outcome is uncertain. It seems likely that in many cases the connection between expenditure and outcome is tenuous at best. There is even some evidence to suggest that the duplication of facilities and lower throughput implied by competitive markets may lead to poorer patient outcomes than might be achieved in a single unit with a higher volume of cases (Luft, 1980; Flood *et al.*, 1984). There is also, of course, reason to suppose that the level of amenity may also be higher than is optimal.

It is important to consider the factors generating these results. On the one hand, comprehensive insurance coverage removes the incentives for consumers (whether patients or physicians) to select suppliers on the basis of cost, and indeed generates pressures for suppliers to compete on a non-price basis. The greater the degree of competition for patients, the greater the extent to which economic rents will be eroded in cost-increasing expenditures (except insofar as rents are taken in the form of, for example, levels of investment in equipment that not only attract patients but provide on-the-job utility, and hence X-inefficiency, for doctors and other hospital decision-makers). Clearly there is some constraint imposed on this process by consumer resistance to increasing insurance premiums, but this constraint appears weak. The existence of tax relief on premiums, the important role of employer contributions, and the fact that costs incurred by an individual patient are borne by all policyholders all serve to blunt the incentive to engage in costly search behaviour, and contribute to the relatively low price elasticity of demand for insurance (Propper, 1989). In addition, it is reasonable to suppose that as the costs of medical care increase so the demand for insurance cover against these costs will also increase, and this will serve to offset the reduction in demand caused by higher premiums.

On the other hand, the basis on which suppliers (notably hospitals) are reimbursed is equally important. Under a retrospective cost-based reimbursement regime hospital suppliers have no incentive to minimise costs in order to protect net revenues. The combination of third-party payment and retrospective reimbursement creates a situation in which the objective of consumers to obtain the highest quality of care available is accommodated by suppliers facing an essentially open-ended budget constraint. In the United States this combination of incentives has been widely held to be responsible for the substantial inflation in hospital costs in the 1970s and early 1980s (Robinson and Luft, 1987).

It is therefore crucial to investigate the ways in which competition between hospitals can be made to work in such a fashion as to ensure (a) that the product-mix, output rates and quality approximate their policy targets and (b) that whatever is produced is produced at least cost per unit.

4. PRICES AND CONTRACTS

The nature of the contractual relationship between provider and payer is evidently crucial if the problems discussed in section 3 are to be avoided. Before addressing these issues in the context of the UK health care system, we develop the theory further and review some more empirical experience in the United States, focusing in particular on the role of competition in 'cost-containment'.

Leaving aside attempts to sharpen consumer incentives by the introduction of increased co-payments or user-charges, policies in the United States to constrain the rate of hospital cost inflation have concentrated on two broad strategies: changes in the basis of hospital reimbursement accompanied by price controls on hospital charges, and the introduction of a greater degree of explicit price competition into the market through selective contracting (Arnould and De Brock, 1986).

Two specific legislative initiatives, one at state the other at federal level, have sought to introduce price controls into hospital markets. By the mid-1970s a number of States had introduced regulatory commissions with responsibility for approving hospital charges for Medicaid patients, and four States had extended regulation to cover all payers. Although details differ between States, most current schemes seek to restrain the rate of hospital cost inflation by setting rates on the basis of historic cost and utilisation patterns adjusted for inflation and changes in patient volume. The objective is to impose pressure on hospitals to contain cost increases within targets. Rates are set prospectively and operate in a similar way to the price controls prevalent in the US airline industry up to 1978.

Legislation enacted in October 1983 changed the basis of reimbursement for patients under the federal Medicare programme from a retrospective cost-based reimbursement to a prospective payment system (PPS) with different fixed rates for each of 467 diagnosis-related groups (DRGs). Under PPS, Medicare reimburses hospitals on the basis of a fixed price per case according to initial diagnosis. Hospitals whose costs exceed the fixed rate receive no supplementary financing and hospitals with lower costs are able to retain the surplus.

The logic of a scheme of this kind is straightforward. A payment system which establishes a direct link between levels of payment and the costs incurred by individual suppliers provides weak incentives to contain costs. In principle, setting a fixed price based on the average (or even the minimum) cost of all suppliers in the industry breaks the link and generates incentives for producers to minimise costs.

In assessing the likely impact of a change to PPS reimbursement, it is important to bear in mind that the underlying nature of demand from consumers is unchanged and, in particular, that in a competitive market non-price competition will continue to exert a significant influence on final outcomes. Bearing this in mind the main determinant of the effects of PPS on hospital costs is likely to be market structure.

(i) *Monopoly in the Product Market.* Under a fixed-price payment system a profit-maximising monopoly supplier will continue to minimise costs, and will continue to provide the minimum level of amenity consistent with demand. Any surplus of reimbursement over costs will be converted to profit (if the supplier is constrained to maximise profit) or on-the-job rents in the non-profit case.

(ii) *Competition in the Product Market.* A competitive supplier will also have an incentive to minimise the costs of production but the predicted effect on levels of amenity and revenue-promoting expenditure is ambiguous. In the unlikely event that the PPS rate is greater than the average cost of treatment, competition for patients will drive up expenditures on amenity and hospital resource use until any surplus of payment over costs is eroded. This result follows from the fact that in a competitive market all excess profits are transferred to consumers, in this case in the form of higher levels of amenity. On the other hand, if the PPS rate is less than current costs, as seems likely if the scheme is to have any impact on controlling costs, then all competing hospitals within a local market will reduce expenditures per case up to the point at which costs are exactly equal to the PPS rate. In this case, the level of amenity and resource use are reduced.

It is clear, therefore, that if a fixed-price system of reimbursement is to generate savings in costs it will do so only for those hospitals for which the fixed rate is less than current costs. In addition, since the observed costs are expected to be higher in more competitive markets, the impact of PPS should also be greatest in those markets. Before reviewing the evidence on the impact of the change in Medicare reimbursement, it is useful to consider the means by which cost-savings may be achieved. One possible response of hospitals to PPS would be to change the characteristics of inpatient admissions.

Hospitals may for example select-out those patients within each DRG who will be most costly to treat. The rationale here is clear. So long as payment is on a fixed-price basis, a patient who promises to impose cost on the hospital in excess of the average cost for the relevant diagnosis group will cause the hospital to incur losses. Without regulations preventing this sort of selection these patients may remain untreated.

Hospitals may also have an incentive to select-out the less severe DRGs and treat patients on an outpatient basis where previously these patients may have been admitted as inpatients. The Medicare PPS contains specific incentives for hospitals to behave in this way because of the limited coverage of DRGs.

If it is assumed that the total demand for inpatient care is fixed, at least in the short-run, then this process of patient selection may be expected to lead to a fall in total inpatient admissions, with a consequent *increase* in the recorded average cost per case. This increase in cost occurs partly because the short run fixed cost per case increases as the number of cases treated falls, and partly because of changes in the intensity of case-mix (which may also expect to be observed in the long run). As the relatively cheaper DRGs are treated on an outpatient basis, so the inpatient mix contains a higher proportion of more expensive (more severe) cases, and this leads to an increase in the recorded cost per case.

The impact of reduced admissions on costs can be partly or wholly offset by reductions in resource use within the hospital. For example, savings could be achieved by:

a. reducing length of stay and discharging patients earlier, and/or
b. reducing the resource intensity of treatment during the hospital stay.

Whether savings achieved in this way are the result of genuine improvements in efficiency or whether they represent a reduction in the clinical quality of care is primarily an empirical question to which we turn later.

Both rate regulation and Medicare PPS attempt to control hospital charges by establishing a maximum rate tariff. An alternative approach is to encourage price competition between suppliers by *selective contracting*. In 1982 the state-financed Medicaid programme in California was empowered to solicit bids from suppliers to provide hospital care to Medicaid beneficiaries. By 1984, 68 per cent of the State's eligible hospitals had submitted bids, of which 70 per cent were successful (Johns, 1985). In Arizona, the Arizona Health Care Cost Containment System (AHCCCS) has established a selection process in which health care providers are invited to bid for Medicaid enrollees in prepaid group plans at an all-inclusive capitation rate. Unlike the California scheme, in which bidding is on the basis of per diem rates for hospital care, one of the objectives of the Arizona scheme was to encourage the development of comprehensive prepayment plans. In the first year of the scheme (1982), 113 bids were received from 50 separate organisations, many of them created in response to the invitation to bid. In the fourth year of the programme, 46 bids were received from 15 organisations (McCall *et al.*, 1987).

Compared with the cost containment benefits of fixed prospective reimbursement, selective contracting offers a greater degree of flexibility. Benefits of this flexibility include the opportunities afforded to hospitals with excess capacity to fill empty beds by selective price discounting, and the opportunities for payers to exercise control over the range and quality of contracted services. In a genuinely competitive environment with contracting, a fixed-rate payment schedule becomes an effective upper-bound to prices rather than the norm. However, an important disadvantage of contracting is the fact that cost-containment depends crucially on the existence of genuine competition between suppliers. Without competition, contracting becomes impotent.

Bearing this important qualification in mind, the precise incentives for suppliers generated by competition depends on the nature of the contract between suppliers and payers and, in particular, on the extent of risk-sharing between the two parties. One of the inescapable features of financial cover for health care costs is the presence of uncertainty. An insurance carrier faces uncertainty about both the number of cases requiring treatment in a given period and the costs of treatment. The nature of the contractual relationship between payer and supplier determines the incidence of the financial consequences of these uncertainties.

From the point of view of the payer, the 'ideal' contract will be one in which total expenditure is fixed in advance. A *capitation* contract, in which risk exposure for medical costs is shifted from the payer to the supplier, meets this requirement. Under a capitation arrangement, as in the AHCCCS, the supplier agrees to provide medical care for a specified population for a specified period of time, irrespective of the number of cases treated and the costs of treatment (which may be expected to depend on case-mix).

In the face of a fixed revenue constraint, a hospital has an incentive to minimise the costs of treatment, and also to minimise admissions since additional workload merely adds to costs without adding to revenues. The obvious downside for the payer is the need, as with all contracts, to establish quality review procedures to discourage excessive cost-cutting, and to maintain acceptable levels of patient access and throughput. The costs of specifying and monitoring these crucial aspects of hospital performance must be set against the potential savings. In the Arizona prepayment experiment quality assurance and customer (patient) satisfaction form a significant part of the AHCCCS management function. Primary responsibility for quality control and contract compliance rests with the provider, but AHCCCS also carries out regular financial reviews and medical audits. In the most recent phase of the experiment, concern for the financial viability of provider plans has assumed increasing importance because of the potential disruption (and administrative cost) of bankruptcy or insolvency. During the first three years of AHCCCS operations, four plans experienced serious financial difficulty. As a result of these concerns for financial stability and quality assurance, price has come to play a relatively minor role in the selection of winning bids. For example, in the fourth programme year bids were evaluated on a 200 point scoring scheme in which only 40 points were related directly to bid price (McCall *et al.*, 1987, p.87).

At the other end of the spectrum, suppliers will prefer an *open-ended* contract with prices related to specific costs which protects total revenues while at the same time rewarding additional workload as well as generating incentives to maximise the range of services offered. To the extent that competitive pressures enable payers to negotiate a discount on normal rates, cost per case or per day may be reduced but in the absence of strict (and costly) utilisation review procedures the impact on total expenditure is uncertain. In the UK, where such charges are uncommon except in the private hospital sector, a possible option will be some form of *case-based* contract with a negotiated price per case differentiated according to a DRG-type classification of patient diagnosis.

This type of system will be similar in its impact to the Medicare DRG-based PPS, with the important exception that in competitive markets, payers may be expected to be able to negotiate rates below the standard price schedules. As with Medicare PPS, a hospital has an incentive to reduce costs per day and per case, although depending on the relative profitability of out-patient and inpatient care, there may also be an incentive to increase inpatient admissions to maintain total revenues. One way around this problem is to include an agreed annual case load in the terms of the contact, but 'DRG-creep' (the incentive to reclassify patients into more lucrative diagnostic categories) remains a problem (Carter and Ginsburg, 1985). Apart from this need to monitor admissions, the major incentive problem for payers is in enforcing agreed standards of care in the face of reduced resource use, shorter length of stay, and earlier discharge. In addition, any comprehensive use of case-rate payments based on patient diagnosis will require an extension of the existing DRG classification system, which has been developed specifically for the purposes of Medicare and which is, as such, geared primarily to the classification of the elderly. Except for a limited set of clearly defined procedures, this could prove to be a costly exercise.

In view of the administrative and monitoring costs of other contractual arrangements, the most widely observed arrangement in the Medicaid system in the US is to contract on a per diem basis for a given number of hospital days, irrespective of case-mix. Under this system a hospital is assured of higher revenues for more costly (that is lengthier) procedures without the need to negotiate separate rates for each possible diagnosis.

The risk to the payer, however, is that while hospitals have an incentive to reduce costs per day of treatment, the incentives to reduce length of stay are weaker than under a case-based reimbursement system. So long as the negotiated price per day exceeds marginal cost, the hospital will seek to use all of its contracted days in order to maximise the contribution of revenues to fixed costs and further, if the marginal cost per day of treatment declines as length of stay increases, this can be achieved more cheaply by increasing length of stay at the expense of the number of cases treated. The monitoring costs for payers are obvious.

It seems fairly clear then that specific contractual arrangements differ not only in the specific incentives generated for suppliers, but also in the monitoring costs imposed on payers and in the incidence of risk-bearing between the two parties.

Both price controls and selective contracting are designed to place a constraint on the level, or the rate of increase, of hospital costs and an obvious way to evaluate the effectiveness of these policies would seem to be in terms of their impact on costs. However, a couple of important points should be borne in mind in assessing this evidence.

4.1 Which costs?

Consider the following simple accounting identity:

Total hospital costs= no. of cases x (length of stay x cost/day)
= no. of cases x (cost/case)

The first point to note is that control of one or more specific components of cost does not necessarily lead to a reduction in the total level of payee expenditure. For example, a reduction in cost per day may be offset by an increase in total inpatient days, just as a reduction in cost per case may be readily offset by an increase in the number of cases treated, or by selection of cases in higher reimbursement categories. Offsetting changes of this sort are not necessarily undesirable, but a comprehensive evaluation of the impact of policy should, ideally, include evidence on changes in total costs, cost per day and cost per case, as well as changes in admissions and length of stay.

Reducing costs through reduced lengths of stay, earlier patient discharge, or reduced in-hospital resource use enhance efficiency only to the extent that patients are not adversely affected and that additional costs are not imposed on other suppliers such as primary care physicians. In assessing evidence on costs, some attention must also be given to the way in which savings are achieved and in particular to the possibility of adverse patient outcomes and cost-shifting.

5. EMPIRICAL EVIDENCE

5.1 Cost per case

Available evidence of the impact on average cost per admission (cost per case) of a shift to PPS for Medicare patients is inconclusive. Some studies

(Melnick and Zwanziger, 1988; Carter and Ginsberg, 1985) have failed to detect any significant effect, while others have reported a reduction in the rate of increase in cost per case following the introduction of PPS. For example, Feder *et al.* (1987) conclude that while cost per case continued to increase for all hospitals (including those still paid on a full cost reimbursement basis in 1984) in the period to 1984, the rate of increase was significantly lower for hospitals paid on a PPS basis. More generally, the *rate of increase* of costs is found to be inversely related to a PPS 'impact-index', an index designed to measure the relative importance of Medicare revenues in total hospital income. Between 1982 and 1984 Medicare costs per case increased 7.6 per cent in hospitals paid by PPS compared with 18.1 per cent in other hospitals. For hospitals with the greatest reliance on Medicare revenues the increase was 3.2 per cent.

This evidence is confirmed by Robinson and Luft (1988) who conclude that a shift to prospective reimbursement exerted a significant downward impact on the rate of increase in costs per case, an impact which was greatest in those hospitals most heavily reliant on Medicare revenues. It is worth noting that there is reason to suppose that hospitals in more competitive markets will also be those with a higher reliance on Medicare patients (partly because these hospitals tend to be located in urban areas), so that evidence that the effect of PPS is greatest in hospitals with a high PPS impact-index is consistent with the view that this effect will also be greatest in hospitals in more competitive markets which are, in any case, those with the highest initial levels of cost.

Direct evidence of the effect of competitive contracting on hospital costs is restricted to the experience of Californian hospitals following the introduction of selective contracting in 1982. Although the Arizona experiment offers some important insights into the contracting process (see, for example, Hillman and Christiansen, 1984; Brecher, 1984; McCall *et al.*, 1987), there is no good empirical evidence on the effect of the AHCCCS scheme on hospital costs or other performance variables.

Controlling for the effect of the introduction of Medicare PPS in 1983, Melnick and Zwanziger (1988) found that for Californian hospitals in markets with a high degree of competition, costs per discharge declined (in real terms) by just less than 2 per cent between 1982 and 1985 compared with an increase of 8.3 per cent in hospitals in low competition markets. Both of these changes are significantly less than the average 12 per cent increase in costs in the period 1980 to 1982. They conclude that the rate of increase in costs per discharge in hospitals in high competition markets was 3.5 per cent lower than the rate of increase in hospitals in low competition markets. There is also some evidence that costs per day, while continuing to increase in real terms after 1982, increased at a slower rate in hospitals in highly competitive markets (see also, Zwanziger and Melnick, 1988).

In a comprehensive study which compared the cost experience of hospitals in California with hospitals in other states, Robinson and Luft (1988) conclude that selective contracting exerted a significant downward impact on the rate of increase in costs per admission in hospitals with more than ten neighbours within a 15 mile radius, compared with similar hospitals in other states. For these hospitals the rate of cost inflation was 21.7 per cent lower in the period 1982 to 1986. The slower rate of cost inflation was sufficient to reverse the historic tendency for costs to be higher in more competitive markets. In 1982 average costs were 13.3 per cent higher in the most competitive markets in California compared with the least competitive. By 1986 this cost difference had disappeared.

In summary, there is some evidence that, for hospitals in markets in which competition is vigorous, selective contracting has been successful in reducing the rate of increase in costs per case. It is important to note, however, that in their study of hospitals in California, Robinson and Luft found no significant effect of selective contracting on hospitals with less than ten neighbours. The evidence on the effects of PPS appears less conclusive, but this is not unexpected. The main determinants of changes in cost per case will be changes in admissions (which on balance will be expected to increase costs) and changes in length of stay. The ambiguous evidence of trends in costs per case merely reflects the potentially offsetting impact of these two variables. Although evidence on the effect of selective contracting offers the most direct insight into the likely effect of provider markets in the NHS, we also include discussion of the effects of Medicare PPS because of the insight which it offers on the likely effect of cost containment (whether by prospective payment or by contracting) on hospital behaviour.

5.2 Admissions

Between 1981 and 1985 the trend across all hospitals in the United States has been for a reduction in total inpatient admissions. Total hospital admissions declined at an average annual rate of 2.3 per cent in the years to 1985. However, within this overall trend there is evidence that admissions of Medicare patients had been increasing up to 1982 and then declined significantly (at around 12 per cent per year) after the introduction of PPS. Using a sample of 729 US short-term general hospitals, DesHarnais *et al.* (1987) compared the actual number of admissions in 1984 with expected admissions projected on the basis of trends in the period 1980–83. In 1984 the actual number of Medicare and non-Medicare admissions decreased. However, Medicare admissions had been increasing in each of the years to 1983 and then declined by 5.4 per cent in 1984, a statistically significant difference. Non-Medicare admissions on the other hand were not significantly different from expected levels in 1984. In a separate sample of Californian hospitals, Melnick and Zwanziger (1988) report a significant decline in patient admissions in the period 1983–85 compared with the years 1980–82. Using data for 1982 and 1984, Feder *et al.* (1987) examined the effect on hospital behaviour of the introduction of Medicare PPS. Total Medicare admissions declined in hospitals paid by PPS compared with a sharp increase in other hospitals. It should be said, however, that for this sample of hospitals the decline in non-Medicare admissions, which occurred in all hospitals, was consistently greater than the fall in Medicare cases.

This evidence is consistent with the hypothesis that the introduction of PPS for Medicare patients has been accompanied by a decline in total inpatient admissions, and within this by a proportionately greater reduction in Medicare cases. There are a number of reasons why these changes may have occurred, including the increasing use by funders of second opinions and pre-authorisation before admission, a shift of patients from inpatient to outpatient care, and a tendency for hospitals to be more selective in the types of cases treated. The overall impact of reduced admissions has been to increase case-mix severity and hence average cost per case.

5.3 Length of stay

In those studies in which costs per case are found to decline with the introduction of PPS, the main contributory factor appears to be a significant decline in average length of hospital stay. Guterman and Dobson (1986) reported an average decline of 9 per cent (0.9 days) in length of stay for Medicare beneficiaries in the first year of PPS, and DesHarnais *et al*. (1987) reported an average reduction of 1.12 days (12 per cent) for all Medicare patients in 1984. Taking a sample of five DRGs in 501 hospitals in the United States, Morrisey *et al*. (1988) found evidence of significant reductions in length of stay in all diagnostic groups (except in DRG 89–91, pneumonia) after the introduction of PPS in 1983.

In the Feder (1987) study, which identified a significant impact of PPS on cost per case, the most important determinant of changes in cost appeared to be changes in length of stay. Between 1982 and 1984 average length of stay declined for all patients and for all types of hospitals, but the reduction for Medicare patients in hospitals paid on a PPS basis was substantially greater. Average length of stay declined by 14.6 per cent for these patients compared with 5.4 per cent for non-Medicare patients in hospitals paid on a cost reimbursement basis. The observed reduction in length of stay was also positively related to the PPS 'impact-index'.

5.4 Total hospital costs

The impact of PPS and pro-competition policies on the rate of increase of total inpatient costs depends primarily on changes in hospital admissions and on changes in cost per case. In the case of PPS, the evidence suggesting a fall in admissions is fairly clear, while the effect on cost per case remains equivocal despite evidence of reductions in length of stay. Most studies detect a reduction in the rate of increase in total in-patient costs following the introduction of PPS for Medicare patients but the possibility that all of this effect is due to a reduction in the rate of Medicare admissions cannot be dismissed. For example, Carter and Ginsberg (1985) argued that the reduction in length of stay induced by PPS had been offset by a substantial increase in case-mix severity with no discernible change in cost per case, so that any saving in total expenditure had been achieved by a reduction in the volume of patients treated. This conclusion was confirmed by Melnick and Zwanziger (1988) who found no significant effect of PPS on costs per admission but nonetheless concluded that hospitals under greater financial pressure from PPS had slower rates of increase in total in-patient costs between 1983 and 1985. Analysing the independent effects of selective contracting on Californian hospitals, Melnick and Zwanziger reached a similar conclusion. In the period 1982 to 1985, total inpatient costs *declined* by 11.7 per cent for hospitals in the most competitive markets compared with a slight increase (0.3 per cent) in hospitals in less competitive markets. However, taken together with evidence that cost per discharge declined only 1.65 per cent in competitive hospitals, this suggests that the bulk of savings in total costs may have been due to a reduction in the volume of admissions.

Clearly, a fall in inpatient admissions is consistent with an increase in the proportion of cases treated on an outpatient basis, and this may be an efficient response to competitive pressure. In the California study, Melnick and Zwanziger recorded a number of significant changes in the behaviour of hospitals following the introduction of selective contracting in 1982. In particular, while total inpatient days declined by 5.0 per cent in the period 1983 to 1985, the fall in total inpatient costs was only 1.8 per cent because of an increase in both cost per case (+1.3 per cent) and cost per day (+3.7 per cent) over the same period. Total hospital costs declined by less than 0.5 per cent and this was primarily the result of an increase in outpatient costs of 5.5 per cent in the period, an increase which was greater than in the period 1980 to 1982 before the introduction of selective contracting. Surprisingly, Feder *et al.* (1987) found a *reduction* in outpatient visits for all hospitals in the period 1982 to 1984 following the introduction of PPS for Medicare patients, accompanied by an increase of over 30 per cent in total outpatient costs. This study offers an interesting perspective on the potential cost-saving effects of prospective payment. While the authors concluded, quite correctly, that the rate of increase in both total hospital costs and cost per Medicare admission was lower in hospitals paid under PPS than in hospitals paid on a cost reimbursement basis, it was nonetheless the case that in the period 1982 to 1984 in hospitals paid by PPS, total costs increased by an average of 12.9 per cent, despite a reduction of 15.2 per cent in total inpatient days (mainly achieved through shorter length of stay) and a reduction of 6.1 per cent in outpatient visits. Part of the reason lay in an increase of 7.6 per cent in inpatient cost per case and a substantial increase in total outpatient costs of 30.2 per cent.

5.5 Patient outcomes

One of the most robust results to emerge from studies of cost-containment policies in the United States is the incentive for hospitals in competitive markets to reduce costs by reducing length of stay. There are a number of possible means by which the average length of inpatient stay may be reduced, any of which *could* be consistent with enhanced efficiency. On the one hand, inpatient days may be reduced by carrying out diagnostic tests and pre-operative investigations on an outpatient basis. Alternatively, patients may be discharged earlier in order to reduce the costs (to the hospital) of post-operative recovery and rehabilitation.

To the extent that earlier discharge is also associated with a lower average level of health status, one implication of reduced length of stay should be that patients are discharged more frequently to sub-acute care facilities rather than to self-care at home. In order to test this hypothesis, Morrisey *et al.* (1988) examined changes in the probability of discharge to sub-acute care after the introduction of PPS in 1983. On the basis of a sample of patients in five DRGs from 501 hospitals in the United States, the authors concluded that for each of the DRGs studied, the probability of discharge to sub-acute care increased significantly after 1983. Similar results were reported by DesHarnais *et al.* (1987) who found a significant decline in discharge to self-care at home (–3 per cent) accompanied by a 2 per cent increase in discharges with home nursing help. Discharge to other facilities (for example, mental and rehabilitation facilities) also increased (0.4 per cent). The observed decline in the probability of discharge home (without nursing help), which is also emphasised in the Morrisey study, is indicative of the fact that earlier discharge does not necessarily correspond to earlier (quicker) return to full health, and this should be kept in mind when assessing the impact of cost-containment on the full *social* costs of medical care.

Additional evidence on patient discharge is provided by Sager *et al.* (1989) who looked at changes in the location of death between 1981 and 1985. This study found evidence of a significant decline in the proportion of deaths occurring in hospital and a corresponding increase in the proportion of deaths in nursing homes, evidence which is consistent with earlier discharge of the terminally ill. Sager *et al.* also reported evidence that the relationship between reductions in length of stay and the proportionate decline in hospital deaths was stronger in more competitive markets, where competition was measured in this study by the proportion of a state's population enrolled in health maintenance organisations (HMOs).

Most of the evidence discussed so far relates to the impact of cost-containment policies on input use and hospital costs but ultimately any reduction in resource use must be weighed against the possibility of poorer patient outcomes. There is some evidence that the use of intensive care units (ICUs) and coronary care units (CCUs) by Medicare patients has declined since 1983, but this did not appear to be associated with any change in in-hospital mortality or re-admission rates (DesHarnais *et al.*, 1987).

However, other studies (American Society of Internal Medicine, 1985; Shortell and Hughes, 1988) have raised serious doubts about the effects of cost-containment policies on inpatient mortality. On the basis of a sample of over 200,000 patients in 16 diagnosis related groups, Shortell and Hughes (1988) identified a significant positive relationship between inpatient mortality rates (corrected for case-mix) and the stringency of state programmes to review hospital rates, the stringency of certificate of need (CON) regulation, and the intensity of market competition as measured by enrolment in health maintenance organisations. Hospitals in States with stringent rate review procedures experienced mortality rates 6–10 per cent higher than expected, and hospitals subject to the most stringent cost regulation had mortality rates 5–6 per cent higher than predicted.

The effects of competition in local markets was measured in two ways: by the presence of more than two hospitals within a 15 mile radius, and by the proportion of a State's population enrolled in health maintenance organisations. Competition among hospitals, as measured by the presence of other hospitals, was not associated with mortality but market penetration by HMOs was significantly correlated with higher in-hospital mortality rates. The rationale for these results is based on the presumption that as regulation and competition become more intense, so pressures to reduce costs by reduced length of stay, by reduced use of diagnostic or therapeutic facilities, or by the complete elimination of some services, may push hospitals beyond the point at which the costs of producing a given improvement in health are minimised.

These results provide food for thought, but it is possible that the effects of cost-containment policies on patient mortality identified by Shortell and Hughes are actually understated. Changes in observed in-hospital mortality rates may be the result of three factors: (i) changes in admissions which affect case-mix severity, (ii) changes in hospital resource use which affect the clinical quality of care, and (iii) changes in length of stay associated with earlier discharge to sub-acute care. The decline in Medicare admissions following the introduction of PPS in 1983 is well documented, but if, as seems likely, this decline in admissions is associated with an increase in average case-mix severity (as less severe cases are treated on an outpatient basis), then hospital mortality rates would be expected to increase for this reason alone. However, this effect may be masked by the tendency of hospitals in more stringently constrained markets to discharge patients earlier. Evidence of changes in the location of death and of increased probability of transfer to sub-acute care, suggest that in-hospital mortality may be an incomplete indicator of the effects of cost-containment on patient outcomes. Observed increases in mortality corrected for case-mix, as in the Shortell and Hughes (1988) study, may then be consistent with either reductions in the quality of care brought about by less intensive use of resources within the hospital, or with a reluctance to transfer patients early to sub-acute care. Without further detailed study, and in particular without evidence of post-discharge mortality rates, the true impact on patient outcomes of cost-containment remains unclear.

6. HOSPITAL COMPETITION IN THE UK: WHAT SORT OF REGULATION IS NEEDED?

We now return to the issues raised in section 1. The adverse effects of competition observed elsewhere in the hospital sector seem to arise from three root causes:

a. absence of an effective budget constraint on purchasers/consumers because of the absence of co-payments; this leads to a lowering of the price-elasticity of demand and encourages non-price competition,
b. retrospective hospital reimbursement by third-party payers (government agencies or insurance firms) which simultaneously allows demands at low prices to be met and which reimburses cost as defined by the service provider; this encourages activity and simultaneously increases unit cost,
c. poor information about quality whether interpreted in process terms (e.g. input intensiveness) or outcome (e.g. effective impact on health status), and a failure to embody agreement about these in the contract between supplier and demander.

In the UK, since both purchasing GPs and purchasing Health Authorities will be expenditure capped, the first of these sources will be absent. Moreover, under the proposed contracting arrangements, providers will be paid prospectively according to mutually agreed contracts, so the cost-inflationary implications of retrospective reimbursement will also be absent. The proposed arrangements in the UK remain vulnerable, however, on three counts: first, the currently available information about quality is extremely poor; secondly, since prices will be particular to the terms of specific contracts, their 'reasonableness' will be hard to assess in relation to the prices embodied in other contracts or in relation to recorded cost information. The third vulnerability relates to the absence of monopsony on the purchasing side. Although no single hospital is necessarily forced into making contracts with only one authority, in practice most of the custom for most hospitals will come from the local DHA. In addition, however, there will be GP purchasers whose buying power may weaken the ability of DHAs to hold prices down (which may be to the advantage of the providers but which will probably lead to higher overall expenditure) and which also brings the threat of fragmentation of services and the continuity of care. There will be a need for some local arrangements to integrate and monitor the movement of patients between points of care.

The concern in the Department of Health (1989b) about 'openness' in costing and/or pricing (where 'openness' refers to the availability of information about recorded costs and contract prices to purchasers and providers across the entire system) is one way of responding to these difficulties. The issue at the heart of the problem can be put very simply: how is a purchaser to know whether, for contracted volumes and quantity of packages of services, the offer price is at or close to the 'competitive' level?

Our judgement is that the 'competitive' level is most likely to be identified when three conditions are met:

a. the competitive bidding *environment* is as competitive as it can be;
b. methods for *specifying and monitoring* quality with acceptable accuracy are in place; and
c. there is a *logical structure in terms of which purchasers may evaluate bidders' offers.*

6.1 Making the environment more competitive

The penalty/reward environment for suppliers should reward 'success' and penalise 'failure'. In particular, units that fail to win contracts should not be protected. In practice this ought to mean that management and clinical teams that are unsuccessful should cease their activity and either be hired elsewhere in the health care system or in the rest of the economy. In short, there should be *exit* for the inefficient.

Conversely, there should be ample opportunities for both existing or potential new providers (both public and private) to bid for custom.

There is no mention in the current public documents relating to hospital competition of franchising. Much of the concern about a need for regulation arises from a postulated existence of district, regional or national monopoly. If a producer has such a monopoly and the level of demand, or economies of scale or scope, indicate that in any market area there is likely to be only one surviving producer under competitive bidding—which may typically be the existing producer—then it seems to follow that monopoly pricing (plus X-inefficiency, etc.) will result.

This result comes about, however, only if there is *only one bidder for the contract.* It does not depend upon there being only one producer. There is no reason in general for supposing that a monopoly price would result in a market in which at least two bidders could offer to provide a service of specified quantity and quality at a price schedule (per unit of service such as the inpatient case) which may be a decreasing function of scale in the case of 'natural' monopoly. In such a contestable market, any current incumbent hospital enjoying a 'natural' monopoly would be unable to ignore the threat of entry without incurring the risk of being replaced by a new producer.

What is crucial is that there be competition for the franchise (right to provide a service) and that collusion between bidders be made unprofitable, for example by having the terms offered by the successful bidder not published to the unsuccessful. In this way, the enforcement of any cartel-like collusion will become extremely difficult. This seem to us to be the single most important argument *against* openness in pricing. However, whether it will be seen as decisive depends upon the strength of the other argument *for* openness described below, and this argument for *not* publishing the terms of successful bids applies only when the danger of monopoly is considered real.

One might imagine two alternative mechanisms for achieving competitive pricing and output under monopoly:

a. freedom for current non-producers to bid for a contract, with the implication that an existing provider may lose his business, or
b. self-governing Hospital Trusts (SGHTs) or district hospitals themselves creating a competition between potential teams of physicians or managers for the right to use their resources, with the criteria by which bids will be judged being determined by potential demanders (authorities, GPs) of the suppliers' services.

This mechanism would simulate the behaviour of the capital market when the ownership of enterprises is cheaply transferable and new owners can acquire existing firms that are believed to be inefficient by 'takeover', replace the existing with new management that is believed to be better able to identify and rectify the sources of inefficiency, and make capital gains in the process (if the strategy proves successful).

It would also make the hospital market more contestable. Although the idea of contestability refers normally to the ease of entry of new firms which can see profitable opportunities at lower prices than those currently prevailing amongst incumbent firms (Baumol *et al.*, 1988), it is useful also to extend the notion to that of 'managements' which can see similar opportunities. The industrial ownership structure of the NHS lends itself conveniently to this sort of strategy, whether the hospitals whose management may be put out to tender are under the direct control of health authorities or trusts. The implication is, of course, that some managements may disappear altogether, others may be recycled (probably in reconstituted form) elsewhere in the system, while, for *all* incumbent managements, there will be the continuing threat of their replacement.

One might think in terms of having either regular recontracting of franchises or of periodic recontracting when, for example, regional (or Departmental) judgement was that performance by a particular incumbent team ought to be put to a market test.

The contestability of the hospital market ought probably, however, to be much wider than this. The possibility should also exist for entirely new suppliers of service (viz. the complex of managers, health workers and capital called the 'hospital'), whether publicly or privately owned, to enter the contacting process. This would also entail the possibility of incumbent hospitals which cannot satisfy demanding health authorities and GPs disappearing (with the capital stock either being disposed of or itself franchised to joint teams of managers or other staff). In practice, such exits are unlikely to be frequent mainly because the fact of contestability is itself a spur to efficiency that bears on incumbent hospitals. However, for it to work, the possibility that incumbents who cannot gain contracts will cease business altogether must be something that every management and health care team recognises as the ultimate penalty of failure, for they will then have an incentive to offer demanders the same (or better) net benefit that actual new entry would bring.

Perfect contestability implies not only least cost production when there are many incumbents. It implies also least cost production and 'competitive' prices (roughly, the lowest prices consistent with financial independence) even when cost conditions are such that only a single producer is the expected outcome ('natural monopoly'). The major problem that is likely to constitute an entry barrier in this case is not fixed cost (which would be borne both by incumbent and new entrant) but sunk cost. This might take the form, for example, of the irretrievable loss of value of capital represented by the difference between capital purchase price and discounted 'scrap' value over a possibly short period of time in which a potential new entrant hospital may find that the pre-entry assessment of risk was too optimistic. In markets where there is only one incumbent hospital or at any rate only a few, one of the ways in which such *sunk* costs can be reduced by public policy is by inviting *long-term* contracts from both incumbents and potential entrants so that the differential risk to the latter is reduced. In markets with few incumbent hospitals and where there is the fear of monopoly, regulatory policy should in general be so designed as to make entry so far as possible reversible without cost.

The essence of the solution is that the market itself is harnessed as an effective substitute for regulation (Demsetz, 1968). Like all other competitive solutions, however, this one also depends on the embodiment of quality specifications (or at least procedures for quality control) in the bidding process and, subsequently, in performance monitoring.

6.2 Specifying and monitoring quality

The issue of quality assessment is central but as yet unresolved. We would expect that, at least to begin with, the focus will be on *process* (for example, purchasers requiring providers to show evidence of a peer-review system within the hospital and evidence of arrangements with FPC and community services for proper aftercare) though it is much to be desired that providers will also be required to develop (over time) measures of outcome quality that can be compared with the performance of other providers. The onus should be on the providers to develop such methods, perhaps within a centrally promulgated framework that specifies the kinds of quality dimensions that are likely to be of interest to most purchasers (hospital infection rates, readmission rates, operative fatality rates, outpatient waiting times, inpatient waiting times, linkages with community after care services, quality aspects of 'hotel' facilities, are some possibilities). Their interpretation will need considerable care in order to avoid undesired (by purchasers) 'cream skimming' (treating only the 'easier' cases) and other well-known hazards. Dangers of abuse of indicators, however, should not be allowed to become reasons for not developing quality indicators at all. We expect much experiment and learning in this difficult but challenging and important area.

6.3 Evaluating the 'competitiveness' of prices

While one way (the standard way in the textbook model) of testing the competitiveness of prices is by making direct price comparisons between competitors offering similar services, it is unlikely to be sufficient. There is, however, a clear case for making the bid prices of successful provider contractors publicly available in addition to the bid prices offered by the other bidders for similar contracts. Such information would be particularly useful in the case of purchasers for whose contracts there is only one bidder, or only a few. However, because prices are dependent, as discussed above, on many factors that will be specific to the particular contracts in question, it is often argued that cost information should also be available to prospective purchasers. The crucial cost information for this purpose is, in our view, the cost structures of the *bidding* providers rather than that of other providers, on the grounds that the information about costs will relate to the right to supply the particular package of services being sought. In this case, it becomes highly desirable for purchasers to have some means of assessing the relation between recovered or anticipated costs and the bid prices. A framework is needed that enables sensible judgements to be made by the potential purchaser about the 'competitiveness' of the bid prices. The following (probably incomplete) checklist summarises some of the characteristics of such a framework.

a. are higher costs justified by an asserted higher quality?
b. are higher costs justified by the shortness of the proposed contract?
c. do the proposed prices reflect a reasonable allowance for the risk borne by the provider under the contract terms, and is estimated revenue sufficient to ensure the long run viability of the provider?
d. are the input prices embodied in the provider's cost estimates reasonable?
e. if costs are sensitive to scale (for example, if a higher short run contract price is specified as a capacity constraint is reached) is this reasonable? Relatedly, have economies of scope been adequately reflected in prices?

f. how likely is demand to cause the provider to reach or exceed optimal capacity?

g. have joint costs and overheads been reasonably allocated across the services being priced?

h. have uncertain contingencies that may arise in the future been thought about and reasonably included in future cost estimates and the price schedule?

i. are expectations about inflation agreed between providers and purchasers and reasonably incorporated into the bid?

j. do the suppliers' specifications of real inputs required (e.g., staff, length of stay) reflect 'best' practice?

k. has allowance been made for technological change over the contract period (e.g., as foreseen by experts at the 'leading edges') and has it been reasonably assessed and reflected in bid prices?

6.4 Incentives for purchasers

The foregoing deals with the desired incentive generating market environment as far as providers are concerned. DHAs will not be in competition with one another, nor will they be directly accountable to their client populations for the effectiveness and efficiency of their own performance. There is plainly an important role for the regions in monitoring DHA performance, in ensuring that purchasing decision (and the soliciting of bids) are not corrupted by provider interests (especially where hospitals are directly managed by the DHA), and in providing advice and help to districts in inviting, evaluating and monitoring bids and contracts and the subsequent performance of providers. There may well be value in developing checklists of requirements/desiderata similar to those outlined in the previous paragraph by which district performance would be evaluated, with an eventual development of such lists into comprehensive 'how-to-do-it' manuals similar to the requirements already laid down for option appraisals of major capital developments, which are exemplary in their embodiment of sound economic principles and their encouragement of an imaginative approach to the identification of options.

We turn finally to some of the specific questions that have recently been raised.

6.5 Leaving things to the invisible hand

While monopoly exploitation is certainly one danger of the *laissez-faire* approach a second danger is in our opinion far more serious: absence of information. This is the more serious problem for two main reasons:

a. it enables monopolistic practices to proceed more easily by virtue of the difficulty in detecting them;

b.   whereas quality (at least of inputs) was probably overpromoted under
the retrospective reimbursement systems that predated DRGs and
contracting in the US, and costs were themselves unduly inflated, the
danger under the proposed UK system is that the focus would be
excessively on price competitiveness with quality of outcome and
after care put at risk.

Information about quality of care as well as about the expected costs that
underlie price schedules is therefore of central importance under the White
Paper's arrangements. While literal *'laissez-faire'* is therefore undesirable, a
high degree of decentralisation, with the centre (Department of Health and
RHAs) offering powerful support to purchasing authorities (and provider
bidders) that enables them systematically to structure and evaluate bids for
contracts (section 6.3) should become an essential part of the competitive
framework along with an enhanced scope for competitiveness along the
lines mentioned in section 6.1. This 'modified' *laissez-faire* approach seems to
be both consistent with the principles that underpin the White Paper and to
offer the best route by which to approximate the outcome of a competitive
process.

6.6 Central price schedule

In our view such a mechanism, whether based on existing average specialty
costs or on DRGs, would be fundamentally destructive of the purpose of the
internal market, which is that prices would simultaneously guide resources
to their most productive use (in the eyes of demanders) and reward cost-
effective services of the sort demanded by client authorities and GPs. A fixed
price schedule simply cannot do that.

It is *not* an advantage of a central price schedule that it will control
monopoly abuse. As has been seen above, one of the ways in which
monopoly rents are captured by monopolists (especially non-profit making
ones) is via cost-increases. If these become embodied (and enshrined) in
average specialty costs or DRG costs, then the schedule has the effect of
building abuse into the system by ensuring that (average) X-inefficiency is
not penalised. Yet a principal rationale for the internal market lies in a
perception that, on average, there is already X-inefficiency in the system.

If this option were pursued it would render valueless most of the exercise,
and effectively deny any of the potential benefits of enhanced competition.

6.7 Openness in costing

Historical (recorded) cost data have several important limitations when used
to assess the 'competitiveness' of bids. First, they are at best a record of the
(financial, not opportunity-) cost consequences of *past* decisions. These past
decisions may have been erroneous (embodying, for example, the effects of

unanticipated changes in patient flow, technological change, or political pressures). Secondly, the cost data relate only to the institution in question and do not take account of the cost consequences that past decisions may have had for other parts of the NHS, local authority social services, environmental health, or family carers. Thirdly, they are available only as either total or average costs, whereas what is more usually relevant is *marginal* cost—where what is being bid for is only a *part* of the hospital's total activity and there may be economies of scale and scope. Fourthly, they embody an unknown amount of X-inefficiency, which will normally vary from hospital to hospital but which is not easily identifiable, even in relative terms, in a comparison of inter-hospital cost variation. Apparently low unit costs may mask still high X-inefficiency (being compensated, for example, by low quality care). Finally, the relevant costs for *current* planning and evaluative purposes are the *anticipated* costs over the up-coming contract period, which will reflect managers' judgements about future input prices (which are likely to vary much more in the future), future embodied technology, risk-sharing between purchaser and provider, and a host of other cost-affecting factors.

It cannot be emphasised too strongly that 'costs' are not 'immutable facts scattered about waiting to be gathered and processed. What is a relevant cost in one context is not so in another' (Williams, 1974). Cost in short, is context dependent. It is also attitude (for example to risk) dependent. In contracting, cost is also expectational, reflecting current expectations of the supplier about a host of future contingencies that may affect the ways in which things are best done and the ways in which (and terms on which) it is expected they actually will be able to be done. The search for regulatory environment that focuses on cost and is at one remove from the bargaining relationship of suppliers and demanders is, therefore, a will-o'-the-wisp.

Too strong a focus on historical unit costs seems to us to be the wrong focus. The correct focus is on a competitively priced package of services whose characteristics are sufficiently specified and monitorable for clients themselves to be satisfied that they are getting the best available value for money. The crucial financial variable here is not the supplier's unit cost but his unit *price*. The relationship between unit cost and price is for the supplier to determine in a *competitive* environment made as efficient as it can be rather than a regulatory environment that tends to destroy the power of competitive pricing.

6.8 Openness in pricing

Openness in pricing has a potentially significant disadvantage alluded to above in section 6.1. This is that open (in the sense of published) contract prices makes collusion between bidders easier to enforce. The sort of openness in pricing that is required is an openness for bidders to propose prices of their own determination, open information about prices to the decision makers in client authorities, and (of course) openness about successful bids to auditing agencies.

6.9 Yardsticks

Openness in costing and pricing is clearly an idea whose purpose is to provide yardsticks. This is particularly so in situations where there is only one bidder and pricing information on similar contracts made elsewhere may serve as a useful starting point for discussion with the single bidder, or where there is again only one bidder but there are no comparable contracts elsewhere, in which case cost information about other suppliers may serve a similar purpose. Each of these problems is most likely to arise in the transitional period from the old to the new economic environment.

Since the value of historical cost information is limited (as argued above in section 6.7) and the disclosure of price information may be seen as a threat to the managerial independence of providers, and may also inhibit innovative and entrepreneurial behaviour by SGHTs, it becomes highly desirable to ensure that the probability of there being only one bidder for a contract be made as small as possible. Maximum contestability is one environmental feature that is conducive to this goal. Strong regional pressure should also be exerted on health authorities to seek multiple bids for their contracts. In general, health authorities ought to be required to engaged in market research to try to identify potential bidders, for example by conducting travel time studies to seek out both current incumbents and possible new entrants who may be eligible to provide core and non-core services. There are few districts, even those of low population density, in which there are not several potential suppliers within a reasonable distance, even if they are located outside the district's formal boundary. This is particularly to be encouraged in health authorities which retain a provider role.

Nonetheless, there may still be a role for openness in the provision of cost and price information, particularly in the transitional phase as purchasers and providers learn how to operate under the new conditions. It would therefore be wise to continue with the present system of cost returns and continue the work on DRGs, which may at least provide some bases for discussion between a purchaser and a single bidder. In this situation, the exposure of the bidder's own past costs will be valuable as well as the availability of others' costs. If the availability of the prices in other (successful) contracts of a similar kind to that under negotiation is also considered useful, but possibly disadvantageous to such successful bidders, an appropriate strategy might be to require the information demanding Authority to compensate the information supplying provider(s) for such valuable information. Presumably, such trading in price information would be accompanied by a contractual agreement that specified who was entitled to see the information purchased. In principle, we see no reason why a market in this sort of information might not be developed to complement and enhance the contracting process. This will, of course, require public availability of information about who has contracted with whom and, in broad terms, for what, but without the public disclosure of the pricing details.

6.10   Cross-subsidisation

An open contracting process does not require specific central monitoring for cross-subsidisation, monitoring whose effectiveness must anyway be in doubt (without the most careful case-by-case research) in view of the judgements and discretionary decisions that managers on the supply side necessarily have to make in setting prices *now* for services to be delivered in the future. Cross-subsidisation is a feature predicted *not* to be observed in competitive or contestable markets. Thus, given the right environment, the problem should be of small significance.

6.11   Long-run contracts

The nature of contracts of a long-run character inevitably involves an assessment of risk and some allocations of it between demanders and suppliers (see above in section 4). Long-term contracts are satisfactorily made in the private sector without the 'aid' of regulation. The parties involved make the best 'guesses' they can (aided where appropriate by relevant experts). It would be expected that short-term contracts would be priced higher than longer term contracts (which enable, say, a better—or more certainly —planned use of capital) and higher than contracts in which the buyer bore more risk. But these are matters for negotiation rather than regulation and there is no reason to expect that a successfully concluded bidding process would be biased towards a unit cost that was needlessly (or monopolistically) high. Long run contracts (see above section 6.1) assist in combatting any barriers to entry taking the form of sunk costs.

Suppliers may find themselves with temporary over- or under-capacity, and demanders may find themselves with temporary over- or under-forecast demand. It will be natural for contracts to take account of such factors (whatever their source) and to contain the possibility of renegotiation (with penalties, perhaps) specified in an initially acceptable fashion *before the event* (including the possibility of multi-price tariffs). Such variations in contract terms may result in differential pricing but again the process of (competitive) bidding will help to keep such prices close to the relevant *ex ante* marginal cost and would reflect the various parties' attitudes to risk.

Although we have not discussed in much detail the short term problems of transition from the present to the future arrangements, we have identified some issues (particularly regarding a single bidder for a contract) which are likely to be more prevalent in the short than the long term. Whatever special arrangements are adopted to ease the transition, we would urge that they be neither so protective of current incumbents nor (if they are protective) so permanent in character that they prejudice the future working of a contestable market in hospital services. To embody *now* any measures that may featherbed existing providers for the indefinite future would do much to undermine the entire rationale of the White Paper.

7. CONCLUSIONS

Much of the discussion of the need for regulation is predicated on the potential failure of the competitive process. In our judgement this is a wrong presumption and we are mindful of the dangers, amply referred to above, that regulation can *itself* prejudice the proper working of the competitive process.

At the heart of the issue of regulation lies the matter of information and its accessibility. In our view it is *essential* in *both* market processes *and* regulatory schemes that volume and quality (both of process and outcome) are specifiable with sufficient precision for either to do its job properly. But if information about these is sufficient for efficient contracts to be made between suppliers and demanders, it is unnecessary to have regulation; and if information is insufficient for efficient contracts to be made, then regulation cannot work either.

We therefore conclude that maximum decentralisation of contracting decision-making power be coupled with substantial provision of advisory resources (probably at regional level) and that a thorough-going how-to-do-it manual be publicly available for all potential contractors from either side. It is, in our view, much to be preferred that resources which would otherwise be swallowed up by a regulatory agency (of anyway doubtful efficacy) be devoted to the promotion of the genuine *evaluation* and *monitoring* role that is inherent in the new contracting process and which is so conspicuously absent at present in the UK (as well, needless to say, as elsewhere). The aims should be to focus effective evaluation and monitoring at the decentralised level of health authority, GP and suppliers and to create a bidding and contract enforcement environment that is most likely to meet competitive efficiency criteria.

A final admonition: neither internal markets nor regulatory systems are likely to be perfect. We think that the internal market is more 'perfectible' than the regulatory function mainly because no regulatory body can evaluate the appropriateness of (historic) unit costs reflecting previous uncertain judgements made by contractors about volume and quality in a forward contract. While the market is unlikely to be perfect either, the best chances of squeezing X-inefficiency arising from monopoly, non-profit motives etc, lie in ensuring open competition in the bidding process, the careful monitoring of purchaser behaviour by regions, cost assessment by purchasers and as much attention to specifying and monitoring volume and quality as seems optimal to the parties to a contract. This does not imply *full* information, though it almost certainly implies *more* information than currently exists. It is the job of markets to determine what this optimum should be and, in negotiations, the contracting agents will have a mind for the costs of procuring and acting on the sort of information they have a demand for. So one must not let the perfect become the enemy of the merely good, one should not identify the optimum with *complete* information and one should, above all, not fall victim of the fallacy that costs are uniquely and unambiguously observable to regulators.

Given an appropriate environment that rewards and punishes as it should, and a contracting process that embodies the features we have outlined, there is every reason to expect that the provider market in the NHS will contribute much to improved performance, choice and value for money. The need, we suggest, is less for regulation than for ensuring an environment that is as competitive (or contestable) and open as it can be made and for the provision of central and regional support services that require and enable purchasers to seek out and scrutinise bids in the most searching way possible.

References

American Society of Internal Medicine (1985). *The Impact of DRGs on Patient Care*, Washington DC

Arnould, R.J. and De Brock, L.M. (1986). Competition and market failure in the hospital industry: a review of the evidence. *Medical Care Review*, 43,2,253–292

Baumol, W.J., Panzar, J.C. and Willig, R.D. (1988). *Contestable Markets and the Theory of Industry Structure*, Harcourt Brace Jovanovich, New York

Brecher, C. (1984). Medicaid comes to Arizona: a first year report on AHCCS. *Journal of Health Politics, Policy and Law*, 9, 3, 411–425

Carter, G and Ginsburg, P. (1985). *The Medicare Case Mix Index Increase: Medical Practice Changes, Ageing and DRG Creep*, R-3292-HCFA, The Rand Corporation, Santa Monica

Culyer, A.J. (1988). *Health Care Expenditures in Canada: Myth and Reality; Past and Future*, Canadian Tax Foundation, Toronto

Davis, K. (1971). Relationships of hospital prices to costs. *Applied Economics*, 4, 115–125

Demsetz, H. (1968). Why regulate utilities? *Journal of Law and Economics*, 11, 55–66

Department of Health (DoH) (1989). *Working for Patients*, Cm. 555, HMSO, London

Department of Health (DoH) (1989b). *Contracts for Health Services, Prices and Openness—A Discussion Document*, Department of Health, London

DesHarnais, S., Kobrinski, E., Chesney, S. *et al.* (1987). The early effects of the prospective payment system on inpatient utilization and the quality of care. *Inquiry*, 24, 7–16

Evans, R.G. (1982), Health care in Canada: patterns of funding and regulations. In McLachlan, G. and Maynard, A. (eds.), *The Public/Private Mix for Health*, Nuffield Provincial Hospitals Trust, London, 369–424

Feder, J., Hadley, J., Zuckerman, S. (1987). How did Medicare's prospective payment system affect hospitals? *New England Journal of Medicine*, 317, 867–73

Feldstein, M.S. (1974). The quantity of hospital services: an analysis of geographic variation and intertemporal change. In Perlman, M. (ed.), *The Economics of Health and Medical Care*, Macmillan, London, 402–419

Flood, A.B., Scott, W.R. and Ewy, W. (1984). Does practice make perfect? I: The relation between hospital volume and outcomes for selected diagnostic categories. *Medical Care*, 22, 98

Glaser, W.A. (1988). Politics of cost control abroad, *Bulletin of the New York Academy of Medicine*, 56, 107–114

Glaser, W.A. (1984). Hospital rate regulations: American and foreign comparison. *Journal of Health Politics, Policy and Law*, 8, 702–731

Guterman, S. and Dobson, A. (1986). Impact of the Medicare prospective payment system for hospitals. *Health Care Financing Review*, 7, 97–114

Hillman, D. and Christianson, J. (1984). Competitive bidding as a cost-containment strategy for indigent medical care: the implementation experience in Arizona. *Journal of Health Politics, Policy and Law*, 9, 427–451

Johns, L. (1985). Selective contracting in California. *Health Affairs*, 4, 32–48

Joskow, P.L. (1980). The effects of competition and regulation on hospital bed supply and the reservation quality of the hospital. *Bell Journal of Economics*, 11, 421–447

Joskow, P.L. (1983). Reimbursement policy, cost containment and non-price competition. *Journal of Health Economics*, 2, 167–174

Luft, H. (1980). The relation between surgical volume and mortality: An exploration of causal factors and alternative models. *Medical Care*, 18, 940–959.

Luft, H., Robinson, J. and Garnick, D. *et al.* (1986). The role of specialized services in competition among hospitals. *Inquiry* 23, 83–94

McCall, N. *et al.* (1987). Evaluation of Arizona Health Care Cost Containment System, 1984–85. *Health Care Financing Review*, 9, 79–90

Melnick, G.A. and Zwanziger, J. (1988). Hospital behaviour under competition and cost-containment policies. *Journal of the American Medical Association*, 260, 2669–2675

McLachlan, G. and Maynard, A. (eds.) (1982). *The Public/Private Mix for Health*, Nuffield Provincial Hospitals Trust, London

Morrisey, M., Sloan, F. and Valvona, J. (1988). Medicare prospective payment and post hospital transfers to subacute care. *Medical Care*, 26, 685–698

Newhouse, J.P. (1970). Towards a theory of non-profit institutions : an economic model of a hospital. *American Economic Journal*, 60, 64–74

OECD (1987). *Financial and Delivering Health Care: A Comparative Analysis of OECD Countries*, OECD, Paris

OECD (1987). *Health and Pensions Policies under Economic and Demographic Constraints*, OECD, Paris

Propper, C. (1989). An econometric analysis of the demand for private health insurance in England and Wales. *Applied Economics*, 21, 777–792

Rice, R.G. (1966). An analysis of the hospital as an economic organism. *The Modern Hospital*, 106,87–91

Robinson, J. and Luft, H. (1985). The impact of hospital market structure on patient volume, average length of stay, and the cost of care. *Journal of Health Economics*, 4, 333–356

Robinson, J. and Luft, H. (1987). Competition and the cost of hospital care, 1972 to 1982. *Journal of the American Medical Association*, 257, 3241–3245

Robinson J. and Luft, H. (1988). Competition, regulation and hospital costs 1982 to 1986. *Journal of the American Medical Association*, 260, 2676–2681

Sager, M.A., Easterling, D.V., Kindig, D.A. and Anderson, O.W. (1989). Changes in the location of death after passage of Medicare's Prospective payment system. *New England Journal of Medicine*, 320, 433–439

Shortell, S.M. and Hughes, E.F. (1988). The effects of regulation competition, and ownership on mortality rates among hospital inpatients. *New England Journal of Medicine*, 318, 1100–1107

U.S. Senate (1976). *Cost and Utilization Control Mechanisms in Several European Health Care Systems*, Report to the Committee in Finance, US Senate, February

Williams, A. (1974). The cost-benefit approach. *British Medical Bulletin*, 30, 252–256

Wilson, G. and Jadlow, J. (1982). Competition, profit incentives and technical efficiency in the provision of nuclear medicine services. *Bell Journal of Economics*, 13, 472–482

Woolley, J.M. (1989). The competitive effects of horizontal mergers in the hospital industry. *Journal of Health Economics*, 8, 271–291

World Health Organisation (WHO) (1981). *Control of Health Care Costs in Social Security Systems*, Euro Reports and Studies 55, Copenhagen

Zwanziger, J. and Melnick, G.A. (1988). The effects of hospital competition and the Medicare PPS program on hospital cost behaviour in California. *Journal of Health Economics*, 7, 301–320

CHAPTER 2

Whither the Private Health Care Sector?

Carol Propper and Alan Maynard

1.   INTRODUCTION

The effects of the 1989 White Paper, *Working for Patients* (DoH, 1989), on the private health care sector in Britain are likely to be marginal and distorting in terms of efficiency and equity. The purposes of this chapter are to examine the structure of the markets for private health insurance and private hospital care, to describe the White Paper proposals which will affect these private markets and to analyse how these proposals are likely to affect the finance and provision of private health care in the 1990s. Throughout, our concern will be with the private market for cold elective acute care (that is, non-emergency care, much of it surgical repair).

2.   THE PRIVATE HEALTH CARE SECTOR

Relative to the National Health Service (NHS), the market for private health care is small. In 1988 the market for non-profit health care was £733 million. As this represents about 90 per cent of the total (for-profit and not-for-profit) market, the overall market size was £814 million (Fitzhugh, 1989, p.23). If private (out of pocket) funding is added to this total, which may add 30 per cent of the market size, the total market size was only just in excess of one billion, £1058 million. In comparison, the revenue budget for hospital and community health services (HCHS) in the NHS in England alone for 1988–89 was £12,640 million and the capital budget was £380 million (HM Treasury, 1989, p.1).

However, this aggregate comparison is misleading because the private sector is highly specialised. The market consists of private insurers who finance mostly elective surgery and of private suppliers who specialise in this type of activity. These products are sold with emphasis on the lack of queues, the quality of the hotel facilities, the greater access to information and the personal choice of hospital and clinician. It is these attributes which are not seen as present in the NHS where managers ration demand for elective care with waiting lists. These time barriers to care and the greater consumer orientation of the private sector create its revenue by offering its managers an opportunity to remedy the perceived defects of the NHS.

2.1 Private health care insurance

In 1988, 10.5 per cent of the population were estimated as covered by private health insurance (Forman, in Fitzhugh, 1989, p.17), that is there were approximately 2.742 million subscribers and 5.784 million people were covered by private health care insurance (Laing, 1989). Total premium income for the four largest not-for-profit providers (the providents) is set out in Table 2.1, as are the benefits paid. It can be seen that British United Provident Association (BUPA) is the market leader, even though its market share has declined to just 60 per cent of the not-for-profit market or, in 1987, 55 per cent of the total market (Maynard, 1989).

Table 2.1: The Providents: the income and expenditure of the major insurers

	Subscriptions £m (%)		Benefits payable £m
	1984	1988	1988
British United Provident Association (BUPA)	277.7 (65.9)	439.4 (60.0)	375.6
Private Patients Plan (PPP)	109.6 (26.0)	212.8 (29.0)	175.5
Western Provident Association (WPA)	27.6 (6.6)	58.5 (8.0)	52.1
British Contributory Welfare Association (BCWA)	6.4 (1.5)	22.1 (3.0)	22.1

Source: Fitzhugh, 1989, 287.

The number of subscribers has grown steadily in the last five years. With many subscribers having cover for themselves and dependants, the number of people covered by private health care insurance exceeds the number of subscribers by a factor in excess of two. Subscribers may have one of three types of contract: individual, group and corporate. At present the largest category is corporate, accounting for about 56 per cent of subscribers. Individual and group schemes account for 27 and 17 per cent of subscribers respectively. In the recent past the corporate sector has grown the most rapidly as employers used cover as a fringe benefit to attract workers in a tight labour market. However, within the corporate purchase category, some premia are paid for in part by employees and it appears that purchases remain individually paid in the majority of cases. The 1986 General Household Survey indicated that 50 per cent of purchase is wholly paid by individuals and a further 12 per cent is partly employee paid, whilst Propper and Eastwood (1989) indicated that in 1987 the proportion paying individually in the 25–70 year old age group was 56 per cent.

The benefits paid are divided largely between room charges and surgeons' fees. The share of expenditure going to surgeons over the last ten years has been relatively stable at 23 per cent of the total. The share of room charges, over the same period, has fallen from 50 to 44 per cent. The other large item is miscellaneous inpatient and outpatient fees of around 15 per cent of total expenditure (Laing, 1988, 1989). Unlike health care insurance in other markets, the UK private sector tends usually to offer full cover for the direct costs of specified types of private health care, consumed either in the private sector or NHS pay beds. Rather than using cost saving mechanisms such as coinsurance or deductibles, as in the USA, the major UK insurers attempt to control costs by restricting cover to particular types of acute care, excluding maternity care, long-term psychiatric and nursing care and care of the elderly.

This behaviour is the product of market leadership by BUPA, which recently introduced a new policy for first time buyers aged 65–74 (previously people in this age group were only insured if they had previously purchased cover). This policy covers a restricted set of benefits and offers buyers lower premia in association with two levels of deductible.

The negotiation of reimbursement rates for hospitals and clinicians is a private activity whose nature has changed during the 1980s. In the early 1980s cost containment pressures were not a major problem for insurers (Maynard, 1982) and the market leader tended to control fees for the then relatively small number of providers by moral suasion. Thus the insurers were, in practice, price takers with their premiums set in relation to charges made by providers. However, since the mid-1980s, the growth in benefits paid has exceeded the growth in subscriptions in some years, particularly in 1985 and 1988 (Fitzhugh, 1989, p.287). Thus, whilst the market grows, 'surplus' margins have been squeezed. In 1988 PPP contributed over half the total growth in the market but had much narrower margins; BUPA, WPA and BCWA made operating losses (Forman, in Fitzhugh, 1989, p.17).

Two consequences of the volatility of this market are apparent. First, new forms of contracting between purchaser (insurer) and provider are emerging, such as the preferred provider type of arrangements between BUPA and BUPA hospitals, and Crusader and Nuffield Hospitals, and these are being used to direct insurers' traffic to providers with known and agreed fees. Other insurers are negotiating detailed protocols with clinicians, whereby cost reducing activities, such as hotel rather than hospital stays during pre-surgery work-ups and fixed rates of care, are being agreed with providers of care. Secondly, operating margins may have to be augmented by premium increases which are in excess of inflation. Such increases are likely to affect the growth rate of the total market and the shares of the individual insurers. Thus, the benefits of aggressive cost containment policies may be considerable for individual insurers.

2.2 Private hospital provision

As noted above, the private health care market is highly specialised with less than two dozen procedures accounting for over 70 per cent of expenditure. These procedures are generally not life threatening but reduce considerably the quality of life of the potential patients who are often on NHS waiting lists. Such patients can be referred directly to the private sector by their general practitioners or may choose this care route after a NHS referral to a hospital consultant. The care is provided in either a private hospital or NHS pay beds and generally the medical care is provided by NHS doctors working part-time in the private sector, who by so doing increase their annual income, if they are surgeons, by about £17,000 on average (Laing, 1988).

The distribution of private acute care facilities (that is, in hospitals with an operating theatre) is set out in Table 2.2. Between 1979 and 1989 the number of private acute hospitals in England increased from 134 to 192 with little growth in the rest of the UK. The growth in the hospital stock over the period was very uneven: there was a net increase of 51 hospitals in the period 1979–84 but of only nine hospitals between 1985–89 (Independent Hospitals Association, 1989). This increase of over 43 per cent in the number of private hospitals in the 1979–89 period has resulted in an increase in the private acute bed stock in England of nearly 60 per cent but again, the time trend over the period is uneven, with the bed stock declining in 1985 (by 112 beds) before resuming its upward but uneven growth path subsequently (Table 2.2).

These time trends reflect the excessive optimism about the future of the private health care sector in the first half of the 1980s which resulted in low utilisation rates, sometimes barely over 50 per cent, and very low rates of return on investments (Fitzhugh, 1987). The more modest growth rates in the second half of the decade reflect the consolidation resulting from hospital competition and more vigorous cost containment policies. However, rates of return remain low and American chains are withdrawing from the UK market. BUPA, for example, bought ten hospitals and seven nursing homes from Hospital Corporation of America in July 1989.

Competition in Health Care

Table 2.2: Private acute hospital beds

NHS Region	Number of hospitals			Number of hospital beds			Beds per 100,000 population in 1989
	1979	1985	1989	1979	1985	1989	
Northern	1	3	5	30	144	165	5
Yorkshire	9	14	15	341	535	581	16
Trent	9	14	11	286	524	467	10
East Anglia	5	9	10	123	332	400	20
N.W. Thames	13	16	17	837	1225	1265	36
N.E. Thames	24	25	23	1383	1704	1631	43
S.E. Thames	15	18	19	609	893	1066	30
S.W. Thames	12	16	14	762	1001	860	29
Wessex	7	15	13	191	630	574	20
Oxford	7	12	13	232	470	498	20
South Western	9	10	11	345	425	472	15
West Midlands	13	17	20	419	606	789	15
Mersey	5	6	7	273	312	354	15
North Western	5	10	14	283	616	650	16
ENGLAND (TOTAL)	134	185	192	6114	9417	9772	21
Wales	4	5	5	202	239	248	9
Scotland	9	9	9	265	414	398	8
Northern Ireland	2	2	3	82	86	128	8
Rest of UK (TOTAL)	15	16	17	549	739	774	8
UK (TOTAL)	149	201	209	6663	10156	10546	19

Source: Independent Hospitals Association (1989) page 2.

In part, cost containment policies are the result of a change in ownership patterns. In 1979 less than 30 per cent of beds were owned by for-profit hospitals. By 1989, 59 per cent of hospitals and 56 per cent of beds were in the for-profit sector. The pressures for greater economy induced by this changed pattern of ownership are being enhanced by the actions of the insurers, some of whom (for example BUPA) own hospitals, in an effort to reduce cost pressure on the rate of growth of their premia.

The private sector makes, as noted above, a considerable contribution to the treatment of elective patients. Overall, an estimated 16.7 per cent of all residents in England and Wales who had non-abortion elective procedures were treated in the private sector in 1986 (Nicholl *et al.*, 1989b). In addition, 10.5 per cent of all day case surgery was carried out in the private sector. Uneven geographical distribution of facilities means the contribution in some areas is over 30 per cent (Table 2.3). As can also be seen from Table 2.3, the proportion of private sector activity increased in all regions except Trent and Wales in the period 1981 to 1986.

Table 2.3: Estimated percentage of patients
receiving elective surgery in england
in 1981 and 1986

Region	1981	1986
All Regions	13.2	16.7
Northern	5.2	6.3
Yorkshire	10.8	11.4
Trent	10.2	9.8
East Anglia	12.3	13.9
N.W. Thames	21.8	31.2
N.E. Thames	12.8	22.0
S.E. Thames	13.6	19.0
S.W. Thames	21.7	30.8
Wessex	14.6	19.0
Oxford	18.5	21.8
South Western	13.6	15.1
West Midlands	13.1	16.8
Mersey	13.3	15.0
North Western	9.3	14.2
Wales	10.3	8.7

Source: Nicholl, Beeby and Williams (1989b)
Table IV, p.245.

An alternative supply of private beds is provided by NHS pay beds. After restriction by the Labour Government in 1976, which contributed substantially to the growth of investment in private sector beds, the level of the NHS pay bed stock in England has grown since 1979 by over 23 per cent to 2970 beds in 1987/88 (Fitzhugh, 1989), but throughout this period utilisation has been uneven and sometimes low. The growth in the pay beds stock and the efforts to increase utilisation reflect the drive in the NHS for 'income generation' by NHS District managers and the preference for pay beds of insurers, a preference arising from the shorter lengths of stay (and hence costs) of private patients in these beds (Williams *et al.*, 1985).

3. REFORM AND THE PRIVATE HEALTH CARE SECTOR

The White Paper *Working for Patients* will have both direct and indirect effects on the behaviour of the private health care sector in the 1990s. There are relatively few direct reforms of the private sector. However, it is expected that the radical reform of the public sector will alter its relationships with the private sector. We outline those changes expected to have most impact on the private sector.

The first direct change is the establishment, from 1 April 1990, of tax relief for non-corporate purchase of private health insurance for the over-60s (*Working for Patients*, Section 9.8). The purchaser, whether recipient or not (for example family), will get tax relief at his or her marginal rate, so that the maximum relief could be up to 40 per cent (at 1989–90 rates). Secondly, the White Paper contains enhanced encouragement for the NHS to contract out care to the private sector and to enter into joint ventures with it (*Working for Patients*, Sections 9.12–9.15). This could lead to the increased use of private providers in waiting list initiatives and could provide further comparators against which NHS performance can be assessed.

The more general effects of the White Paper on the private sector will arise from the radical reform of the 'rules of the game' in the NHS market place. We identify four sets of reform which may affect the private sector. First, the fundamental reform is the separation of the purchaser (budget holder) and provider roles with explicit contracting for all service provision. This contracting will oblige the purchasers (both District General Managers and GP budget holders) to be transparent (that is explicit) about their portfolio of patient services and the prioritisation of these activities. Similarly, both public and private providers will have to be transparent: service obligations will be explicitly agreed with prices, volumes and quality controls to be agreed between purchaser and provider.

The second set of reforms in the White Paper will augment or redirect NHS revenues. The extension of the Waiting List Initiative, the proposal to direct revenue at those Districts which 'show they can use money effectively' (*Working for Patients*, Section 4.26) and the changes in the budget allocation formula, RAWP, which will place more emphasis on population weights, allow for the relative costs of service provision and augment the funding of the Thames regions by 3 per cent. The intended increase in the number of new consultants by about 0.5 per cent will presumably be targeted at 'shortage' areas where waiting times and hence the attractions of private care are greater. With the more careful specification of consultants' duties, more regular review of their behaviour and the linking of pay (distinction awards) to managerial performance envisaged in the White Paper, local NHS managers may be able to increase activity rates, especially in those areas in which the private sector is operating.

The third set of reforms will facilitate the creation of NHS self-governing Hospital Trusts. These opted out hospitals will have greater freedom in setting the conditions of employment for labour and capital and a capacity to raise income within the (liberal) scope of the Health and Medicines Act 1988. This will create potential new provider competition for the private sector.

The fourth area in which the reforms will affect the private sector is the encouragement of local managers to differentiate their NHS products and supply a wider range of amenities for which NHS patients can be charged (*Working for Patients*, Sections 2.23–2.24).

At their broadest, the White Paper changes may affect the type of care offered in the NHS, the prices of factor inputs, the geographical distribution of facilities, the development of private facilities within NHS hospitals and the use of the private sector suppliers of care. All these changes may affect the private sector. Further, the results will not necessarily have the same impact upon insurance suppliers as on the independent hospital sector.

The demand for private health insurance is a demand derived from the demand for private health care. Thus, any factor which decreases the demand for private health care will also decrease demand for private health insurance. It will also reduce the extent to which the private sector supplies private health care, but will not necessarily reduce the extent to which the private sector supplies facilities to the NHS (for example, the provision of beds under the Waiting List Initiative). Conversely, an increased demand for private health care may be met from within the NHS by the increased provision of NHS pay beds. This will probably increase the demand for health insurance but decrease the demand for independent hospital sector facilities. In the long run, most changes would appear to affect both the finance and the delivery sides of the private market. However, to identify effectively the separate demand and supply effects, each will be dealt with separately.

4. IMPLICATIONS FOR PRIVATE INSURANCE MARKET

4.1 Tax relief on health insurance purchase

In the short run, the proposal to give tax relief on insurance policies for the elderly will have a positive effect on sales and on insurers' revenues, assuming insurance prices remain unchanged. The impact on the revenue of the sellers of insurance and on the levels of tax lost by the Exchequer depends upon the price elasticity of demand for private health insurance, the size of the price cut that results from the tax relief and the average cost of a health insurance policy.

There are currently no estimates of the price elasticity of demand for the over-60 age group. In fact, the only elasticity estimate available at present is an aggregate estimate, derived from data for all subscriber types (that is individual and corporate cover) and all age groups for the period 1955 to 1986 (Propper and Maynard, 1989). These data suggest a short run price elasticity of –0.6 (95 per cent confidence interval –0.5 to –0.7) which is within the range suggested by North American data (Pauly, 1986).

The size of the price cut depends on how many of the over-60s are tax payers, or will have their insurance purchased for them by tax payers, and the marginal tax rates of the tax payers. Obviously, the proposed changes give an incentive to higher marginal rate tax payers to purchase insurance for a relative aged over-60 who was previously personally covered, as well as increasing total purchase for or by the over-60s but the likely size of a switch between purchasers is not known. In the population as a whole it is estimated that one-third of the over-60s are tax payers. Thus, at its lowest, assuming all policies are bought by the over-60s, the tax relief could amount to an average cut in price of 8.3 per cent (1/3 x 25 per cent). At its highest, assuming all policies were paid for by working individuals with income subject to the highest tax rate, the fall in price would be 40 per cent.

The predicted increase in the number of subscribers, the increase in insurance company revenue and the revenue loss to the Exchequer under three different assumptions about the size of the effect of the tax relief on price are given in Table 2.4. The three assumptions are labelled Scenarios A, B and C respectively. In calculating the changes presented in the table, it is assumed that tax relief is treated as a price decrease by all those who are eligible for relief.

The table shows that the predicted growth in the number of subscribers is relatively small. Under Scenario A, in which one-third of the purchasers of health insurance claim tax relief at a marginal rate of 25 per cent and all others are non-tax payers, the predicted increase in subscribers is just under 30,000. Under Scenario B, which assumes all policies are purchased by individuals whose marginal rate of tax is 25 per cent, the increase in subscribers is 90,000. Under Scenario C, in which all purchasers claim tax relief at 40 per cent, the predicted increase is 144,000.

As a consequence of the relatively small increase in the number of subscribers, the immediate revenue implications for the suppliers of insurance are limited. The revenue implications obviously depend on the price of the contracts purchased. Under the fairly conservative estimates of the price of insurance given in Table 2.4 (£100–£1000 per annum), the increase in revenue ranges from £3 million to £144 million per annum. This first figure assumes the lowest average policy cost (£100 per annum) and smallest extent of tax relief, and the second figure assumes a policy price of £1000 per annum and highest possible take up of tax relief. The higher the price of insurance the higher the revenue gain (assuming the price elasticity of demand does not change).

The final section of the table presents the fall in tax revenue resulting from the tax relief. Under the assumptions used to construct the table, this loss is estimated to be between £5.2 million and £297 million per annum. It should be noted that this loss in Exchequer revenues is greater under each price of insurance and extent of tax relief assumption than the revenue gain for the sellers of insurance. The reason for the difference is that the insurers gain revenue only from new subscribers but tax relief is given to both existing and new subscribers. The divergence between the revenue loss for the Exchequer and the revenue gain for the insurance suppliers is greater the higher the tax relief and the higher the price of insurance.

Table 2.4: Estimated effects of tax relief for numbers of new subscribers, insurance supplier revenue and cost to the Exchequer

Increase in number of subscribers aged 60 and over

	Scenario A	Scenario B	Scenario C
New Subscribers	29,800	90,000	144,000

Increase in insurance sales revenue (£m)

Average Price of Policy	Scenario A	Scenario B	Scenario C
£100	2.98	9.0	14.4
£250	7.5	22.5	36.0
£500	14.9	45.0	72.0
£1000	29.9	90.0	144.0

Cost to Exchequer (£m)

Average Price of Policy	Scenario A	Scenario B	Scenario C
£100	5.25	17.25	29.8
£250	13.12	43.13	74.4
£500	26.25	86.25	148.8
£1000	52.5	172.5	197.6

Assumptions:
The data used assume:
1. Number of current subscribers over 60 = 600,000
2. Price elasticity of demand for insurance = -0.6

Estimates calculated under three assumptions as to impact of tax relief on insurance purchased for over-60s
Scenario A: 1/3 of purchasers pay tax at standard rate (25%); remaining 2/3 pay no tax.
Scenario B: All purchasers pay tax at the standard rate.
Scenario C: All purchasers pay tax at highest rate (40%).

Sources:
Number of subscribers over 60: BUPA Press Release 2/2/89.
Estimate of price elasticity: Propper and Maynard (1989).
Cost of insurance: £100 p.a. is approximate cost of lowest BudgetBUPA policy (Press Release 2/2/89); £250 p.a. is approximate cost of WPA Health Contract Scale 3; £500 p.a. is approximate cost of WPA Health Contract Scale 1; £1000 p.a. is approximate cost of BUPA care London Scale.

The analysis presented in Table 2.4 is a short-run analysis, based on the assumption that suppliers respond passively to an increase in demand by offering more of the same type of contracts and that the nature of demand does not change. It also does not take into account any increase in sales to the under-60s which may result from the publicity about private health insurance in the debate around the White Paper. But it also does not take into account limits to purchase.

At present, the private sector does not treat a high proportion of the elderly (Nicholl *et al.*, 1989a). This may be because of a lack of demand resulting either from restricted access to finance (until recently, no new policies were sold to the over-64s) or from the high cost of finance. It is possible that in response to tax relief, insurance suppliers will respond by issuing new types of lower cost contracts aimed specifically at the over-60s. One such contract is currently on the market (BudgetBUPA) and new contracts may increase purchase. It is worth noting that in any attempt to increase purchase, contracts will have to be designed carefully to avoid adverse selection and the devices used to achieve this may mean sales are fairly limited. For example, restrictions on the treatments covered by insurance helps keep down costs, but also limits the attractiveness of a policy.

However, low demand may not stem only from high cost of insurance. Low demand by the over-60s may be the result of the lack of provision of treatment within the private sector for chronic medical conditions. If low purchase of insurance and/or low usage of the private sector by the over-60s is the result of a lack of supply of appropriate private sector facilities, then changing the price of contracts which provide care of the type currently supplied by the private sector will not result in a large increase in demand by the over-60s. In other words, even if restrictions on access to finance are relaxed, the increase in demand for private health insurance will be limited unless there is a large increase in the demand for private sector care.

In terms of the impact on welfare, subsidisation of health insurance purchase will move the market away from, rather than towards, greater efficiency. Subsidisation results in a distorted (lower) price for insurance, that is, consumers do not face market prices which reflect opportunity costs. *Ceteris paribus*, this will lead to overconsumption of insurance relative to the efficient level. In addition, it has been argued in the North American market that tax subsidisation of health insurance has resulted in cost escalation in the medical care market (Pauly, 1986). The argument runs as follows. Full cover insurance reduces the price of medical care at point of demand, thereby increasing consumption of medical care. This increase in consumption is passed on into higher premia but because of tax relief, demanders of health insurance are relatively insensitive to increases in the price of premia. Thus they continue to buy health insurance and a cost spiral occurs, enhanced by government tax relief.

Although the price of insurance will be lower than the efficient price, the effects of this type of cost escalation will be limited in the UK while the private sector remains a small provider of health care. The limited nature of private sector provision means that any cost escalation that arises from increased provision of full cover health insurance will be confined to acute care and so will be small in relation to the whole of the medical care market. Nevertheless, the price of insurance remains distorted by tax relief, thus encouraging over-consumption of health insurance.

Tax relief on health insurance would also not appear to promote equity, defined either in terms of an after-tax income distribution which is more pro-poor than the pre-tax distribution (vertical equity) or in terms of equal access to medical care for those in equal need or ability to benefit (horizontal equity). Social surveys show that the insured tend to be of higher average income than the uninsured (General Household Survey, 1986). Thus, as tax relief represents a transfer to all purchasers of health insurance for the over-60s (that is, to existing as well as new subscribers), it will go predominantly to those with higher incomes. Thus tax relief will decrease rather than promote vertical equity. As the over-60s covered by health insurance are currently of higher income than the over-60s who are not, tax relief will permit greater access to health care by a higher income group and so, unless this group are sicker, will decrease horizontal equity.

4.2 The effect of changes to the NHS

The introduction of GPs as budget holders may alter the incentives of GPs to promote private insurance and private sector health care which may result in increases in insurer costs and premia. At present, GPs perform a gatekeeper role for private care financed by private health insurance in much the same way as they do for NHS care. Reimbursement for private care is not given unless such care was authorised by a medical practitioner, generally the GP. Currently, a GP has no financial incentive to refer a patient to the private sector, though there is some evidence that private patients are being referred more often (Gillam, 1985), perhaps because referral to the private sector has fewer time or reputational costs for the GP. If GPs become budget holders these incentives will change.

A GP with a limited budget has an incentive to encourage patients to take out insurance in order to reduce outgoings from his/her own budget. For example, diagnostic tests will be included in the GP's budget. If the GP can persuade practice patients to use the private sector, paid for by insurance, then the GP will use less of the practice budget. If GPs respond in this manner to the new incentives, insurers will no longer be able to use these GPs as their gatekeepers and will have to seek new methods of cost containment. This will probably raise administration costs, as GPs currently receive no remuneration from insurance suppliers for their gatekeeping role. The implications for supplier profitability depend on whether such costs are passed on to premia and the price elasticity of demand.

Waiting lists, or more properly, waiting times, are argued to be a key determinant of insurance purchase (Laing, 1988; Propper and Eastwood, 1989). While the White Paper extends the current Waiting List Initiative, which reduces lists if suppliers do not respond to shorter lists by increasing referrals (see for example Cullis and Jones, 1985), in the short run it does not seem likely that this will much affect the demand for private health insurance. It has been argued, both in North America (Neipp and Zeckhauser, 1986) and in the UK (Propper and Eastwood, 1989), that individual insurance buyers are slow to respond to marginal changes in their purchase of insurance. Corporate buyers appear to use insurance, at least in part, as part of a package to attract employees (Stockwell, 1988). Thus neither individual nor corporate subscribers appear likely to reduce purchase in the short run simply because the Waiting List Initiative is extended.

In the longer run, the NHS Review will lead to some type of internal market. Whether this will reduce the long-term equilibrium level of lists depends on the willingness of patients to travel to receive care and the response of consultants to shorter lists. If waiting times are significantly reduced by the development of an internal market then the demand for private insurance may fall but if there is no perceived fall in waiting times then the demand for private insurance may rise because the expectations about a better NHS service have not been met.

Changes in the nature of NHS provision will provide competition for the private sector. This may decrease the demand for insurance. For example, the increased use of amenity beds and the provision of more 'consumer orientated' care in the NHS sector may reduce the long-term demand for wholly private care. The creation of NHS Hospital Trusts may create direct competition for the private sector, particularly if these hospitals raise their level of amenity provision. Any increase in the geographical imbalance of better NHS facilities that favours the south east (due, say, to distribution of NHS Hospital Trusts and better funding for the Thames regions) will result in a pattern where better NHS facilities will be in the same areas as the insurance buyers. Thus, potential purchasers have some incentive not to move out of the NHS. Again, the extent of change will depend on the responsiveness of both individuals and corporate purchase to these factors and the ability of NHS managers to increase the provision of amenities. The stricter the cash constraints on the NHS, the smaller may be the ability of managers and clinicians to increase consumer orientated provision, thus the smaller will be any fall in demand (or the greater the growth in demand) for private sector care and so for health insurance. The development of an internal market may also lead to greater provision and marketing of NHS pay beds. If demand for these increases, so will the purchase of private health insurance.

Finally, unless efficiency increases, any increase in costs in the private sector will be passed on into insurance premia. In the short run, there will be cost increases from the nurses pay award of 1988 (Laing, 1988). Additionally, there will be costs associated with administering tax relief on behalf of the Inland Revenue via MIRAS. Other longer term possible private sector cost increases are discussed in the next section. It is worth noting that as demand appears to be inelastic, the affect of an increase in premia, at least in the short run, will not reduce insurance revenues as a whole. However, it may encourage switching to lower cost suppliers if there are substantial price differences between suppliers. In the long run, any cost increases in the private sector are unlikely to be beneficial for the health insurance market, particularly if NHS hospitals increase their provision of amenities. Finally, the increased provision of such amenities at a positive price may stimulate the growth of other forms of medical insurance, for example, Health Cash Insurance, which provides cash in the event of a hospital inpatient stay.

5. IMPLICATIONS FOR THE INDEPENDENT HOSPITAL SECTOR

The implications for the independent hospital sector depend on changes in the demand for private care and in the costs of private provision relative to NHS costs. Certain proposals in the White Paper may benefit the private independent sector.

5.1 Proposals which positively benefit the private sector

First, given the amount and/or extent of spare capacity in the private hospital sector, the extension of the Waiting List Initiative and the development of a provider market should provide opportunities for greater use of private sector capacity. In the short run, the private sector can price at marginal cost. If this is below NHS costs, the private sector would attract patients and so increase revenue. There is very little evidence as to the relative costs of the NHS and the private sector, though isolated examples suggest the costs charged to the NHS by the private sector are not necessarily lower than NHS (marginal?) costs (see, for example, the report in the *Health Service Journal*, 21 January 1988, p.69). The use of private sector facilities under the Waiting List Initiative to date has been relatively limited. In 1986 for example, 10,655 surgical and medical NHS patients were treated in non-NHS facilities and just under 40 per cent of these were resident in one regional health authority (Nicholl *et al.*, 1989a). However, this may reflect political unwillingness to use the private sector. Under the type of provider market system that may emerge from the White Paper, such political reluctance may diminish in the face of cost incentives.

Incentives for health authorities to engage in joint capital projects with the private sector are clearly of benefit to the private sector. To date such ventures have been limited in number but have extended in 1988 from partnerships in prestige hospitals to joint ventures in district services and facilities. Despite evidence of considerable interest in the private sector in such activities, it is too early to assess their profitability. In addition, rules to include capital costs in NHS pricing will lead to a fall in the relative price of the independent hospital sector and so benefit the private sector.

5.2 Proposals which have either positive or negative effects

The long-run implications of provider markets for the private sector appear to be less clear-cut. In the long run, a private supplier must cover fixed as well as variable costs. Given the amount of excess capacity in the industry, it seems as if the private sector will have to have significant cost advantages relative to the NHS in order to avoid some decline.

The White Paper probably increases the incentives for NHS managers to re-introduce NHS pay beds. While little costing data are available (and the independent sector argues that the NHS does not calculate costs correctly (Randall, 1988)), the amount of day surgery is greater and length of stay in NHS pay beds is shorter than length of stay in the independent sector (Nicholl *et al.*, 1989b). If charges are related to length of stay then NHS pay beds will be cheaper. On the other hand, prices may be higher in the NHS because of 24 hour cover by doctors, though the findings of Nicholl *et al.* (1989a) indicate that the amount of medical cover in the private sector is rising. If there is a price difference in favour of NHS facilities, cost containment measures by insurers may lead to encouragement of subscribers to use NHS pay beds rather than the independent sector. Limited evidence from the corporate purchasers of insurance suggests that cost containment is a concern for corporate purchasers (Stockwell, 1988), so moves to lower premia would have the support of this group of purchasers.

While the independent hospital sector may not face competition from all NHS hospitals (particularly since the cash constraints on the NHS seem likely to continue) the NHS Hospital Trusts may present competition for the private sector. This could be competition for patients (inside and outside pay beds) and/or for labour. If these hospitals are predominantly located in south east England, in the absence of a substantial increase in the demand for private sector care, the demand for care in the independent sector may diminish.

5.3 Long-term effects of increased competition

In general, any long-term boost to demand from the divorce of service provision and budget receipt will depend on how the private sector costs or efficiency compare with those of the NHS. It is not clear that the attempts to increase the amount of competition in the health care market will necessarily be beneficial to the private sector. It will face competition for patients, factor inputs and insurance finance from NHS hospitals, NHS pay beds and the new NHS Hospital Trusts. All of these will probably be cash constrained and seeking ways of increasing their revenue within the wide ranging powers offered by the 1988 Health and Medicines Act. First, relative costs in the two sectors are currently unknown, though as noted above, length of stay for similar elective treatments is lower in the NHS pay bed sector than in the independent sector. If this reflects costs, then total costs per case may be higher in the private sector.

Secondly, as the private sector currently has very limited training facilities, it has to compete with the NHS for staff. Nicholl *et al.* (1989b) have commented that there is probably no spare labour capacity in the health care sector at present. Any increase in staff in the private sector must come from a shift from the NHS. If consultants see their NHS wages as fixed, then the effect of an increased demand for consultant staff in the private sector will probably be to increase wages in this sector.

Thirdly, any general increase in wage costs that results from the NHS reforms will be passed on to the private sector, although costs relative to the NHS may remain unchanged. The NHS is presently a monopsonistic purchaser of medical labour. This labour is itself, to some extent, monopolistically organised. The fragmentation of the NHS may lead to a reduction in NHS monopsony power. The consequences of a breakup of a monopsonist are difficult to predict when the prior situation was one in which the monopsonist faced a monopolist (Pauly, 1988) but, given that medical inputs remain monopolistically organised, wage increases may be expected following the development of internal markets. Any increase in wages will increase the costs of the private sector. Even if there is only a small increase in costs on average, the ability of NHS Hospital Trusts to set their own pay scales will probably raise the costs of labour to hospitals in the same location. If these Hospital Trusts are predominately located in the south east, the private sector will again face higher input cost in a region which already has considerable over-capacity.

Fourthly, there is evidence from North America that increased competition by hospitals to attract physicians increases hospital costs. Robinson and Luft (1985) suggest that the more competitive the market for physician inputs, the higher hospital costs. Under a system in which physicians are not full-time hospital employees but bring patients to the hospitals (as in the UK private sector) hospitals must compete for physicians. To compete they tend to introduce capital equipment and procedures which raise patient demand for physicians' services, so attracting physicians. However, this introduction of increased capital and diagnostic procedures increases the hospitals' costs. If NHS hospitals do not have to compete for physicians to the same extent as independent hospitals, or consultants in NHS hospitals are unable to increase their capital to the same extent as the private sector, the impact on costs of competition for consultants will be greater for the independent sector.

Finally, the aim of the White Paper is to improve efficiency. In order to achieve this, the NHS budget holder should not seek merely to reduce costs, but to obtain lowest cost for a certain level of quality. Freeland *et al.* (1988) argue that it is extremely difficult, even within the American health care market in which better data on outcomes is available, to issue contracts which simultaneously monitor price, quantity and quality. One response to this problem is to increase regulation. Robinson and Luft (1985) have argued that increased regulation is associated with higher health care provider costs. Thus, this type of regulatory response will decrease the long-run profitability of the private sector unless these costs can be passed on. Another response to the problem of measuring quality is to set minimum volume requirements, as volume appears to be associated with (crude) measures of better outcome

(Hughes *et al.*, 1987). Bed sizes vary in private hospitals, but a minimum volume measure would probably have greatest adverse consequences for the not-for-profit hospitals which have tended to operate smaller units. If non-pay bed NHS volume was taken into account in assessing volume, then it would be expected that such regulation would have greater impact on the independent than the NHS private sector.

6. CONCLUSIONS

Many of the changes outlined in the NHS Review are not spelt out in any detail and hence predictions about the impact of these changes on the private sector are inevitably speculative. However, the following broad conclusions may be drawn.

The effect of tax relief on private health insurance purchased to cover the over-60s will be to increase sales of private health insurance. The increase depends upon the size of the tax relief and the elasticity of demand with respect to the tax cut. Preliminary estimates suggest that demand appears to be price inelastic. Even under the assumption of 40 per cent tax relief for all purchasers of health insurance for the over-60s, the increase in sales would appear to be below 150,000. The loss in tax revenues following tax relief is greater than the gain in insurance supplier revenue from higher sales. The increase in revenue from new sales is insufficient to outweigh the tax loss consequent on relief for both existing and new subscribers. Under the assumption that insurance is currently priced at marginal cost, tax subsidisation of insurance reduces welfare because it reduces the price to the consumer to below marginal cost.

The effects of the Review on the independent hospital sector depend first upon the change in demand for private sector care and second upon the relative costs of this sector compared to the NHS. In the short run, an extension of the Waiting List Initiative would appear likely to benefit a sector with over-capacity. Encouragement of joint public-private sector ventures will expand a developing area of activity. In the longer run, on the demand side, the private sector is likely to face competition from the NHS, particularly if there is increased provision of amenities either in all NHS hospitals or in those located close to provide sector hospitals. On the supply side, the independent sector may face greater competition from NHS pay beds for private patients (and perhaps insurance finance) and with the NHS as a whole for staff. The breakup of the NHS as a monopsonist may increase the average level of wages in the health care sector, so generally increasing private sector costs. Competition for staff may raise independent sector costs more than those of the NHS; competition for patients may be accompanied by increased regulation which, if volume-based, would have greatest impact on the smaller not-for-profit segments of the independent sector. Given the current low occupancy rates, it appears likely that the independent sector must have a significant cost advantage over the NHS to avoid rationalisation and perhaps greater concentration of ownership.

The private sector has developed to fill a perceived gap in NHS provision. Given that the dominant mode of financing health care is not altered by the Review, to the extent that the Review sets in motion changes which improve NHS acute services, at least in regions with higher per capita income, then the private sector is likely to face more competition. If the overall level of demand for private care does not increase very much or most of the growth in demand is for amenity beds and consumer extras to NHS care, then the scope for the private sector is diminished rather than boosted by the Review. On the other hand, if there is a large demand for private care as the result of higher incomes and expectations and the private sector is more efficient (or lower cost), then the incentives for increased competition between providers that the introduction of budget holders is designed to give will increase the demand for private provision and for private insurance. Finally, NHS Hospital Trusts may increase competition for the private sector, particularly if they are consumer orientated in their activities. It has been argued that the debate over pay beds initiated by the Labour Government in the mid-1970s sharply increased the opportunities for the private sector. Paradoxically, if the scope for increasing the number of players is limited, the reforms of a Conservative Government may reduce opportunities.

References

Cullis, J. and Jones, P. (1985). National Health Service Waiting Lists. *Journal of Health Economics*, 4, 119–135

Department of Health (DoH) (1989). *Working for Patients*, Cm. 555, HMSO, London

Freeland, M.S., Hunt, S.S. and Luft, H.S. (1988). Selective contract for hospital care based on volume, quality and price: prospects, problems and unanswered questions. *Journal of Health, Politics, Policy and Law*, 12, 3, 409–426

Fitzhugh, W.A., (1989). *The Fitzhugh Directory of Independent Hospitals and Provident Associations, Financial Information*, Health Care Information Services, London

General Household Survey (1986). OPCS, London

Gillam, D. (1985). Referrals to Consultants—the NHS versus private practice. *Journal of the Royal College of General Practitioners*, 35, 15–18

HM Treasury (1989). *The Government's Expenditure Plans 1989–90 to 1991–92*, Cm. 614, Chapter 14 (The Department of Health), HMSO, London

Hughes, R.G., Hunt, S.S. and Luft, H.S. (1987). Effects of surgeon volume and hospital volume on quality of care in Hospitals. *Medical Care*, 25, 6, 489

Independent Hospitals Association (1989). *Survey of Acute Hospitals in the Independent Sector*, IHA, London, p.2

Laing, William (ed.) (1988). *Laings Review of Private Healthcare 1987*. Laing and Buisson Publications Ltd, London

Laing, William (ed.) (1989). *Laings Review of Private Healthcare 1988/89*. Laing and Buisson Publications Ltd, London

Maynard, A. (1982). The private health care sector in Britain. In McLachlan, G. and Maynard, A. (eds.), *The Public/Private Mix for Health*, Nuffield Provincial Hospitals Trust

Maynard, A. (1989). Whither private health care. In *Implications of the New Thinking on the National Health Service*, Crusader Insurance plc and the Foundation for Business Responsibilities, London

Neipp, J. and Zeckhauser, R. (1986). Persistence in the Choice of Health Plans. In Scheffler, R. and Rossiter, L. (eds.), *Advances in Health Economics and Health Services Research Vol. 6*, 47–72. JAI Press Greenwich, C.T. and London

Nicholl, J.P., Beeby, N. and Williams, B. (1989a). Comparison of the activity of short stay independent hospitals in England and Wales, 1981 and 1986. *British Medical Journal*, 298, 239–42

Nicholl, J.P., Beeby, N. and Williams, B. (1989b). Role of the private sector in elective surgery in England and Wales, 1986. *British Medical Journal*, 298, 243–7

Pauly, M. (1986). Taxation, Health Insurance and Market Failure in the Medical Economy. *Journal of Economic Literature*, 24, 629–675

Pauly, M. (1988). Market power, monopsony and health insurance markets. *Journal of Health Economics*, 7, 111–128

Propper, C. and Eastwood, A. (1989). *The Reasons for Non-Corporate Health Insurance Purchase in the UK*. Discussion Paper 52, Centre for Health Economics, University of York

Propper, C. and Maynard, A.K. (1989). *The Market for Private Health Insurance and the Demand for Private Health Insurance in the UK*. Discussion Paper 53, Centre for Health Economics, University of York

Randall, J. (1988). Service Provision Reviewed. *Health Service Journal*, Vol 98, 5084 (21 Jan), p. 94

Robinson, J.C. and Luft, H.S. (1985). The impact of hospital market structure on patient volume, average length of stay and the cost of care. *Journal of Health Economics*, 4, 333–356

Stockwell, M. (1988). *The Role of Private Health Care as an Employee Benefit*. Paper given at the Financial Times Conference on Private Health Care, London, 29–30 November 1988, Speakers Papers

Williams, B.T., Nicholl, J.P., Thomas, K.J. and Knowelden, J. (1985). For Debate: differences in duration of stay for surgery in the NHS and private sector in England and Wales. *British Medical Journal*, 290, 978–980

CHAPTER 3

NHS Resourcing: a Financial and Economic Analysis

David Mayston

1. INTRODUCTION

This chapter contains an analysis, against the background of the NHS Review proposals (DoH, 1989a), of a number of key aspects of NHS resourcing, paying particular attention to the importance of labour and capital resource inputs into the NHS. Since the financing of health care provision is likely to remain a subject of continuing interest, the chapter seeks to examine several of the underlying economic factors that are likely to affect NHS financing.

The NHS Review was in many ways a response to the build-up of financial pressures that have quite deep economic causes. If a worried patient is to be effectively cared for, it is important that there be both a correct diagnosis of the underlying causes of the observed symptoms and a well-founded prognosis of the likely future courses of events, with and without different possible forms of treatment. We therefore seek first to diagnose several of the underlying factors which have generated current concerns over the health of the NHS, before then assessing the likely impact of some of the key changes proposed by the NHS Review.

2. FINANCIAL PERSPECTIVES

A prime cause of the frustration of the present Government with the NHS is that despite very large increases in funding since the Conservative Government came to power in 1979, the NHS still has problems in meeting the demands made upon it and shows several apparent signs of inefficiency in meeting these demands. However, there are several factors which are central to any diagnosis of the real impact of this increase in funding on service delivery and upon politicians and their constituencies.

Table 3.1: NHS Hospital, Community Health and Related Services Gross Current Expenditure in England

HCHS Current Spending	1978/79	1979/80	1980/81	1981/82	1982/83	1983/84	1984/85	1985/86	1986/87	1987/88	1988/89
Cash terms (£m)	4421	5333	6886	7688	8284	8882	9386	9886	10623	11730	13007
% Increase		20.6	29.1	11.6	7.8	7.2	5.7	5.3	7.5	10.4	10.9
General Inflation (%)		15.8	17.3	10.4	7.7	4.7	5.0	5.4	3.5	5.3	7.5
Growth Ahead of General Inflation (%)		4.8	11.8	1.2	0.1	2.5	0.7	-0.1	4.0	5.1	3.4
Specific Inflation (%)		20.5	28.0	8.1	6.5	5.1	5.8	5.2	6.9	8.5	10.5
Growth Ahead of Specific Inflation (%)		0.1	1.1	3.5	1.3	2.1	-0.1	0.1	0.6	1.9	0.4
New Cost Improvements (%)		0.0	0.0	0.2	0.5	0.5	1.1	1.4	1.4	1.3	1.3
Margin Available for Service Development (%)		0.1	1.1	3.7	1.7	2.6	1.0	1.5	2.0	3.2	1.7
Demographic Demand Growth (%)			0.9	0.3	0.5	0.5	0.6	1.1	1.0	0.9	0.9
Net Margin (%)			0.2	3.4	1.2	2.1	0.4	0.4	1.0	2.3	0.8
General PP terms (£m)	4421	4605	5068	5125	5127	5250	5284	5280	5482	5749	5930
Specific P&P terms (£m)	4421	4426	4464	4611	4665	4759	4754	4759	4784	4869	4886
New Cost Improvements (£m)		0	0	12	36	39	105	138	153	153	169
Cumulative Real CIs (£m)		0	0	7	27	48	101	168	237	300	364
Total Specific Position (£m)	4421	4426	4464	4618	4693	4807	4855	4927	5021	5169	5249

Source: DHSS, 1988; DoH, 1989.

2.1 Growth in spending

As in Figures 3.1 and 3.2 and Tables 3.1 and 3.2, the increases in the funding of the NHS Hospital and Community Health Services (HCHS) and the Family Practitioner Service (FPS) since 1979 have indeed been very large in money terms. In the case of total current expenditure on the HCHS, it has increased from £4.4 billion in 1978/9 to £13.0 billion in 1988/9. In the case of total current spending on the Family Practitioner Service, it has increased from £1.4 billion in 1978/9 to £4.9 billion in 1988/9. Whilst the annual increases ahead of general inflation are less dramatic, they have none the less been positive increases. The second highest curves in Figures 3.1 and 3. 2 show the increases in such general purchasing power (General PP) terms, measured at 1978/9 prices.

Figure 3.1: NHS hospital and community health services total current spending in England

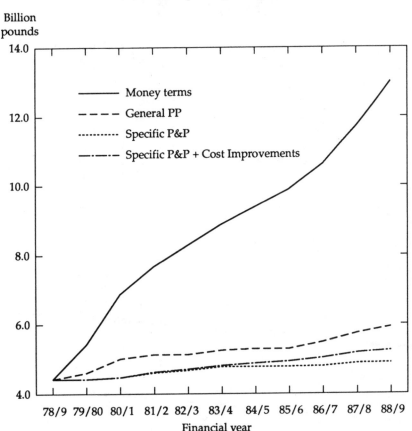

Source: DHSS: 1988; DoH, 1989

Table 3.2: NHS Family practitioner services gross current expenditure in England

FPS Current Spending	1978/79	1979/80	1980/81	1981/82	1982/83	1983/84	1984/85	1985/86	1986/87	1987/88	1988/89
Cash terms (£m)	1434	1684	2114	2504	2894	3110	3421	3604	3878	4229	4917
% Increase		17.4	25.5	18.4	15.6	7.5	10.0	5.3	7.6	10.9	14.4
Growth Ahead of General Inflation (%)		1.6	8.2	8.0	7.9	2.8	4.7	-0.1	4.1	5.6	6.6
Specific Inflation (%)		17.0	25.5	13.1	11.6	5.4	7.2	5.0	5.1	6.8	10.3
Growth Ahead of Specific Inflation (%)		0.4	0.0	4.7	3.6	2.0	2.6	0.0	2.4	3.8	3.7
General PP terms (£m)	1434	1457	1576	1703	1837	1888	1977	1975	2056	2171	2315
Specific P&P terms (£m)	1434	1439	1440	1508	1562	1592	1634	1639	1678	1742	1806

Source: DHSS, 1988; DoH, 1989.

Figure 3.2: Family practitioner service total current spending in England

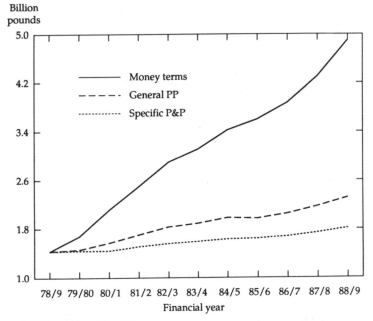

Billion
pounds

Money terms

General PP

Specific P&P

78/9 79/80 80/1 81/2 82/3 83/4 84/5 85/6 86/7 87/8 88/9

Financial year

Source: DHSS, 1988; DoH, 1989

However, in terms of the increases in the prices of the specific items of resource inputs that the NHS actually purchases, the growth in real expenditure is more modest. When measured against the rise in the specific NHS pay and prices index, total current spending on the HCHS shows only a 10.5 per cent increase over the whole 11 year period (that is, less than one per cent per annum) from £4.421 billion in 1978/9 to £4.886 billion in 1988/9 in constant 1978/9 specific price terms. This is show by the lowest curve in Figure 3.1, where Specific P & P refers to expenditure deflated by the NHS specific pay and prices index. When the cumulative effect of Cost Improvement Programmes are added into this real expenditure growth, total current spending on the HCHS shows a total growth of 18.7 per cent over the 11 year period to £5.249 billion, being equivalent to a 1.7 per cent average real annual growth rate.

The picture is slightly more encouraging for the Family Practitioner Service in Figure 3.2 and Table 3.2. When deflated by the relevant specific pay and prices index, current expenditure on the FPS shows an increase from £1.434 billion in 1978/9 to £1.806 billion in 1988/9, representing an average annual increase over the period of 2.3 per cent. However, for the NHS as a whole, the overall picture in Figure 3.3 and Table 3.3 is one of an increase in real expenditure, ahead of the specific pay and prices index, from £11.182 billion in 1981/2 to £12.344 billion in 1988/9 at constant 1981/2 prices, representing an average annual increase of 1.4 per cent.

Figure 3.3: Total NHS expenditure in England

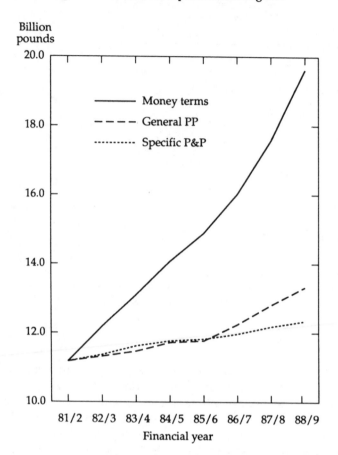

Table 3.3: Total NHS expenditure in England

NHS Total	1981/82	1982/83	1983/84	1984/85	1985/86	1986/87	1987/88	1988/89
Cash Terms (£m)	11182	12197	13116	14077	14889	16023	17598	19639
% Increase		9.1	7.5	7.3	5.8	7.6	9.8	11.6
Growth Ahead of General Inflation (%)		1.3	1.2	2.3	0.3	4.1	4.6	4.1
Specific Inflation (%)		7.4	5.0	6.1	5.2	6.3	7.9	10.2
Growth Ahead of Specific Inflation (%)		1.6	2.4	1.2	0.5	1.2	1.8	1.3
General PP terms (£m)	11182	11327	11463	11727	11762	12244	12808	13333
Specific P&P terms (£m)	11182	11357	11631	11765	11829	11975	12189	12344

Source: DHSS, 1988; DoH, 1989.

2.2 GEOGRAPHICAL REDISTRIBUTION

The effect of the limited total growth in NHS real expenditure ahead of the specific pay and prices index has been amplified in many key areas by a geographical redistribution of resources. Since 1979, the funding formula of the Resource Allocation Working Party (RAWP) for individual NHS regions has had a significant re-distributive effect in reducing the relative shares of several major NHS Regions in the south east of England. This is illustrated in Figure 3.4. Figure 3.5 shows the closing of the gap towards their RAWP targets of the RAWP-gaining regions further from London. Whilst such a steady progression of all NHS regions towards their target allocations was indeed the fundamental objective of the RAWP process (DHSS, 1976), it has tended to emphasise even more strongly within the politically important south east constituencies the problems associated with the limited total growth of the NHS budget ahead of the specific NHS pay and prices index.

Figure 3.4: RAWP losers

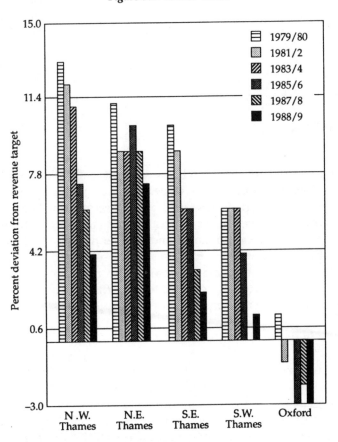

Source: DHSS, 1988

Competition in Health Care

Figure 3.5: RAWP gainers

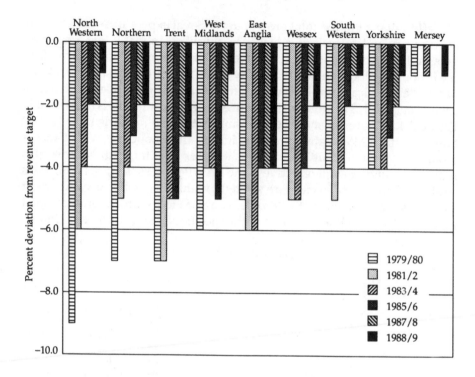

Source: DHSS, 1988

In addition to the decline in their relative share of total NHS funding, south east NHS regions are likely to experience further difficulties due to stronger than average labour market pressures. South east regions have tended to experience lower than average levels of unemployment, higher than average earnings in competing occupations, and frequently greater than average housing market pressures, both from a scarcity of rental accommodation and from rapidly rising house prices in several past years in excess of the national average. All of these factors have added to the difficulties south east regions have faced in attracting medical, nursing and supporting staff.

2.3 Growth in demand

The limited increases in real expenditure ahead of the specific NHS pay and prices index must also be weighed against the growth in demand for NHS services. A major cause of growth in demand is that of demographic change, particularly from an ageing population. As in Table 3.1, the impact of demographic change on the demand for HCHS services in recent years has been to put significant further pressure on the remaining net margin of real resource growth available to meet other elements of increasing demand. These other elements include technological change, which the DHSS have estimated to require some 0.5 per cent increase per annum in available expenditure (see Maynard and Bosanquet, 1986), as well as other major special factors, such as AIDS.

2.4 Increases in productivity

To some extent offsetting these pressures on the available resources have been increases in productivity within the NHS. As in Table 3.4, within the above limited growth in HCHS resources, there have been substantial increases in hospital activity and the number of cases treated. This is due principally to an increase in day cases and a reduction in the average length of stay for inpatients.   Both of these trends represent substantial improvements in productivity, particularly for the capital resources invested in beds and similar resources in the NHS.

The increase in activity has occurred at the same time as a fall in the average daily number of available beds, which in England has fallen from 424,000 in 1970 to 359,000 in 1980 and to 297,000 in 1987/8 (DHSS, 1982–89). The significant increase in the productivity of capital, in the form of beds, is reflected also in the rise in throughput, that is inpatient cases treated per available bed. For acute specialties in England it has risen from 31.6 in 1980 to 40.2 in 1987/8, and for all specialties from 15.9 in 1980 to 22.3 in 1987/8. As in Table 3.4, the average length of stay for acute, geriatric and younger disabled patients has similarly fallen steadily from 13.3 days in 1978 to 9.8 days in 1988/9.

The magnitudes of the above increases in activity and productivity are large compared to the growth in HCHS funding ahead of the specific pay and prices index. Day-case admissions have risen by an average of 5.8 per cent per annum between 1978 and 1988–89, and the average length of stay for inpatients in the acute, geriatric and younger disabled sectors has fallen by an average of 2.9 per cent per annum over the same period.

However, particularly because of the lack of available data on re-admissions, it is difficult to assess precisely the effect of the reduction in length of stay on the quality of care or on total costs per continuing case. In addition, a reduction in the length of stay, or a move from an inpatient to day-case treatment, is likely to save marginal costs that in the short-run are below the average cost of treatment per patient day. In the longer run, some saving in unit capital cost is also likely as the number of patient days per case is reduced. However, this is still likely to be less than a saving at average cost, with time spent in an operating theatre typically the most expensive item per unit time, both in capital and revenue terms, compared to time spent recovering in bed.

A further relevant feature of the change in hospital activity in Table 3.4 is the substantial fall in the numbers of occupied bed days for the mentally

Table 3.4: Hospital Activity Data for England

	1978	1979	1981	1983	1985	1986	1987-8	1988-9	Annual Average % change 1978 to 1988-9
ACUTE, GERIATRIC AND YOUNGER DISABLED:									
Inpatient cases treated (million)	4.356	4.423	4.749	4.892	5.155	5.198	5.383	5.342	2.0
Average length of stay (days)	13.3	13.1	12.1	11.6	10.8	10.4	10.0	9.8	-2.9
Outpatients (new attendances) (m)	6.708	6.686	7.003	7.302	7.651	7.737	7.622	7.560	1.2
ACCIDENT AND EMERGENCIES:									
New attendances (m)	9.170	9.197	9.464	9.950	10.403	10.532	10.880	10.984	1.8
MATERNITY									
Obstetrics outpatients (new attendances) (m)	0.678	0.709	0.695	0.681	0.698	0.696	0.652	0.611	-1.0
MENTAL HANDICAP:									
Inpatient cases treated (m)	0.731	0.783	0.796	0.803	0.852	0.862	0.899	0.894	2.0
Occupied bed days (m)	17.020	16.558	15.697	14.703	13.297	12.436	11.660	11.080	-4.1
Outpatients (new attendances) (000s)	3.200	2.600	2.500	2.600	3.300	3.000	4.100	3.400	0.7
MENTAL ILLNESS:									
Occupied bed days (m)	28.534	27.908	26.793	25.312	23.647	22.448	21.540	20.990	-3.0
Outpatients (new attendances) (m)	0.187	0.180	0.188	0.192	0.201	0.202	0.207	0.192	0.3
ALL SPECIALTIES:									
Inpatient and day cases (m)	5.932	5.992	6.474	6.832	7.317	7.464	7.500	7.580	2.4
Outpatient, accident and emergencies (m)	16.747	16.774	17.352	18.127	18.959	19.171	19.366	19.351	1.4
Day case admissions (m)	0.562	0.570	0.692	0.813	0.963	1.050	0.881	0.998	5.8

Source: H. M. Treasury, 1990

handicapped and mentally ill, due principally to the programme of run-down of long-stay mental institutions under the Care in the Community policy. However this is again likely to involve a resource saving at less than average cost, with the least disadvantaged (and hence typically least costly) patients usually transferred first. Moreover the total cost of community care facilities, including those borne by local authorities and informal carers, can often exceed the direct cost saving to the NHS from reduced institutional care. The transitional costs of running existing long-stay institutions alongside new community care facilities are particularly great, with recent falls in land prices from the eventual sale of long-stay sites adding to the overall financial pressures.

2.5 Expansion in activity

Whilst there have been increases in the productivity of the NHS through reducing the average length of stay and increasing the number of day cases, the expansion in the total number of inpatients treated by 2.4 per cent per year, and of day cases by 5.8 per cent a year, has also added to total expenditure pressures. Again, the savings at marginal cost in recovery days as the length of stay is reduced, are likely to be more than offset by the higher average cost of the additional treatment time incurred as the total number of patients treated expands.

The net effect of the expansion in activity, the demands for higher cost treatments through new technology and the limited increases in revenue budgets ahead of the specific pay and prices index has been to place increasing pressure on available funds. In some District Health Authorities, this has been compounded by the acquisition of capital assets, such as new general hospitals, as 'free goods' from the Regional Health Authority, without an adequate anticipation of the revenue consequences of running them within the new tighter budgets. In a significant number of authorities, the result has been a restriction on the use of capital resources of beds and operating theatres below their maximum capacity, together with a deferment of expansion plans for future capital facilities (NAHA, 1989).

3. ECONOMIC PERSPECTIVES

This section examines a number of important economic features of the NHS, and their interaction with the financial problems noted above.

3.1 Sensitivity to wage increase

By far the most important economic feature of the NHS in many ways is that it is a *labour intensive* industry. Salaries and wages themselves account for 73 per cent of total HCHS gross revenue expenditure and 68 per cent of total

HCHS expenditure (CIPFA, 1989). The total NHS cost and resource position is therefore very sensitive to changes in the level of these salaries and wages.

Figure 3.6: Indices of average weekly earnings, based on 1979 = 100

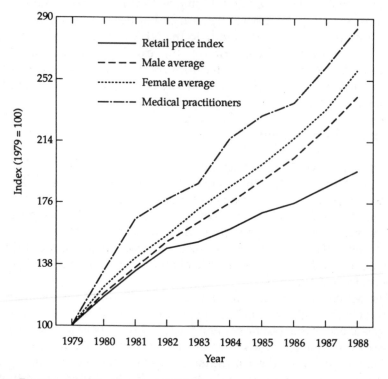

Source: Department of Employment, 1979–88

Across the economy as a whole since 1979, salaries and wages have tended to more than keep pace with general inflation, reflecting a rise in average real earnings in general purchasing power terms. This is illustrated in Figure 3.6. As in Figure 3.7, the salaries and wages of key NHS staff and professionals have also tended to increase ahead of the retail price index, reflecting in part the growth in real earnings that has occurred in the economy at large since 1979. In several important cases, such as those of medical practitioners and qualified nurses and midwives, the real increase has been even greater than that for the average of all occupations. With the exception of hospital porters, the earnings of all NHS workers illustrated in Figure 3.7 have more than outpaced general inflation.

3.2   Relative price effect

The increase in the overall level of NHS salaries and wages ahead of general inflation, against the background of a growth in real earnings in the economy at large, is then clearly a major factor in bringing about the rise in the NHS specific pay and prices index ahead of general inflation. This in turn tends to push up the share of GDP at market prices that must be spent on such a labour intensive service in order to maintain output constant. This is particularly so where the scope for *labour productivity growth* tends to be smaller than in manufacturing and similar industries and where the scope for the *substitution of capital for labour* in response to rising real labour costs tends to be limited.

Figure 3.7: Indices of average weekly earnings in the health care sector based on 1979 = 100

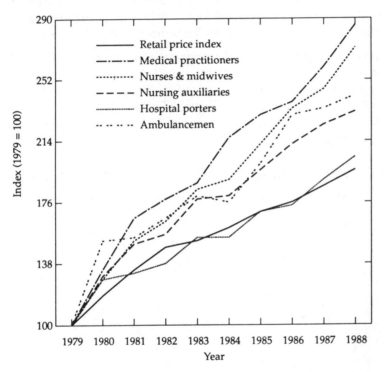

Source: Department of Employment, 1979–88

As in Figures 3.1 to 3.3, increases in NHS funding ahead of general inflation will then not necessarily bring about any increase in real output. Yet this is indeed precisely what we would expect from the *relative price effect* of public expenditure economics (see Baumol, 1967; Brown and Jackson, 1986). As a consequence principally of the arithmetic relations of national income accounting, the relative price per unit of output of a labour intensive service will tend, *ceteris paribus*, to rise with increases in real wages across the economy at large. Changing the structure of the NHS will only be able to overcome this basic economic trend to the extent that re-organisation yields large offsetting increases in the productivity of labour, capital and other resources.

3.3 Demand pressures

The relative price effect and Figures 3.1 to 3.3 more generally imply that any productivity gains or improvements in efficiency that can be cost-effectively obtained become increasingly desirable, as the NHS comes under increasing financial pressure from the relative price effect in any attempt even to maintain existing output constant. There are, of course, strong reasons why simply maintaining existing NHS output constant is itself likely to be an undesirably low policy target, and hence why this financial pressure is likely to become even greater in the future. These are principally two-fold:

i. the demographic trends of an ageing population that will continue beyond the period 1979–1988. As in Figure 3.8, the size of the population over 65 years of age will continue to increase substantially in the coming decades. As in Figure 3.9, the costs imposed on the NHS budget by this older age group are significantly above those of younger age groups.

Figure 3.8: Demographic trends 1986–2025 for England in relevant age groups

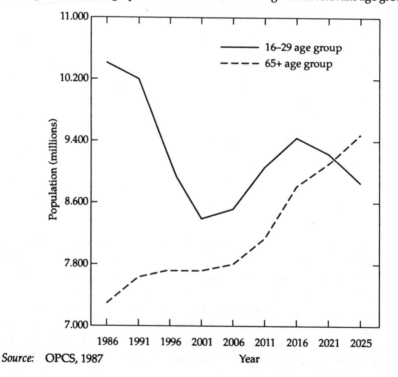

Source: OPCS, 1987

Figure 3.9: Gross current expenditure per head by age group in England

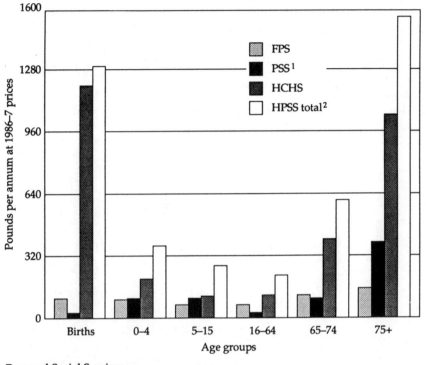

1. Personal Social Services
2. Health and Personal Social Services
Source: H.M. Treasury, 1990

Figure 3.10 shows the effect of applying these cost differences to the changing age structure of the population predicted by the Office of Population Censuses and Surveys (1987). Whilst these rises are substantial, they still on average represent less than a 0.5 per cent annual increase in expenditure demands. However, if one assumes real *per capita* benefits to increase at the same rate as over the earlier period 1974–84, the OECD (1988) have estimated that a 162 per cent increase in real funding of health care in the UK will be required over the period 1980–2040 as a result of the demographic trends, implying an annual average growth rate of some 1.6 per cent per annum.

ii. A large part of this increase in real *per capita* benefits results from advances in medical technology which expand the possibilities of new forms of treatment, though often at a high cost of more resource input from labour, capital equipment and/or expensive drugs. Thus rather than facilitating the substitution of capital for labour, the introduction of more capital equipment, such as CAT scanners, into the NHS may require additional skilled labour both to operate it and to process the additional cases for treatment that the new technology can detect. Whilst technological change has been estimated in recent years by the DHSS to have added 0.5 per cent to HCHS real funding needs, its future impact in precise terms is uncertain, with some potentially significant offsetting factors, such as the development of more healthy life-styles.

Figure 3.10: The effect of demographic trends on current expenditure in England

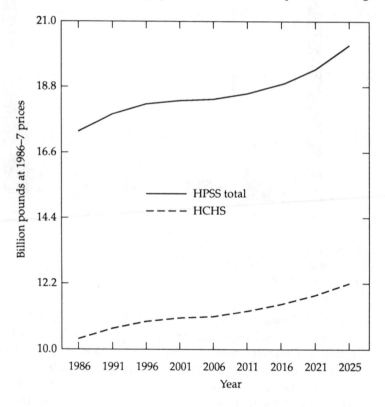

3.4 Willingness to pay

In identifying existing sources of inefficiency in the NHS, or scope for further efficiency improvements, one must be careful to distinguish those apparent inefficiencies which are induced by problems in funding pay settlements from those which are not due to these problems. When the relative price effect is combined with a governmental demand and willingness to pay for labour and for funding pay settlements that is not completely inelastic, the pressure for higher wages and salaries in the NHS will be met by an under-funding of these settlements compared to that necessary to maintain the labour force at its existing level.

Individual hospitals and DHAs, when faced with the budgets that are associated with such a funding situation, will then tend to find themselves with a mixture of an inability to hire as many staff as previously, cutbacks in service levels, and their planned budgets used up before the financial year-end, with resultant financial deficits. This itself will tend to lead to ward closures, longer waiting lists, under-utilisation of operating theatres and an under-working of existing specialised staff, particularly towards the financial year-end.

3.5 Future levels of funding

An assessment of the direction that policy actions should take in the face of the above problems and opportunities will depend upon the amount of funding likely to be available across the system as a whole. If it will be sufficient to maintain or improve existing service levels, then the above short-run inefficiencies due to a temporary under-funding of pay settlements can be removed relatively straight-forwardly. If it will be insufficient, then ward closures may become more permanent and a general rationalisation of capacity required to achieve efficiency at the new level of real funding. Again the relative price effect implies that, *ceteris paribus*, funding will have to increase ahead of the general price index in order simply to maintain output, unless substantial improvements in labour productivity are going to occur at the same time.

3.6 Labour and capital inputs

An important further economic feature of the NHS is that of the *complementarity* which exists between the productivity of different resource inputs, including labour, capital and medical supplies. As in reducing length of stay, some increase in labour productivity, in terms of the numbers of patients treated, may be possible. However, the productivity of capital resources, such as NHS operating theatres, depends critically upon the availability of labour in each of the required categories. The National Audit Office study (1987) on theatre utilisation found one major cause of low utilisation rates to be that of cancelled sessions due to staffing difficulties. The financial consequences for revenue budgets of increased theatre utilisation were also cited by several DHAs as a reason for not increasing the current rates of theatre utilisation.

Complications arise in the NHS due to short-run responses to under-funding of pay settlements and differences in labour market pressures, service priorities, capital endowments and the age structures and geographical dispersion of the local population that exist in different parts of the country. Variations in such published NHS *performance indicators* as waiting lists and length of stay over the country as a whole will not necessarily be reliable indicators of the extent of existing inefficiencies and of the scope for future improvements in outputs without additional resources.

Whilst techniques exist (see Mayston and Jesson 1988; Mayston *et al*, 1987) to identify the extent of such feasible improvements, given adequate data, the NHS represents one of the most complicated areas for drawing such conclusions. This is particularly so given the large number of relevant variables and parameters that are typically involved in different NHS services, and about which adequate data are often not readily available. This problem is discussed at greater length in Smith (1989), using the example of maternity services.

3.7 Improved resource management

Nevertheless there is evidence that, given sufficient staffing availability and revenue funding, the improved management of the key capital resources of NHS beds and theatres can substantially increase NHS output and productivity. Thus Bath DHA has been able to achieve a 32 per cent increase in the rate of elective admissions and a 24 per cent increase in the use of scheduled theatre operating time through the use of bed managers, with similar examples to be found elsewhere (NAO, 1987).

In other cases, there may be substantial savings in revenue expenditure possible through the improved utilisation of the NHS estate. Thus one study in Merton and Sutton found revenue savings from estate rationalisation of the order of £300 million to £500 million a year if applied on a national basis (NAO, 1988). The issues involved in the improved management of capital resources in the NHS are further discussed in Chapter 5 of this book. The importance of such improved utilisation of NHS capital assets can be seen when considered alongside the existing Cost Improvement Programmes in the NHS, shown in Table 3.5 below.

Table 3.5: Cost Improvement Programmes

	1986–7 Achieved (£m)	1987–8 Achieved (£m)	1988–9 Planned (£m)
Rationalisation of patient services	31.9	35.4	50.6
Competitive tendering	39.4	35.4	43.2
Other reductions in labour costs	33.4	3.6	8.1
Rayner Scrutiny savings	6.7	10.2	8.8
Supply cost savings	10.4	8.5	10.1
Energy savings	11.7	29.1	36.4
Other savings	19.8	30.6	12.1
TOTAL	153.3	152.8	169.4

Source: DoH, 1989b

There are two notable features of such Cost Improvement Programmes. The first is that they may well be subject after some point to a *law of diminishing returns*, whereby the most easily obtainable cost improvements are reaped early on and remaining further cost improvements become increasingly difficult to achieve without reducing patient services. A recent King's Fund Institute study (1989) has also argued that the precise magnitude and impact on service levels of existing Cost Improvement Programmes have been insufficiently monitored to conclude that they have all been achieved with no effect on service levels.

Finding new sources of revenue savings, such as through estate rationalisation, is likely to become of increasing importance whenever these can maintain or enhance existing service levels. Again this is likely to be particularly so in the face of a specific pay and prices index that tends to increase faster than the general price level.

The second, and in many ways most important, feature of such new annual Cost Improvements is that they are relatively small in size, totally only about £150 million a year nationally, and equivalent to only 1.3 per cent of the annual HCHS revenue budget. More importantly in the present context is the fact that *it would require only a 1.9 per cent annual increase in the salaries and wages bill of the NHS to completely eliminate these new annual cost improvements resulting from greater internal efficiencies.* Clearly, over time, the significance of such annual cost improvement programmes becomes cumulatively greater. However, so too does the impact of accumulated wage increases on the NHS wages and salaries bill, so that a total increase of less than 9.5 per cent in the NHS wages and salaries bill would completely offset the cumulative total of Cost Improvement Programmes of £778 million estimated to have been achieved up until April 1989.

3.8 Demographic trends

What happens in the labour market, and the impact of the proposed NHS reforms on the labour market, remain of paramount importance to the future financial position of the NHS, and to its ability to deliver patient services out of any given level of funding. This conclusion becomes of even greater importance when the influence of demographic factors is taken into account. As in Figure 3.8, the coming decades, and especially the 1990s, will see a dramatic fall in the population of the 16–29 year old age group from whom many recruits for the NHS labour force, particularly nursing staff, are drawn. The demographic change becomes even more dramatic when viewed against the accompanying rise in the 65 year-old-and-over age group, with the ratio between the two populations dropping from 1.43 in 1986 to 0.93 in 2025.

3.9 Increased competition

As in Enthoven (1985), there may be a strong case for an appropriate form of increased competition in an NHS internal market that can achieve gains from specialisation, improved use of capital assets and a reduction in inefficiencies where these do exist. In principle this is in line with the proposals in the NHS Review (Cm. 555) for a separation of the purchaser and provider roles for DHAs and their supplying unit hospitals.

However, the number of local hospital suppliers for acute services in many areas is often small and typically much fewer than the number of residential homes for elderly patients. The separation of purchaser and provider roles for acute care will then typically involve more problems of *bilateral monopoly* than in the case of the market for residential care for the elderly. Fortunately, the NHS White Paper (para. 3.9) recognises the problems of such a local monopoly, though their solution may need detailed price regulation that will require careful implementation.

However, competition in the *product market* must be distinguished analytically from competition in the *labour market*. The only direct reference that the NHS White Paper makes to the all-important labour market is by proposing increased labour market competition through abandoning any requirement for self-governing hospitals to adhere to national pay agreements. Rather they will 'be free to settle the pay and conditions of their staff, including doctors, nurses and others covered by national pay review bodies. Subject to their contractual obligations, NHS Hospital Trusts will be free either to continue to follow national pay agreements or to adopt partly or wholly different arrangements' (para. 3.12).

The following sections assess, from the perspective of economic analysis, the likely financial impact on NHS labour costs of a more competitive labour market. Given that expenditure on the NHS itself accounts for some 15.9 per cent of all central government expenditure, this question is of interest not just for the real future funding position of the NHS but also for the control and management of public expenditure at large.

4.   THE GAINS FROM MONOPSONY

As in Figure 3.11, we will assume a linear total supply curve for such labour, of the form

$$L_s = -a + b.\hat{w} \tag{1}$$

where L_s is the total supply of labour to the health care sector, a and b are positive constants, and $\hat{w}$ is the total reward per unit of labour supply. In order to allow for the possibility of any differential willingness of medical and nursing staff to work in either the public or private health care sectors at a given monetary wage, we will assume

$$\hat{w} = w_N + s \tag{2}$$

where w_N is the monetary reward which the health care worker receives in the NHS and s ($\lessgtr 0$) is the extent of any additional non-pecuniary satisfaction that a health care worker receives through working in the NHS rather than in the private sector.

Equilibrium in the labour market will require an equalisation of net rewards between the public and private sectors, that is

$$\hat{w} = w_p = w_N + s \qquad (3)$$

where w_p is the monetary reward paid to a health care worker in the private sector. The wage variables will be measured here in real inflation-adjusted terms, that is after deflation by a relevant cost-of-living index, such as the Retail Price Index.

Before the implementation of the NHS Review, the private sector is taken to be a small part of the total demand for health care labour, with the NHS acting as a leader in the determination of health care wages and the private sector as follower. The demand for health care labour from the private sector, L_p, is assumed to be a decreasing linear function of the private sector unit cost of labour, w_p, and associated unit costs, k_p, of associated medical supplies and capital equipment, with

$$L_p = \alpha - \beta.(w_p + k_p) - \theta.Q_N \qquad (4)$$

where α, β, and θ are positive parameters. The private sector demand for health care labour is also assumed here to be a decreasing linear function of the quality-adjusted magnitude of the supply, Q_N, of health care made available by the NHS. Thus any reduction in the quality-adjusted supply of health care available to patients through the NHS will tend to boost demand for private sector health care. As we shall examine in more detail later, the magnitude of the parameter θ will reflect in part the cross-elasticity of demand for private sector health care with respect to the supply of health care in real terms made available by the government, both in quantity and quality terms. A fall in either the quantity of NHS health care made available, as measured by the numbers of patients treated, or its quality, will then tend to increase the demand to the private sector to an extent that is reflected in the size of the parameter θ.

The size of this parameter itself is likely to be increased by any greater introduction of user charges into the NHS that reduce the differential between the direct cost to the patient of treatment in the NHS compared to the private sector. In addition, the size of θ will also depend upon any differences in the labour-output ratio in the private sector compared to the NHS, as discussed below.

In order to calculate the supply of labour function facing the NHS, we need to net off the private sector demand for health care labour from the total supply of health care labour function. Thus at any given level of the total unit reward, $\hat{w}$, to health care labour, the total supply of health care labour to the NHS, L_N, is equal to the difference between the total supply of health care labour, L_s, to both sectors and the demand, L_p, for health care labour absorbed by the private sector at the corresponding unit wage w_p in (3) and (4), that is

$$L_N = L_s - L_p = n.Q_N \qquad (5)$$

The second equality of (5) reflects the assumed relationship between the supply of labour to the NHS and the resultant output of health care, Q_N, that the NHS is able to produce from this labour. The positive constant, n, in (5) equals the labour–output ratio in the NHS, being the reciprocal of the average productivity of NHS labour in producing health care output.

Before the implementation of the NHS Review proposals, the dominant position of the NHS as an employer of health care labour may give it an effective monopsony position which implies that it must take into account the effect of its actions on the equilibrium level of wages in the health care labour market. It must then take into account in its hiring and wage determination decisions not just the wage, w_N, that it must pay a marginal employee, but rather the total marginal cost of hiring an additional employee. This latter term reflects the increase in the total NHS wage bill $w_N.L_N$ of marginal changes in labour usage by the NHS, given by

$$MCL_N = \frac{\delta(w_N.L_N)}{\delta L_N} = w_N + L_N.\frac{\delta w_N}{\delta L_N} \qquad (6)$$

being equal to not simply the wage, w_N, but also the additional wage, $\delta w_N / \delta L_N$, required to attract additional employees that must be paid to each of the existing labour force under a uniform wage constraint. Since the existing labour force of the NHS is large by any standards, at 789,000 whole time equivalents in the HCHS in England alone, including 392,000 nurses, the second term of (6) represents a significant additional consideration in NHS finance.

From equations (1) to (5), we may show that

$$w_N = \frac{(1 - \theta/n).\, L_N + v_o}{(b + \beta)} - s \qquad (7)$$

where $v_o = a + \alpha - \beta.k_p$

being the equation of the (linear) supply of labour curve, S_N, facing the NHS, as in Figure 3.11. We will assume initially that θ/n is strictly less than one. The significance of this assumption, and of its relaxation, will be discussed below. From equations (6) and (7), we have also

$$MCL_N = \frac{2.(1 - \theta/n).L_N + v_o}{(b + \beta)} - s \qquad (8)$$

as the marginal cost of labour curve facing the NHS. As in Figure 3.11, MCL_N in equation (8) has the same vertical intercept but twice the slope as the NHS labour supply curve, S_N, implied by equation (7).

Figure 3.11: The NHS labour market

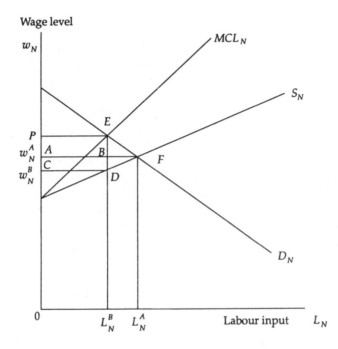

The *demand* for NHS labour will be taken to be a decreasing (linear) function of the wage, w_N, together with any additional costs, k_N, of capital equipment, drug and other supplies associated with the use of health care in the NHS, as in equation (10) below. The effective demand for NHS labour is taken to be derived from the Government's willingness to pay for NHS health care, with an associated governmental demand curve given by

$$Q_N = c - g.u_N \quad \text{where} \quad u_N = (w_N.n + k_N) \qquad (9)$$

where c and g are positive constants and u_N is the total unit cost of NHS health care. From the second equality of (5) we have then the derived demand for NHS labour to be given by

$$L_N^D = c.n - g.n.k_N - g.n^2.w_N \qquad (10)$$

As noted above, w_N and k_N are measured here in real terms, after deflation by any changes in the general price level. Unless there are accompanying changes in the parameters c and g, equations (9) and (10) imply a willingness by the Government to fund monetary wage rises in the NHS in line with *general* inflation, without reductions in staffing levels. Any unwillingness by the Government to fund fully NHS wage rises that simply keep pace with general inflation, as measured by the retail price index, would imply a fall in the value of the intercept parameter c in equations (9) and (10) above.

When it comes to wage increases that are ahead of general inflation, such as have indeed occurred in recent years (see Figures 3.6 and 3.7 above), the responsiveness of government funding to such pay settlements is determined by the parameter g in our above analysis. A low value to g (viz. $g < L_N/w_N.n^2$) implies an inelastic governmental demand for NHS labour, so that higher NHS wages ahead of general inflation would lead to some increase in the total NHS wage bill in real terms and to increased funding from government ahead of the general price level. However, so long as g is positive, this increased funding would not be to the extent necessary to maintain the (government-funded) demand for NHS labour constant in the face of any NHS wage rise that exceeds the general rate of inflation. The result will then be an effective under-funding of any real NHS wage increase, at the given initial size of the labour force, and some required fall in staffing levels.

When the NHS is able to exercise monopsony power in the labour market, equilibrium is achieved in the basic analysis at point E in Figure 3.11. At point E, the willingness to pay, w_N, along the NHS labour demand curve in Figure 3.11 and equation (10), is equated to MCL_N in Figure 3.11 and equation (8). The effective demand for NHS labour is then L_N^B, which in turn equals the willing supply of labour to the NHS at the corresponding wage level w_N^B.

The pre-Review equilibrium, E, may then be compared with the competitive situation which might be expected to prevail after the implementation of the NHS Review proposals. These proposals include in particular a substantial number of 'opted-out' self-governing Hospital Trusts competing with one another for the available health care labour, and 'free to settle the pay and conditions of their staff, including doctors, nurses and others [currently] covered by national pay review bodies' (DoH, 1989, para. 3.12).

Each such self-governing hospital acting alone would represent only a small part of the total health care labour market. In particular, it would find that at the initial level of labour usage, L_N^B, in Figure 3.11, its funded willingness to pay for additional health care, as reflected in the total demand curve D_N, would exceed the pre-Review level of health care wages, w_N^B. Since it can neglect the effect of its own actions on the general equilibrium of the whole health care labour market, of which it is only a small part, it has then an incentive to seek to hire more health care labour. Since the same is true for all such self-governing hospitals, they will all seek to do so up until the point where the funded willingness to pay for an additional unit of health care labour equals the wage that each self-governing hospital must pay to obtain it.

Unless central control is exerted to the contrary, this process would be expected to lead to a new competitive equilibrium in the NHS labour market where supply, S_N, and demand, D_N, are equated at point F in Figure 3.11. This will then be at a new higher equilibrium wage level, w_N^A, but also greater use, L_N^A, for NHS labour compared to the monopsony position E.

It should be noted that competition in the product market, in the form of the supply of health care, will not itself prevent the attainment of such a higher competitive wage in the labour market. The monopsony ability of the NHS without strong competition in the labour market to maintain wages at a lower level represents a *public good* for the finances of all its constituent hospitals. Under free competition in the labour market, each hospital acting alone has an incentive to hire more labour, as above, and to neglect the effect of its own actions on the level of wages in the market as a whole, of which it is only a small part. In other words, as in standard welfare economics the public good, here of wage restraint, will be under-supplied in a de-centralised competitive equilibrium with each individual economic agent acting alone.

The effects on the supply of labour to the NHS and to the private sector are shown in Figure 3.12 below. The increase in the NHS wage from w_N^B to w_N^A increases the supply of NHS labour along the supply curve S_N facing the NHS and increases the total supply of health care labour along the total supply curve S given by equation (1).

As in equations (1) and (4), the rise in w_N raises the wage level, w_p, that the private sector must pay to compete with the NHS and, *ceteris paribus*, reduces the demand to the private sector in equation (4). This is reflected in Figure 3.12 in a reduction in the gap, from $h_0 k_0$ to $h_1 k_1$, between the total supply of health care labour and that offered to the NHS, *thereby reducing the relative size of the private health care sector as a result of the abandonment of NHS monopsony power*. However, this effect would be counteracted by any accompanying fall in governmental demand and funding for the NHS in real terms, as reflected in a downward shift in the demand curve, D_N, for NHS labour in Figure 3.12, that would increase this gap, such as from $h_1.k_1$ to $h_3.k_3$.

We can next examine the net gain to the NHS from its monopsony position at E compared to the new post-Review competitive equilibrium at F. As in Figure 3.11, this will equal

$$Z = ABCD - BEF \qquad (11)$$

where $ABCD$ is the saving in the NHS wage bill for the initial quantity, L_N^B, of labour it employs due to the wage differential AC between the competitive wage, OA, and its monopsonistic level, OC. The small triangle BEF reflects the 'deadweight loss', or foregone benefit, of additional health care labour, $L_N^A - L_N^B$ that would be hired by the NHS in the competitive equilibrium F but not at the monopsonistic equilibrium E. This is valued in BEF at the excess of the Government's willingness to pay for such additional health care labour, as reflected in its demand curve, D_N, over the competitive wage it has to pay for this additional labour in the new competitive equilibrium F.

Figure 3.12: The market for health care labour

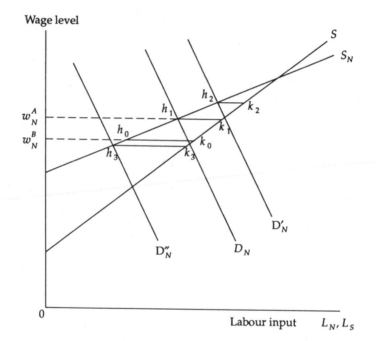

As in the Appendix, we may show that $Z > 0$, that is the gain to the NHS from its monopsonistic position under the above assumptions is positive. Hence the erosion of its monopsony power under the above proposals would lead to a positive loss, equal in magnitude to Z, that would need to be more than offset by positive gains from other NHS Review proposals, such as will be examined in Section 5 below. Such a positive value to Z also implies from equation (11) that the rise, $ABCD$, in the NHS wage bill exceeds the positive magnitude BEF. There is no guarantee in general that this rise in labour costs as a result of the loss of monopsony power will be limited to only 1.9 per cent of the existing wage bill. The offsetting efficiency gains would then need to be greater in magnitude than those so far obtained under the annual Cost Improvement Programmes.

5. COMPARATIVE STATICS

As noted above, there are a number of important trends operating in the health care sector, both independently and as reinforced by the NHS Review proposals, that will have an impact on Z, the loss due to the erosion of monopsony power in the NHS. These include:

i. an expanding demand for health care over the coming years, in response to both demographic trends and advances in treatment, as noted in Section 2 above. This will be reflected in the above supply and demand analysis by an increase in the demand parameter c in equations (9) and (10), whenever at least part of this additional demand is met through an expansion in government funding and planned output for the NHS at a given level of NHS wages. As in equation (A.12) of the Appendix, we may show that the gain from monopsony is an increasing function of c, this demand shift parameter. Hence, *ceteris paribus*, losing the existing monopsony power of the NHS will become increasingly costly as the demand for health care rises.

ii. an improvement in the planned efficiency of the NHS and a consequent reduction in its 'organisational slack' (Cyert and March, 1964) or X–inefficiency (Leibenstein, 1966). To the extent that these organisational improvements are reflected in a fall in the non-labour unit cost parameter k_N in equation (9) above, there will be a consequent increase in the magnitude of Z, as in equation (A.13) of the Appendix. Hence, *ceteris paribus*, losing the existing monopsony power of the NHS will become increasingly costly with a reduction in non-labour unit costs that permits an expansion of the supply of health care within any given initial budget.

iii. an increased commercial orientation of the health care sector and a reduction of the public service ethic, which in the above analysis would be reflected in a fall in the parameter s in equation (2). As in equation (A.14) of the Appendix, this would tend to erode the magnitude of Z.

iv. a fall in the supply of key health care labour, including nursing staff, as the demographic trends shown in Figure 3.8 above work their way through the 16–29 age group, from whom a large proportion of nursing staff are traditionally recruited. This would be reflected here in an inward shift in the total supply of health care labour function (1) and a rise in the intercept parameter a. As in equation (A.14) of the Appendix, this then tends to reduce the value of Z. When this trend is occurring at the same time as the above increase in the demand for health care, whether the *net effect* is to increase Z can be shown to depend upon whether the ratio of the size of the increase in c to the size of the increase in a over time exceeds the ratio of $g.n$ to the sum of the public and private sector slopes of the labour supply functions with respect to wage rises, that is whether

$$\frac{dc}{dt} \Big/ \frac{da}{dt} > \frac{gn}{b + \beta} \qquad (12)$$

as in equation (A.16) of the Appendix.

Whilst the above discussion has concentrated on the effect on the total benefit to the NHS from its existing monopsony power, directly parallel results can be shown to hold for the impact of the above changes on the wage bill for the existing staff that such a loss of monopsony power would bring, as in equation (A.17) of the Appendix.

It can be seen from the above discussion that some factors, such as the expected increase in the demand for health care and increases in organisational efficiency, are tending to increase the size of the advantage Z that is derived from the pre-Review monopsony power. However, other factors, such as the projected fall in key labour supply, may tend to reduce the absolute magnitude of Z. Whilst, as in Figure 3.11, Z is zero when the NHS supply of health care labour curve is infinitely elastic, Z remains positive for any finite positive value to the parameters b and β in equations (1) and (4), causing any loss of NHS monopsony power to remain a subject for concern in any attempt at cost containment for the NHS.

6. ADDITIONAL LABOUR MARKET CONSIDERATIONS

In order for the NHS Review to produce net gains, the loss of Z must be offset by positive efficiency gains elsewhere. These may be achieved from several different sources.

6.1 Local variability

The first of these is greater variability in local wages to match differences in local supply and demand conditions for medical and support staff.

As in Figures 3.13 and 3.14 below, there will be some initial service gains to the NHS from expanding labour use to the point where supply and demand are equated at the local competitive wage. In Figure 3.13, the local supply and conditions for the self-governing hospital i are taken to be such that the local competitive wage, w_i^c, is *less than* the monopsonistically determined national wage, w_N^B. At the nationally negotiated wage rate, w_N^B, the local demand for labour was L_i^B. At the lower competitive level this expands to L_{ij}^C yielding an increased service benefit of TUV. In addition in Figure 3.13 there is a fall in the wage bill of $GHUT$.

However, since the average national competitive wage, w_N^A, in Figure 3.11 is higher than the monopsonistically determined national wage, w_N^B, we would also expect in a significant number of locations that the local competitive wage is *higher than* the monopsonistically determined national wage, as it is for hospital j in Figure 3.14. Here at the lower nationally determined wage, w_N^B, hospital j initially finds itself with a demand for health care labour that exceeds the willing supply, by an amount equal to $L_j^D - L_j^B$.

Figure 3.13: *A locality where the national uniform wage, w_N^B, exceeds the local competitive wage, w_i^C*

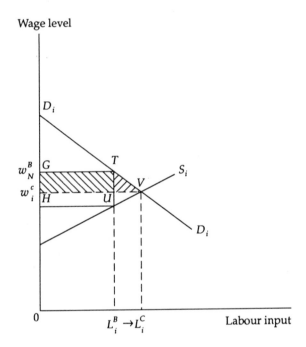

When the wage rises to the local competitive level w_i^C, this has the effect of not only increasing the local supply of health care labour but also of reducing the demand for health care labour that the hospital can afford to finance out of its available budget, which in turn is derived from NHS (cash-limited) willingness to pay for the treatment of patients. Its use of labour then expands only to L_j^C, rather than L_j^D, with a resultant service benefit of *tuv* in Figure 3.14. However against this must be offset the rise in the wage bill for hospital j of *zyhu* that is likely to more than offset the service gain *tuv*, at least measured in terms of the governmental willingness to pay for improved health care provision.

Competition in Health Care

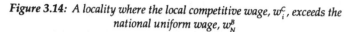

Figure 3.14: *A locality where the local competitive wage, w^c_i, exceeds the national uniform wage, w^B_N*

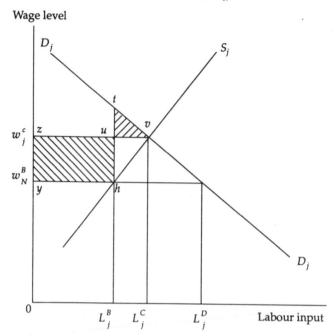

Moreover one must be careful here to avoid double-counting these local gains and losses from local changes in labour use and wage bills with the national changes already taken into account in the computation of Z above. The summation of the local changes from competition in the labour market can be shown to equal the national changes, of the loss Z from losing the national monopsony power, plus a gain Y that to some extent offsets the loss Z. The gain Y results from the additional local flexibility that local competition gives over and above the national average competitive wage w^A_N of Figure 3.11. This gain may be shown to equal

$$Y = \tfrac{1}{2}\sum_i (L^C_i - L^B_i).(P_i - P - f_i) \quad \text{where} \quad f_i = w^c_i - w^A_N \qquad (13)$$

where P_i is the local willingness to pay for additional health care labour at the pre-Review monopsony wage, as determined by the local demand curve, and P the corresponding national demand price in Figure 3.11. L^B_i and L^C_i are the local pre- and post-Review use of labour respectively, and w^c_i is the post-Review local competitive wage.

The flexibility for local competitive wage determination after the implementation of the Review, when a significant number of hospitals will have become self-governing, involves a wage differential of f_i for locality i compared to the post-Review national average wage, w^A_N. This wage differential will be positive in some localities, that is those with large initial excess demand for health care labour, and negative in others. Y then reflects the gain to all localities $i = 1, .., M$ from its flexibility to hire additional labour in excess of the national average willingness to pay, and in excess of the wage differential, f_i, that locality i must pay in comparison to the average national wage to attract this additional labour.

The fact that f_i will tend to be greater in those localities where P_i is large compared to P suggests that the overall size of this local flexibility gain Y may not be strongly positive. In areas of a comparative plentiful supply of labour, the differential, f_i, compared to the average national wage will be negative, and P_i may also then be less than the national pre-Review demand price P. Again the overall size of Y may not be strongly positive.

In addition, a large part of the benefits of local flexibility in response to variations in local supply and demand conditions may well still be obtainable from a system of regional, or sub-regional, guidelines for wage variations determined collectively for all NHS hospitals in the region, or sub-region, whilst still retaining a large element of monopsony power.

6.2 Gains to the labour force

What is capable of offsetting Z is the inclusion of the gains to health care workers from the increased wages and labour use which abandonment of the pre-Review monopsony power would imply. Thus in Figure 3.11 the wage increase of $ABCD$ that the NHS must pay represents a transfer to the labour force, with an additional gain to the labour force of BDF from greater employment and a competitive wage w_N^A paid for these additional hours in excess of the supply price required. When these are included, there is no longer a net loss from relaxing the monopsony power, but rather a positive gain of DEF.

However, it can be seen that there is then a conflict between the objective of cost containment for the NHS, from which the taxpayer is likely to gain, and the inclusion of gains to the work-force from higher wages. A social cost-benefit analysis might put potentially unequal weights on the benefits accruing to each group, with some then offset to Z from any positive weight placed upon the above gains to the labour force. However, if our prime objective remains that of cost containment, Z remains a positive loss from relaxing monopsony power that must be made up from gains elsewhere.

6.3 Countervailing power

A third factor that must be taken into account is the strength of countervailing monopoly power by unionised labour. The precise strength of such countervailing power may indeed vary between the group of health care workers involved. Nurses following a no-strike ethic may exert much less countervailing power than the doctors' union, in the form of the British

Medical Association. To the extent that the latter is able to exert countervailing monopoly power, the theory of bilateral monopoly (see Gravelle and Rees, 1981, pp. 382–398) predicts that the quantity of labour supplied will be equal to that in a competitive situation, as at point L_N^C in Figure 3.15, but with the precise wage determined by their relative bargaining strength. If this were at the competitive level w_N^C in Figure 3.15, the gain to the NHS from its *monopsony power* would result from its ability to prevent the loss of the shaded area in Figure 3.15 that it would otherwise suffer from the *monopoly power* of the BMA or other health service unions. This shaded area results firstly from the additional wage bill it would have to pay on the labour, L_N^M, it would still hire at the higher monopoly wage, w_m. In addition, it results from the loss of service benefit it would suffer from being able to afford less labour under the monopoly outcome, compared to the outcome L_N^C under bilateral monopoly.

Figure 3.15: Bilateral monopoly in the NHS labour market

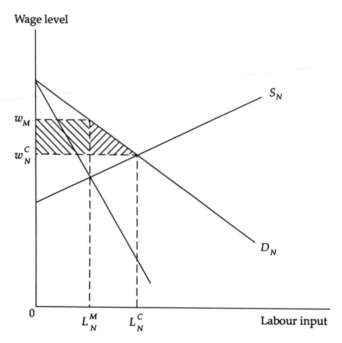

Avoiding the loss of this shaded area again represents a positive gain to the NHS so long as it *does* retain its monopsony power. So long as the countervailing power of the monopsony is positive, so that the final wage deal under the bilateral monopoly is strictly preferred by the NHS to that under unilateral monopoly, there will be a positive gain from the monopsony power of the NHS. Giving up this monopsony power would then involve a corresponding positive loss to the NHS in financial and service benefit terms.

6.4 Non-pecuniary factors

We have included within our labour supply function in equations (1) and (2) a term s which may be positive, negative or zero, to reflect any non-pecuniary satisfaction which health care workers derive from working in the NHS compared to elsewhere. That s may be positive is suggested by a recent study from the Institute of Manpower Studies (1987) which found that the average amount of unpaid overtime supplied by NHS nurses in the survey exceeded one hour a day, suggesting a willingness within the NHS to supply labour at less than the going wage outside. Any reduction in the value of s through a decline in such social motivation would then have a monetary consequence for the size of the NHS wage bill to maintain the labour supply at its former level, with the value of such unpaid overtime in excess of £100 million a year, and comparable in size to the total annual Cost Improvement Programmes.

6.5 Changing working practices

A key question also arises as to the extent to which less well-qualified nursing staff can be partially substituted for the existing standard of nursing staff without loss of quality of patient care. With the projected 18 per cent fall in the total available 16–29 year old population from 1991 to 2001, this question will become of increasing importance during the 1990s. To the extent that they can be substituted, and this has not already taken place, it corresponds to a partial outward shift in the supply of labour curve that can offset to some extent the inward shift due to demographic changes.

However also important here is the question of whether this partial outward shift due to changed working practices will be encouraged at any given wage level by greater competition in the labour market, or could be achieved whilst retaining some degree of monopsony power for the NHS in the labour market. There is a case for arguing that the bargaining power of NHS management in bringing about such changes in working practices will be greater if the management can bargain as a collective entity in negotiations with the Royal College of Nursing. Much of the pressure for changes in working practices may arise in any case through competition on price in the product market between different hospitals, combined with the above demographic pressures. The size of union resistance to such change will also depend upon the extent to which there are opportunities for relieving existing qualified staff of more onerous and less expert tasks.

6.6 Stability considerations

Before turning to the sources of other possible efficiency gains, we may now note the significance of our earlier assumption that θ/n is less than one. From equation (4), we have

$$\theta/n = \frac{-\delta L_p}{\delta Q_N} \cdot \frac{1}{n} = \frac{m}{n} \cdot Q_{pN} \qquad (14)$$

where m is the labour–output ratio in the private health care sector. The term Q_{pN} equals the increase in the demand for private sector health care which results from a unit fall in the available supply of NHS health care. When the available supply of NHS health care is high, both in terms of quantity and quality of care, we would expect Q_{pN} to be relatively small, given the price differential from private insurance premiums or user charges that faces a marginal private health care user compared to a user who relies upon the NHS. Under such circumstances, unless the labour–output ratio, m, in private sector health care is substantially greater than the labour–output ratio, n, in the NHS, our earlier condition that (14) is less that one will be satisfied.

The case where θ/n is precisely equal to one will occur if there is an identical labour–output ratio in both sectors and Q_{pN} is equal to one, that is a fall in the supply of NHS health care available leads to an equal off-setting rise in the demand for private health care as consumers transfer between the two. In these circumstances a fall in the demand for health care labour by the NHS would lead to an equal and offsetting rise for health care labour by the private sector. In such a case, the supply of labour curve facing the NHS, that is S_N in Figure 3.11 and equation (7), becomes perfectly horizontal. The NHS is then effectively a price-taker in the labour market and the gain, Z, from monopsony power would be equal to zero.

A similar result would indeed occur in equation (7) above, whatever the value of θ/n, if the sum $(b + \beta)$ becomes infinite. This would result either from a perfectly elastic total supply of labour to the health care sector, with b then tending to infinity in equation (1) above, or from a perfectly elastic demand for private health care with respect to price increases, with β then tending to infinity in equation (4) above. In both cases the NHS would face a horizontal supply of labour curve, with a zero value to Z, the gain from monopsony power in the NHS labour market.

In general, however, we would expect a finite value to both elasticities, and hence to $(b + \beta)$ in equation (7) above. A problem then arises if θ/n exceeds unity. In such a case, the supply curve facing the NHS in equation (7) would take on a negative slope, causing potential problems in the attainment and maintenance of a competitive equilibrium.

The circumstances under which θ/n will exceed unity, from equation (14), would include those where the labour–output ratio in the private health care sector exceeds that in the NHS and Q_{pN} is greater than or equal to one. The condition of Q_{pN} exceeding one will indeed occur if there is a tendency for patients und r private insurance to receive more tests, medication and/or surgery than would be the case under a quantity-constrained NHS in which doctors have no financial incentive to encourage such additional resource use.

A higher labour–output ratio, m, in the private sector than that, n, in the NHS might arise because of more nursing and medical attention per patient treated for a given case-mix. The likelihood of this condition occuring may increase with any future fall in the real level of NHS funding compared to the greater demands being made upon it by demographic trends. This might then cause the available health care labour to be spread more thinly over patients in the NHS than the staffing levels enjoyed by the private sector.

If θ/n does exceed one over some range, then potential problems arise in the labour market successfully attaining or maintaining a competitive equilibrium, since such a value to θ/n will cause the supply of labour function facing the NHS in equation (7) to slope downwards. In particular, when the supply of labour function facing the NHS cuts the NHS demand for labour curve from below, as in Figure 3.16, any initial wage level above the level w_N^c, at which the supply and demand curves intersect, will be associated with an excess demand for labour by the NHS.

Figure 3.16: Cost escalation in the NHS labour market

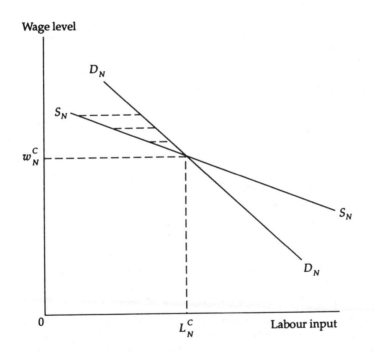

Under competition between hospitals for labour, such excess demand for labour will tend to raise the prevailing wage level still further, tending to move the labour market away from the intersection wage w_N^c. The process may then continue until a new equilibrium is achieved at some higher wage level at which the value of Q_{pN} drops sufficiently far in equation (14) to make

θ/n again less than unity. Such a fall in Q_{pN} would be associated with a lack after some point of any further economic mobility of patients into the private sector at the new higher level of wages and private insurance premiums.

In contrast, retaining the monopsony power of the NHS would enable it to select the point along the supply curve it found most advantageous. A lower wage under monopsony would then have the *self-reinforcing* advantages of avoiding the above labour cost escalation, maintaining the ability of the NHS to hire a substantial quantity of labour within its available budget, maintaining a reasonable quality of health care in the NHS, avoiding a labour-absorbing shift of health care demand into the private sector, and facing a greater quantity of labour supply on offer to the NHS than would be the case under greater competition in the labour market. Again this tends to suggest there may be significant advantages to retaining the monopsony power of the NHS in the labour market.

7. POSITIVE EFFICIENCY GAINS

There are a number of sources of positive efficiency gains outside the labour market from which the NHS Review may succeed in reaping substantial benefits.

7.1 Improved management information

The existing Korner initiatives have already generated a substantial increase in the availability of management information to the NHS, compared to the earlier paucity of information in many directions. The proposed separation of the purchaser and provider roles of DHAs and individual unit hospitals, combined with the extension of the Resource Management Initiative, under the NHS Review will bring with it in addition a large increase in the required data on detailed treatment costs.

However for this to be successfully applied will require reliable data that is adequately adjusted for variations in case mix, and can identify marginal as well as average treatment costs. Moreover, for this information to be reliably produced and correctly interpreted will require an increase in the availability of *sufficient qualified* manpower, particularly given CIPFA's recent identification of 'very acute shortages in those skills needed to see through further managerial changes' in the NHS (CIPFA, 1989). Again labour market considerations, in the form of the availability of sufficient qualified manpower at a reasonable price within the implementation time-scale, become paramount in ensuring the successful implementation of this initiative.

The financial memorandum to the recent NHS and Community Care Bill itself estimates the need for some 3,500 additional permanent staff, particularly in information technology, finance and personnel, to implement this and other initiatives. In order to yield a positive return on the estimated additional labour cost of approximately £200 million a year, and associated capital costs of computer hardware and information systems, there will need to be generated annual benefits well in excess of those currently achieved by the annual Cost Improvement Programmes discussed above. The importance of allowing sufficient development time for these benefits to be realisable has been emphasised by the Brunel (1989) evaluation of the initial Resource Management pilot sites.

7.2 Improved utilisation of human capital

A second source of efficiency gain may arise from the greater concentration and improved utilisation of specialised resources, including human capital in the form of specialised skilled manpower. Given the substantial investment of resources that the NHS incurs in training nurses, medical and support staff, a greater return would clearly be desirable from an improved retention rate, particularly for nursing staff where this rate is currently low.

Even if some degree of monopsony power is retained for the NHS, it is clearly important that the long-run elasticity of supply be taken into account in wage determination, in order to achieve an optimal retention rate for specialised staff that yields a maximum feasible return on the investment in their training. In addition, a problem clearly arises concerning who should bear this initial investment cost if the private sector recruits an increasing percentage of NHS-trained nurses and medical staff.

7.3 Improved utilisation of physical capital

Physical capital in the NHS includes operating theatres, CAT scanners and other hospital facilities. However, as stressed above, securing such improved utilisation of such capital resources depends upon achieving a balance in the availability of capital, labour and other revenue resources. This is particularly so where there is a tendency towards a *fixed proportions* technology in the short run, with the availability of specialised labour, such as anaesthetists, being crucial in achieving the maximum productivity of the capital resources invested in operating theatres.

As noted by the National Audit Office report (1987), the cancellation of theatre sessions due to the non-availability of key staff is a prime cause of the low utilisation rate of operating theatres. Achieving improved utilisation rates then depends on maintaining the ability of the NHS to hire specialised labour in sufficient volume within its available budget. However it also requires their subsequent accountability for performing work at the scheduled time, such as through placing consultants contracts more at unit or district level, rather than at regional level as at present.

Given such factors, there is then scope for the improved co-ordination of the inputs of capital, labour and medical supplies through the appointment of theatre and bed managers. In particular, the National Audit Office (1987) estimated that the full utilisation of scheduled theatre time, even within a five day standard working week, 'could have increased throughput by as many as 11,000 operations in a year' in the three specialties and five district health authorities which the NAO examined. However, the achievement of such greater utilisation of existing capital resources and reduced waiting lists may require additional revenue funding, albeit at a reduced average total resource cost per patient treated than if these capital facilities had remained under-utilised.

Figure 3.17: Health care output under a constant capital–labour ratio

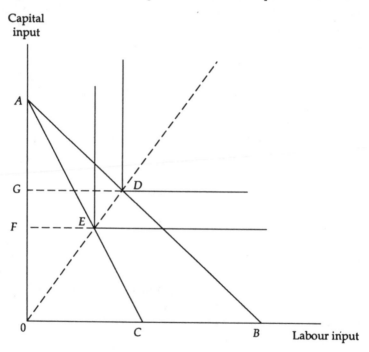

The situation is then consistent with Figure 3.17 above, showing the L-shaped isoquant map of fixed proportions technology in the short-term. Unless it was fully anticipated at the time of initial investment in the capital facilities, the relative price effect will mean a pivoting of the budget line facing the DHA, such as from *AB* to *AC* in Figure 3.17, in the face of a rising relative price of labour.

The optimum feasible production point then shifts down from point *D* to the lower isoquant at point *E*, with excess capacity in the short-run of *FG*. If capital in the specialised facilities involves sunk costs (as defined in Baumol *et al.*, 1982), the slope of the budget line incorporates the cost of maintaining the capital facilities, which is less than the long-run cost of acquiring new capital facilities. Additional output can then be obtained at a positive marginal cost less than average cost by expanding the budget line outwards parallel to AC to restore the original level of output at D.

In addition, securing long-run efficiency in the use of capital resources implies an avoidance of the excess capacity that may be associated with monopolistic competition and unrestricted entry to the health care market. As argued in Chapter 5 below, there is then a case for long-term contracts with assured supply between purchasers and providers to fill the role of *futures markets* that would otherwise be absent from the internal market regime. Without such futures markets or long-term contracts, there will tend to be significantly greater risk placed on investors in new NHS capital resources than would be true even under the system of complete competitive markets envisaged by general equilibrium theory (see Debreu, 1959) in its theorems on market efficiency.

The separation between purchaser and provider roles under the NHS Review also provides the opportunity for DHAs to free themselves from their traditional attachment as providers to a number of historically given sites that may have been accumulated sub-optimally over time. Instead they may with greater freedom seek the least-cost sources of supply from a long-term point of view under such long-term contracts, and have the purchasing muscle to effect accompanying estate rationalisations necessary to achieve this.

Such long-term contracts have the added advantage of avoiding the risk of short-run exposure to price increases by a local monopoly supplier. Under a system of nationally determined wage rates with scope for regional variations, there is much less problem in specifying such long-term contracts than if they were of the cost-plus type with wages set locally. A system of long-term fixed-price contracts in the face of unknown future wage movements determined locally may similarly prove difficult to operate.

In order to accommodate short-term flexibilty to optimise the utilisation rate of the available capital resources, there may also be scope for a Prestel-type of information exchange on capacity availability and short-run variations in demand across the country, within which internal market arrangements may be entered into on a much shorter-run basis as fine tuning to the main long-term contracts between purchasers and providers.

8. CONCLUSIONS

By far the most important element of total NHS costs is that of labour costs. The NHS is therefore particularly susceptible to cost pressure from the *relative price effect*. This implies that an increasing real wage and standard of living for the labour force at large, as measured against the retail price index, will tend to require an increasing proportion of GDP at market prices to be devoted to health care, even to maintain existing output constant.

If the percentage of GDP devoted to health care is to stay at around 6.2 per cent in the UK (compared to 8.1 per cent in West Germany, 8.5 per cent in France and 11.1 per cent in the United States), whilst maintaining quality of care, there is something of a race implied between likely future rises in labour costs and the achievement of planned improvements in productivity.

There is evidence of scope for improvements in productivity, particularly through the improved utilisation of capital resources and rationalisation of the NHS estate. However, such improved utilisation itself depends upon attaining a sufficient supply of specialised staff at a reasonable wage within the total available NHS budget. Under a cash-limited service, there is then an important interaction between rises in labour costs and having sufficient revenue funds to operate capital assets at an efficient level of utilisation.

Whilst greater competition in the health care product market, through the introduction of an internal market, will tend to encourage the improved use of capital assets, greater competition in the labour market will to some extent undermine this process if it results in significant increase in wages ahead of those which are in any case likely to occur. The extent of future wage rises, in comparison to likely increases in NHS funding, is thus of key importance in ensuring the optimal use of scarce capital resources, both for the efficient use of existing capital assets and for the productiveness of new capital investment. The improved utilisation of capital assets, particularly of beds and operating theatres, is itself likely to hold the key to reducing existing waiting lists and increased total output.

The impact of the NHS Review upon labour cost therefore remains critical, particularly in view of the fact that less than a two per cent rise in labour costs would more than out-weigh existing annual Cost Improvement Programmes. There is then a strong case for seeking the benefits of greater competition in the health care product market, without abandoning the advantages to the NHS of some degree of monopsony power in the health care labour market. To do so may involve a system of local wage guidelines, even for self-governing hospitals, that take account of regional variations in supply and demand pressures, without permitting full competition between individual hospitals in setting wages. This is particularly so when no centralised power is to be exerted through an imposed schedule of charges in the product market.

A system of managed competition, rather than unregulated competition, is also likely to have advantages in reducing inefficiencies due to the potential for excess capacity from uncontrolled entry to the health care market. Once such excess capacity arises, the scope for wage wars in an uncontrolled local labour market becomes even greater. Again, therefore, optimal resource management requires a recognition of the inter-dependence between the efficient management of labour and capital resources, if the above race is to be won in favour of the NHS.

APPENDIX

From equations (8) and (10), we have at point E in Figure 3.11:

$$MCL_N = \frac{2(1-\theta/n)L_N^B + v_0}{(b+\beta)} - s \tag{A.1}$$

$$= (c.n - g.n.k_N - L_N^B) / g.n^2 \tag{A.2}$$

i.e. $L_N^B = v_2/v_1$ where $v_1 = \dfrac{2(1-\theta/n)}{b+\beta} + \dfrac{1}{g.n^2}$ $\qquad$ (A.3)

and $v_2 = s + \dfrac{c}{gn} - \dfrac{k_N}{n} - \dfrac{(a+\alpha)-\beta.k_p}{b+\beta}$ $\qquad$ (A.4)

Similarly from equations (7) and (10), we have at point F in Figure 3.11:

$$L_N^A = v_2/v_3 \text{ where } v_3 = \frac{(1-\theta/n)}{b+\beta} + \frac{1}{g.n^2} \tag{A.5}$$

From Figure 3.11 and equations (8), (10), (A.3) and (A.5):

$$ABCD = (w_N^A - w_N^B).L_N^B = \frac{(1-\theta/n)}{b+\beta} \cdot [L_N^A - L_N^B].L_N^B \tag{A.6}$$

$$= \frac{(1-\theta/n)}{b+\beta} \cdot \frac{v_2^2}{v_1^2.v_3} \cdot (v_1 - v_3)$$

$$= \frac{(1-\theta/n)^2}{(b+\beta)^2} \cdot \frac{v_2^2}{v_1^2.v_3} \tag{A.7}$$

$$\tag{A.8}$$

$$BEF = \frac{1}{2}[L_N^A - L_N^B].[MCL - w_N^A]$$

$$\tag{A.9}$$

$$= \frac{1}{2}[L_N^A - L_N^B].[2L_N^B - L_N^A].\frac{(1-\theta/n)}{b+\beta}$$

Competition in Health Care

$$Z = ABCD - BEF = \frac{1}{2} \cdot \frac{(1-\theta/n)}{b+\beta} \cdot [L_N^A - L_N^B] \cdot L_N^A \qquad \text{(A.10)}$$

$$= \frac{1}{2} \cdot \frac{(1-\theta/n)}{b+\beta} \cdot \frac{(v_1 - v_3)}{v_1 \cdot v_3^2} \cdot v_2^2$$

$$= \frac{1}{2} \cdot \frac{(1-\theta/n)^2 \cdot v_2^2}{(b+\beta)^2 \cdot v_1 \cdot v_3^2} > 0 \qquad \text{(A.11)}$$

for $\theta/n < 1$, $L_N^B > 0$, and $b + \beta$ finite.

From (A.3) – (A.5) and (A.11), given $L_N^B > 0$, we have:

$$\frac{\delta Z}{\delta c} = \frac{2Z}{v_2} \cdot \frac{\delta v_2}{\delta c} = \frac{2Z}{v_2 \cdot g \cdot n} > 0 \qquad \text{(A.12)}$$

$$\frac{\delta Z}{\delta k_N} = \frac{2Z}{v_2} \cdot \frac{\delta v_2}{\delta k_N} = - \frac{2Z}{v_2 \cdot n} < 0 \qquad \text{(A.13)}$$

$$\frac{\delta Z}{\delta s} = \frac{2Z}{v_2} \cdot \frac{\delta v_2}{\delta s} = \frac{2Z}{v_2} > 0 \qquad \text{(A.14)}$$

$$\frac{\delta Z}{\delta \alpha} = \frac{\delta Z}{\delta a} = \frac{2Z}{v_2} \cdot \frac{\delta v_2}{\delta a} = - \frac{2Z}{v_2} \cdot \frac{1}{b+\beta} < 0 \qquad \text{(A.15)}$$

$$\frac{dZ}{dt} = \frac{\delta Z}{\delta c} \cdot \frac{dc}{dt} + \frac{\delta Z}{\delta a} \cdot \frac{da}{dt} = \frac{2Z}{v_2} \cdot \left(\frac{1}{gn} \cdot \frac{dc}{dt} - \frac{1}{b+\beta} \cdot \frac{da}{dt} \right) \qquad \text{(A.16)}$$

From (A.7) equivalent results hold for the impact of the above changes on *ABCD*, with *ABCD* replacing Z in (A.12) – (A.16). Thus:

$$\frac{\delta ABCD}{\delta c} = \frac{2 \cdot ABCD}{v_2} \cdot \frac{\delta v_2}{\delta c} = \frac{2 \cdot ABCD}{v_2 \cdot g \cdot n} > 0 \quad \text{etc.} \qquad \text{(A.17)}$$

References

Baumol, W.J. (1967). Macroeconomics of Unbalanced Growth, *American Economic Review*, 415–426

Baumol, W.J., Panzar, J.C. and Willig, R.D. (1982). *Contestable Markets and the Theory of Industry Structure*, Harcourt Brace Jovanovich, London

Brown, C.V. and Jackson, P. (1986). *Public Sector Economics*, 3rd edn., Martin Robertson, Oxford

Brunel University Health Economics Research Group (1989). *Resource Management: Process and Progress—Monitoring the Six Acute Hospital Sites,* Department of Health, London

Chartered Institute of Public Finance and Accountancy (CIPFA) (1989). *Health Service Trends—The CIPFA Database,* (2nd edn), Healthcare Financial Management Association, London

Cyert R.M. and March, J. (1964). *A Behavioural Theory of the Firm,* Prentice-Hall

Debreu, G. (1959). *Theory of Value,* Yale University Press, London

Department of Employment (DEmp) (1979–89). *New Earnings Survey.* Part D: Analyses by Occupation

Department of Health (DoH) (1989a). *Working For Patients,* Cm. 555, HMSO, London

Department of Health (DoH) (1989b). *Public Expenditure on Health Matters,* Memorandum submitted to the Social Services Committee, HC 418, HMSO, London

Department of Health and Social Security (DHSS) (1976). *Sharing Resources for Health in England.* Report of the Resource Allocation Working Party, HMSO, London

Department of Health and Social Security (DHSS) (1982). *Health and Personal Social Services Statistics for England,* HMSO, London (and subsequent editions to 1989)

Department of Health and Social Security (DHSS) (1988). *Public Expenditure on the Social Services,* Memorandum Submitted to the Social Services Committee, HC 548, HMSO, London (and previous editions)

Enthoven, A.C. (1985). *Reflections on the Management of the National Health Service,* Occasional Paper 5, Nuffield Provincial Hospitals Trust, London

Gravelle, H. and Rees, R. (1980). *Microeconomics,* Longmans, Harlow

HM Treasury (1989). *The Government's Expenditure Plans 1989–90 to 1991–92 – Department of Health,* Cm. 614, HMSO, London

HM Treasury (1990). *The Government's Expenditure Plans 1990–91 to 1992–93 – Department of Health,* Cm. 1013, HMSO, London

Institute of Manpower Studies (1987). *Attitudes, Jobs and Mobility of Qualified Nurses,* Royal College of Nursing, London

King's Fund Institute (1989). *Efficiency in the NHS: A Study of Cost Improvement Programmes,* Occasional Paper No. 2, King's Fund Institute, London

Leibenstein, H. (1966). Allocative Efficiency versus X-Efficiency, *American Economic Review,* 56

Maynard, A. and Bosanquet, N. (1986). *Public Expenditure on the NHS: Recent Trends and Future Problems,* Institute of Health Services Management, London

Mayston, D.J., Jesson, D. and Smith, P. (1987). Performance Assessment in the Education Sector: Educational and Economic Perspectives. *Oxford Review of Education,* 13, 249–266

Mayston, D.J. and Jesson, D. (1988). Developing Models of Educational Accountability, *Oxford Review of Education,* 14, 3, 321–339

National Association of Health Authorities (NAHA) (1989). *Annual Report,* NAHA, Birmingham

National Audit Office (NAO) (1987). *Use of Operating Theatres in the National Health Service,* HC 405, HMSO, London

National Audit Office (NAO) (1988). *Estate Management in the National Health Service,* HC 405, HMSO, London

Office of Population Censuses and Surveys (OPCS) (1987). *Population Projections 1985–2025,* HMSO, London

Organisation of Economic Cooperation and Development (OECD) (1988). *Ageing Populations—The Social Policy Implications,* OECD, Paris

Smith, P.C. (1989). Effectiveness of Maternity Services: An Appraisal of the Limitations of Performance Indicators in the Public Sector, mimeo, University of York

CHAPTER 4

Information Systems and the White Paper Proposals

Peter Smith

1. INTRODUCTION

The implementation of many of the proposals in the White Paper depends crucially on the availability of relevant, accurate and timely information. Two particular developments in the White Paper will have significant information requirements (Department of Health, 1989):

a. The establishment of self-governing hospitals (or hospital trusts) requires that the existing system of direct control by district health authorities will be significantly changed, so that control of such hospitals will in future be by means of contract. Hitherto it has been possible for authorities to control resources by pragmatic responses to local pressures. Where work is placed with hospital trusts this will no longer be possible, as control will be by means of explicit contract.

b. The introduction of practice budgets will require a revolution in the management of general practice. Practices will have to introduce budgetary control mechanisms, and will also require explicit information about the costs and quality of care in institutions to which they refer patients.

Moreover, as the spirit of competition is introduced into all aspects of the National Health Service (NHS), managers will rely increasingly on accurate and timely information to ensure that the resources at their disposal are being used efficiently. Indeed, long before the White Paper was published, the pursuit of a high quality information base for the NHS had been an objective of successive British governments. This commitment to investment in information is supported by anecdotal evidence from the private sector which suggests that the 'excellent' companies devote considerable resources to information systems, and expend much effort in ensuring that workers at

110

all levels are made aware of information relevant to their performance (Peters and Waterman, 1980, chapter 8).

Yet information is not a free good. It is a resource the deployment of which should be subject to the same economic criteria as other resources, such as hospitals, personnel and drugs. As with these other resources, the ultimate aim of information is to improve the effectiveness of the health services in terms of the health outcome for patients. This suggests that information should assist doctors, nurses and other professionals in delivering the most efficient service to patients, within resource constraints, and subject to whatever criteria of equity are deemed appropriate.

It is however helpful to consider information more generally as a means of enabling managers throughout the health service to control the resources at their disposal. The key concept in examining managerial control is that of accountability (Stewart, 1984). Various principals, such as the Secretary of State, or district health authorities, devolve responsibility to agents, and the role of information is to enhance the accountability of those agents to their respective principals. In promoting accountability within the health service, a good information system should enhance both decision-making and monitoring. That is, it has both a prospective and retrospective role. We can therefore set out two important roles for information:

a. In its prospective role, information should enable managers to improve current decisions about the allocation of the resources at their disposal between various activities, and to improve the effectiveness with which those resources are employed. The budget is the most formal mechanism whereby information fulfils this role, acting as a framework for future action. More detailed systems, such as financial control mechanisms, can then be used to fine tune decisions as events unfold.

b. In its retrospective role, information acts as a control mechanism, enabling managers to evaluate the performance of aspects of the enterprise for which they are responsible, to learn from experience, to review previous decisions, and to exercise sanctions where necessary. Various systems of performance indicators and peer review have been suggested as means of using information to this end.

These principles are generally applicable to the internal requirements of enterprises of all sorts in promoting accountability within the organization, and it is the management accountant who has played the leading role in making them operational (Maciariello, 1984). However, in the health services, information should play additional external roles.

c. It should enable politicians, patients and citizens to scrutinize the operations which they are financing through taxation. This role of information is analogous to the financial reporting private companies are required to provide to their investors through annual reports.

d. For the individual patient, information acts as the means whereby continuity of care can be secured. That is, after an episode of care, information in the form of medical records will form an important input to any subsequent treatment. As a result, we can consider information as an output of the current episode.

Thus, so far as (d) is concerned, information in the health services acts not just as a control mechanism but also as a product in its own right.

Ultimately the benefits generated by the health service information systems must be judged in terms of the health outcome of patients. However it is possible to consider a variety of intermediate indicators of success, such as:

a. improvements in the appropriate mix of resources used by the organization (input price efficiency);
b. improvements in the extent to which resources are translated into outputs (technical efficiency);
c. a closer match between levels of activity and society's requirements (allocative efficiency);
d. progress towards any equity considerations required by society;
e. improvements in the medical records of individual patients.

Any information system imposes a cost. There are obvious direct costs, such as the purchase of computer systems and the recruitment and training of appropriate personnel. Moreover, all information systems must be imperfect and incomplete. Imperfection can lead to distortions in decision-making and control and therefore impose considerable additional indirect costs. The evaluation of any information system should take all such costs into account, and weigh them against the benefits expected from improved information. The purpose of this chapter is to set up a framework within which such an evaluation might take place, and to assess the implications of the White Paper proposals. The emphasis throughout is on the internal role of information within the health service. It is nevertheless important to remember, as noted above, that there will be important external demands made of any information system, both by individual patients, and by the community as a whole.

The chapter seeks to develop the notion of an efficient level of investment in information in the health services. In examining information itself, it is prudent to distinguish between the various types of efficiency. Thus, in this context, input price efficiency refers to the optimal level of investment in information in relation to all other resources, given their input prices. Technical efficiency refers to the success with which the organization translates information and the other resources into outputs. Allocative efficiency is relevant to information in its role as an outcome of health care, and will be secured if the efficient level of such information is provided in relation to all other outputs.

A model of managerial control is introduced first. This model appears to underlie much of the discussion of information in the NHS. It is based on the use of budgets (to allocate resources) and performance indicators (to review the effectiveness with which they are used). The various problems that arise in trying to implement this model are then examined. A brief review of existing information systems follows. The specific information requirements implicit in the White Paper proposals are then discussed, and the chapter ends with an assessment of the priorities for the future.

2. BUDGETS AND PERFORMANCE INDICATORS

Any centrally planned organization, whether public or private, requires considerable information flows to ensure that resources are allocated efficiently and that management is fulfilling objectives. Indeed, experience in the largest organizations, such as centrally planned economies, suggests that an overwhelming flow of information is required if all decisions are to be made centrally (Nove, 1977, chapter 2). As a result, it has become recognized that it is essential in such organizations to devolve responsibilities, allowing local management a certain amount of discretion concerning the use of resources. If such devolution of responsibility is designed well, it should both reduce the volume of information required by the centre, and create incentives for management to use their resources efficiently.

Nevertheless, devolution only reduces the need for information *flows* between tiers, and there remains a crucial need for accurate information within the devolved units if they are to manage their resources successfully. Moreover, if the central authority (say the NHS Management Board) is to set the devolved authorities (say the Regional Health Authorities) realistic and equitable targets, it still requires a large volume of undistorted information about the performance and needs of the regions. The same principle applies at the detailed level of clinical budgeting. Two tools play an important role in planning and control of complex hierarchical organizations: budgets and performance indicators.

Budgets, in the form of cash limits, have become an intrinsic part of public sector management in the United Kingdom. The best-known budgeting system in the NHS is the Resource Allocation Working Party (RAWP) process, whereby central government funds were allocated to regions (RAWP, 1976). Set by the centre, budgets are not only intended to secure financial control, but also imply a preferred allocation of resources. However, in a devolved organization, it is inevitable that the budgetary process will leave the lower tiers some flexibility in how they use their resources. This should of course encourage input price efficiency, as managers strive to minimize their costs. Thus, for example, areas with high labour costs might adopt capital-intensive solutions to delivering services. Moreover, if managers are thought to be output maximizers, budgets might also be construed as an incentive to technical efficiency, as managers seek to maximize output within resource constraints.

The devolved responsibility will also give the devolved units some freedom to vary outputs in accordance with local preferences and constraints. Thus, although the budget given to, say, a health authority contains an implicit judgement about the level and mix of outputs, it is unrealistic to expect the health authority to adhere to that judgement in the mix of services it actually delivers. If there is a satisfactory local political process to exercise this discretion, then it could be argued that the devolution has enhanced allocative efficiency by allowing outputs to vary with local preferences. However, it could equally be argued that national priorities are the appropriate ones to pursue, and that the local discretion therefore compromises allocative efficiency. It is therefore highly likely that, in a system with devolved budgeting, and with no national inspectorate to ensure that uniform standards are adopted, there will be conflict between the centre and the devolved units.

The traditional budgeting literature presumes that there are certain underlying needs in the community which give rise to demand for health services. It is generally presumed that these needs are not evenly distributed throughout the population, and that they are highly dependent on the demographic and socio-economic characteristics of the community. As a consequence of this underlying demand, the provision of a particular health facility will give rise to a level of realized demand, which will have expenditure consequences. That is, health needs give rise to expenditure needs, the magnitude of which also depend on the priorities and expectations of society, as reflected in government guidelines and less formal pressure from the local population. Depending on the level of services provided, and the technical efficiency with which the services are run, an outcome in terms of the health of the community will arise. Within this framework, information has a central role in the budgeting process, and serves a number of purposes.

a. Information is required to assess the relative health needs of the clientele served by the devolved units. At the most rudimentary level, this information might reflect differences in the size or composition of population being served. However, more subtle determinants of need might obtain. Thus, for example, geographical areas experience different levels of morbidity, and can therefore be expected to require different levels of finance. In the RAWP process, mortality was (controversially) used as a proxy for morbidity, which in turn was assumed to indicate the need for resources.

b. Information is required on costs. In order to translate health needs into the need to spend—or budgets—some measure of the expenditure consequences of health needs is required. There is a difficulty at this stage in deciding whether to allow for differences in relative prices of inputs between areas (or between specialties, say). In practice, most budgeting systems use some form of uniform 'standard' costs determined by reference to national norms, perhaps making some allowance for gross distortions, such as higher staff costs in London.

c. Once budgets have been set, a monitoring system is required to help the devolved unit ensure that it adheres to the budget. This financial control mechanism must incorporate a mundane recording function, to note all activity with an expenditure consequence as it occurs. However, most importantly, the system must also include a forecasting function, to alert management to any potential divergence from the budget, and to facilitate a quick and appropriate response.

The second key tool of managerial control is the performance indicator (Smith, 1990). The principal perspective of the budget is prospective. In contrast, performance indicators have a predominantly retrospective role, indicating the extent to which management has achieved objectives, or satisfied standards. Performance indicators are becoming ubiquitous in the public sector, and the NHS package is currently the most advanced in terms of coverage and presentation (DHSS, 1985). Since 1985 the package has been made available annually in computer readable form, with many aspects of performance in health authorities and hospitals included. The main areas covered include:

- resource provision (such as medical manpower, nurses, operating theatres and beds);
- resource quality (for example, the level of training amongst staff);
- resource costs (staff costs, maintenance costs, total costs);
- process variables (lengths of stay, bed turnover, throughput per bed, waiting lists).

The package does not operate at a more detailed level than broad specialties within hospitals. The main thrust of the existing system is therefore its use at the strategic level, in the review of performance of regions and districts by the Department of Health (Bowen and Payling, 1987). There is nevertheless no reason why the principles of performance indicators should not be applicable at the detailed level of the clinical team, although of course the problems of random fluctuations in numbers and special circumstances become even more acute as the detail becomes finer.

The information required in a performance indicator system for a service as complex as health care is clearly extensive, and can be considered under four headings:

a. Environmental data indicate the demands being placed on the unit being assessed. Clearly population size will be important, as will the epidemiological characteristics of the population. There is an almost total absence of this kind of information in the NHS package, but it is clearly important if valid comparisons are to be made.

b. Cost data are required to examine whether the correct mix of resources is being used. Hitherto detailed information on NHS costs has been unreliable.

c. Outcome data are the ultimate measure of the success of the health services in improving the health of the community. Such information is exceedingly difficult to come by at present. There are only a handful of outcome variables (relating to perinatal mortality) in the NHS package. But it must always be borne in mind that all health service activity should be aimed at improving these indicators.

d. Process data indicate the nature of the resources employed, and how they are used. This information is particularly useful once evidence of exceptionally good (or poor) performance is uncovered, as it may help explain why the results arose, and what lessons could be learned. For example, a first step towards understanding an exceptionally high post-operative mortality rate observed in a hospital might be to examine how its operating theatres are resourced, to determine aspects worthy of more detailed examination.

Thus, although principally a monitoring device, a performance indicator system can of course be used prospectively to set targets, evaluate options, and indicate areas for future action. Such action might take the form of further research into aspects of services giving cause for concern.

The setting of targets and the interpretation of performance therefore appear to have considerable information requirements. So far as budgets are concerned, the principal requirements refer to local needs and costs, and the feasibility of attaining targets. The central authority has to balance the need to encourage managerial efficiency, by setting a reasonably 'taut' budget, with the need to give managers a realistic chance of achieving objectives (Keren, 1972). An excessively taut budget could lead to the breakdown of services, and all the inefficiencies associated with crisis management. A slack budget might encourage managerial inefficiency. The principal role of performance indicators is to offer feedback on levels of attainment so that future activity can be modified if necessary. In order to do this they should ideally be reliable, unbiased, timely and comprehensive.

In practice, the costs of achieving this counsel of perfection are almost certainly prohibitive. As with all resources, in determining the efficient level of investment in information, the benefits flowing from an improved information base must be balanced against the costs. Moreover, the marginal product of investment in information is highly sensitive to the capacity of the organization to use the information to good effect. Thus, for example, the efficient quantity of information might be much higher in an organization with widespread skills in information management than in one with no such skills.

Most of the relevant literature however takes it for granted that managers are able to make full use of information systems. The implementation of budgets and performance indicators arises from a model of managerial control which is based on a crude engineering, or cybernetic, vision of organizational behaviour (Beer, 1966). Information is seen as the key element in an organizational 'thermostat' which enables management to allocate resources in an efficient and sensitive fashion. In practice, modern enterprises are much more subtle and unpredictable than machines, so it is likely that problems will arise in applying the cybernetic principles to human organizations. In other words, there is a widespread danger of the existence of technical (or managerial) inefficiency in the use of information.

3. PRACTICAL DIFFICULTIES

We now therefore consider four areas in which difficulties might arise in implementing budgets and performance indicators in the health sector, with particular emphasis on the role of information. The areas of concern are: measurement problems; the problem of which measures to choose; the role that feedback plays; and the implications of organizational complexity.

3.1 Measurement

Measurement difficulties beset the control of health services. Here we concentrate on just three aspects: needs, costs, and outcome.

As noted above, the measurement of health needs is central to the budgeting process. However it is equally important in the performance review process. Only when adjustment has been made for the different needs which managers or clinicians have been addressing is it possible to make valid comparisons of performance.

In the NHS, much work has been done at the strategic level on measuring health needs, with the RAWP recommendations until recently serving as the basis for budget allocations to regions. The debate surrounding the RAWP system illustrates the difficulty of determining acceptable measures of need even at the relatively simple level of the community, where age structure and socio-economic characteristics of the population play a central role (Mays and Bevan, 1987).

It is, however, at the level of the individual clinician that such considerations become most important. In particular, case-mix is a crucial determinant of clinical needs. The difficulty in measuring case-mix is demonstrated by the massive volume of research into diagnosis-related groups, and the small number of practical applications (Bardsley *et al.*, 1987). Although many patients can of course be readily categorized, it is the more complex cases, possibly with comorbidity and difficult social circumstances, that both defy easy categorization and consume a disproportionately large volume of resources. Any clinical budgeting system must make some allowance for case-mix, and the only realistic source of information on case-mix is clinical records from previous years.

Under these circumstances it is very important that the marginal increment to the budget generated by an extra patient should reflect the marginal costs of treating the patient. If it does not, there is a danger that clinicians will treat only patients for which marginal revenue (to the budget holder) exceeds the marginal cost to the budget holder, resulting in a loss of allocative efficiency if this outcome is not intended. This is why accurate costing information is so important.

Various approaches have been adopted in the attempt to cost NHS services. The RAWP system uses measures such as national average bed occupancies in the acute sector, applying a standard daily bed charge. At the level of hospitals, costing returns have been produced since the inception of the NHS, but rely on arbitrary allocations of overheads. Regression techniques have been used in a variety of guises (Ashford *et al.*, 1981). Yet it must always be borne in mind that many of the services in the NHS have high fixed and low marginal costs, and that the neat attribution of all costs to specific patients, so beloved of accountants, is therefore a highly questionable procedure.

More generally, true opportunity costs will vary substantially between organizations, depending on the configuration of fixed resources they have available. These costs are appropriate for *ex ante* allocation of resources, but are usually not available except in the few cases where techniques such as linear programming can be applied (Fischer, 1981). In practice, most budgeting systems must rely on *ex post* estimates of costs. In these circumstances it is important to focus on resources that may be in short supply, to verify that simple accounting costs are appropriate, and, if this is not the case, to adjust costs where it seems likely that there will have to be rationing.

Finally, it must be emphasized that, until acceptable measures of outcome become available, satisfactory comparison of performance will be impossible. The lack of such measures throws into doubt the validity of the model of control described above. For if no measures of outcome are available, then the control process must concentrate on inputs and costs. Without the necessary data it becomes impossible to appraise fully the relative merits of different modes of treatment, or to assess the benefits of allocating resources to different care groups. Work on Quality Adjusted Life Years (QALYs) is proceeding apace, but much more needs to be undertaken before it becomes universally applicable and acceptable (Gudex and Kind, 1988). This is clearly an area of research that demands a high priority.

3.2 Choice of measures

Even if all aspects of activity in the NHS could in principle be measured, it would not be efficient to record this huge volume of data. As a result it is necessary to make choices about which measures of performance to record. For example, in the maternity services it has become traditional to report outcome in terms of a variety of mortality measures. To take just one, consider the neonatal mortality rate (proportion of infants dying within 28 days of birth). Clearly such a one-dimensional measure cannot convey all aspects of performance of a maternity hospital. Mortality rates cannot possibly measure the outcome for surviving babies, and indeed may be negatively correlated with measures such as handicapped survival. The 28 day limit is clearly arbitrary. Yet ultimately performance will be measured on a small number of indicators such as this, notwithstanding their selectivity and limitations. Managers and clinicians will then have an incentive to concentrate on the aspects of performance that are measured, to the exclusion of aspects excluded from the review process. It is therefore imperative that such summary measures are chosen with care, and that they enjoy widespread acceptance.

In reality, any system of measuring performance, particularly in an organization with health as its output, will be incomplete and imprecise. Excessive reliance on indicators is likely to encourage managers and clinicians to concentrate on the quantifiable at the expense of the unquantifiable. In particular, given the paucity of outcome measures, it seems inevitable that control mechanisms will concentrate on costs. Under these circumstances it is important that, in any system of performance review, full consideration is given to aspects of performance that have not been measured. This is where the Government's notion of peer review will assume considerable importance amongst clinicians.

A widespread problem is that almost all systems work to annual cycles. Budgets are set for (at most) one year ahead. Performance indicators represent a snapshot of one year's performance. Yet many of the outputs of the health services are the result of years of investment in preventive medicine, health promotion and education, and many other influences, possibly outside the control of the health services. There is a danger that the myopic perspective of the managerial model will inhibit activity that does not redound immediately to the credit of the current management. Again, a well-designed review system will be able to accommodate longer term considerations, and at the very least give managers a chance to explain the long term significance of their work.

3.3 Feedback

In simple budgeting systems there is a well-documented incentive for managers in the devolved organization to misrepresent their circumstances. Typically, as in the RAWP system, previous behaviour has a major impact on future budgets. When this is the case, there is an incentive for devolved budget holders to maintain some slack, and not to operate at maximum efficiency. For if they improve productivity in one year, the expectations at the centre will be raised, and budgets in future years may become more taut. This phenomenon, known as the 'ratchet' effect in the Soviet literature, is particularly important when uncertainty about future circumstances is great, as managers strive to maintain some degree of flexibility (Birman, 1978). The temptation will be for managers and clinicians to adopt median behaviour. To be sure, this might improve the performance of hitherto poor performers. But it might also inhibit the innovation, research and pursuit of excellence that result in major improvements in productivity. Weitzman (1976) shows one attempt to overcome this problem, in which budget holders are given incentives not only to satisfy this year's target, but also to improve productivity in future years.

Moreover, if budget holders have control over the data on which budgets are set, there may exist an incentive for them to distort those data. Thus, for example, if historical records of case-mix are used to determine clinical budgets, there is a persistent incentive for clinicians to exaggerate the incidence and severity of clinical complications. In this way they would overstate their apparent productivity, and thereby reduce any pressure for increased *real* productivity in the future. Some sort of independent audit of all data sources would seem to be desirable to overcome this problem.

An associated problem is that managers or clinicians may perceive the control mechanism to be unfair, perhaps in not giving adequate recognition to their performance, or in penalizing them for factors outside their control. If such perceived inequity arises, then the aggrieved managers might become alienated and uncooperative. In order to minimize this risk, it is imperative to involve managers at all levels in the design and implementation of any system of budgeting and performance measurement.

3.4 Complexity

The peculiar nature of health services is likely to exacerbate the problems associated with gaining organizational control. The model set out above presumes a hierarchical organization with clear lines of responsibility. The 1983 NHS Management Inquiry carried out by Sir Roy Griffiths envisaged the NHS moving towards such a structure. However, seven years on, the NHS is still notable for the complexity of its organizational structure. The attempt to place hospital resources under managerial control has left managers with responsibility for budgets, but without direct control over the hospital consultants who are responsible for much of the expenditure. The family practitioner service has a crucial impact on hospital and community services, yet operates largely independently. The accountability of, say, a district general manager remains complex. In different guises he or she is answerable to the Secretary of State, the regional health authority, the local health authority, the community health council, and so on.

From an information perspective, the implication of complex

organizational structure is complexity in the flow of information. First, as the number of accountability links increases so does the number of information transactions. And secondly, because the information system has to serve a variety of users with different requirements, there is a likelihood that the volume of information collected and transmitted is greater than it would be with a simpler organizational structure.

Even if the organizational difficulties could be solved, the complexity of the services provided by the National Health Service suggests that any satisfactory information system will itself have to be exceedingly complex. The most obvious source of complexity is the enormous range of services offered by the NHS, and the fact that, however inconvenient their demands might be, patients cannot be turned away. Associated with this is the importance of individual patient characteristics in determining the service they receive, and the need to maintain integrity of treatment of a patient between one episode of care and the next. Information in the form of medical records should be the link which ensures this continuity.

To take a specific example, consider services for child health, which most commentators would acknowledge should be subject to comprehensive planning and control. The range of services that must be coordinated under this heading is large. Routine services, such as immunization and vaccination, will be provided by general practitioners and health visitors. The school health service also has an important screening and educational role. Hospital services, provided by paediatricians, surgeons and psychiatrists, amongst others, will be used by most children at some stage, although for very different reasons. Support staff, such as speech therapists and physiotherapists, offer important services. Liaison with local authorities, particularly social services and education, is imperative. And children are a target group for health education and promotion.

This incomplete list illustrates the difficulties of applying a simple model of organization and information to such a complex entity as the NHS. A wide variety of services is provided by a wide variety of agencies. Not only is there a fundamental need for information, there must also be a mechanism for sharing the information between agencies. The necessary integration and control is currently achieved by a mixture of formal methods (such as immunization and vaccination recall systems) and informal methods based on local knowledge and experience. In this particular sector of child health, the NHS must take an especially long term view of the benefits of service provision. Many of the benefits of, say, immunization, or health education, might accrue to individual and community only in many years' time. The costs of implementing an information system to ensure continuity and integrity in the services provided to an individual child must be weighed against the costs of not implementing such a system. This latter course of action might impose costs in terms of the poorer health outcome for the children, and additional costs to the health services brought about by a less healthy population and an inadequate records system.

3.5 Conclusion

The manager therefore faces a formidable task in determining the efficient level of investment in information. So far as allocative efficiency is concerned, while the returns from a good system used in an efficient manner would appear to be high, the costs of a good system—brought about by complexity— are also likely to be high. Furthermore, the manager has to ensure not only that the efficient level of information is provided, but also that it is used in a technically efficient manner. Appropriate systems for disseminating and sharing the data must be put in place, and staff must be trained to use the data to full effect.

4. EXISTING INFORMATION SYSTEMS

The NHS has a tradition of large information systems. Before the explosion in the availability of information technology, most of these took the form of statutory manual returns to the Department of Health. Although voluminous, these data sources were highly selective, concentrating on costs and process variables such as length of stay.

The introduction of large mainframe computers in the 1970s gave health authorities the opportunity to collect and analyse more detailed datasets. The tradition throughout the NHS of local initiatives and discretion was sustained in the field of information technology. While some consortia were set up to develop standard systems, many health authorities went their own ways and developed bespoke computer systems. This state of affairs, while allowing flexible responses to local circumstances, made central monitoring and control difficult, and made it impossible to benefit from the potential economies of scale derived from developing nation-wide systems. This section considers existing developments under three headings: administrative; financial; and clinical information systems.

4.1 Administrative information systems

On the administrative side the most universal systems to become available were the Hospital Activity Analysis systems set up to record details of acute hospital inpatient episodes. As with many other batch processing systems, these were plagued by poor accuracy. A major problem was that the originators of the data—doctors and medical clerks—had no incentive to ensure that the data were accurate. There were no perceptible rewards for improving quality, and data were used principally by government and planners for purposes which seemed remote to doctors and nurses caring directly for patients.

Other administrative systems developed in a more piecemeal fashion. As a result, the Government set up a Steering Group on Health Services Information—the Korner working group—to examine the minimum information requirements that new information systems should satisfy (Steering Group, 1982). Their recommendations, which were formulated in great detail, were intended to form the core of any future systems in the hospital and community services, whether developed locally or for universal application in the NHS. The recommendations should now have been implemented by all authorities, even in the hitherto virgin territory of community services. For a number of reasons, such as differences in computer hardware, the desire to preserve local autonomy, and the difficulty of satisfying all users, local initiatives continue to proliferate. However the NHS has recognized the need for coordination and standardization, with initiatives such as the national strategic framework for information management (NHS Management Board, 1986) and the 'common basic specification' for information systems (Molteno and Bishop, 1989).

4.2 Financial information systems

The health service has employed computerized financial information systems for some time. The most common system was until recently the Standard Accounting System (SAS), which was used by about 100 health authorities. It provided a basic system for recording financial transactions, administering the payroll and providing budgetary and manpower information. In common with many systems developed in the early days of mainframe computing, SAS relied on batch processing, and its urgent replacement by more flexible systems has been sought. One such replacement is the Integrated Resource Information System (IRIS), the principal advance on SAS being an online capability and increased flexibility, so that the system can be tailored to the requirements of individual users (Anslow, 1989). The main challenge still outstanding is to integrate these routine financial systems with the administrative and clinical information systems to produce financial planning systems.

4.3 Clinical information systems

With the advent of online computer systems, particularly keen interest has centred on clinical information systems, which attempt to go beyond the administrative level to facilitate the clinical management of patients. Clearly, while administrative systems might be based on events (such as hospital inpatient episodes), the clinical information system must be based on patients. A good system should improve clinical management of patients, for example by ensuring that all necessary tests are requested. The system should also facilitate the automatic transmission of results, say, from laboratories back to wards. This suggests the need for integration with information systems in service departments such as laboratories, and the architects of such systems envisage an electronic hospital in which all significant clinical transactions are logged by a unifying computer system. The ultimate logic of clinical information systems is that the patient's medical record should become computer-based.

An initial attempt to integrate all three types of system was the Government's management budgeting initiative, the cornerstone of which was the allocation of budgets to individual clinicians. This foundered because of the failure to involve clinicians fully in the process (Rippington, 1988). In the light of that failure, the mechanism the Government has since chosen to promote the integration of finance and clinical activity is the resource management project. The central thrust of this initiative is to involve clinical and nursing staff in the management process in hospital and community services. To this end, the provision of information that is relevant, timely and accurate is crucial. If one of these criteria does not obtain then either the data will be ignored, or inappropriate decisions will be made. In either case there is an inefficiency, at the very least in the form of the unnecessary provision of unused information.

In the first instance, six acute hospital sites and thirteen communities (district health authorities) have been selected to test clinical resource management, and there are plans to increase the number substantially over the next few years (Buxton *et al.*, 1989). The first evaluations are suggesting that, even where there is considerable commitment, there are implementation difficulties. For example, many of the solutions being adopted are determined more by available software than by user requirements. And some sites are succumbing to the inevitable temptation to provide more information than can be assimilated by users (Norman *et al.*, 1988). Information is a resource that almost certainly has a negative marginal product beyond a certain level, as managers fail to see the wood for the trees, or simply give up using the information altogether. The other key lesson emerging from the pilots is that much attention should be given to the management structure which the information system is intended to serve. If the information is clear but the means for implementing decisions is not, then the benefits of the information are likely to be diminished.

The idea of resource management is to extend the principles currently operating at more strategic levels—regions, districts and units—to the most basic level of the clinical team. Clinical budgeting, probably based on diagnosis-related groups, will for the first time give doctors explicit financial constraints, where hitherto the principal constraints have been in terms of physical units such as hospital beds or operating theatre time. This will of course entail the identification and costing of all resources used by doctors, whose budgets will be debited for each activity with an expenditure consequence. While suffering from numerous theoretical and practical shortcomings, models developed by the accounting profession at least offer a starting point for devising a technology to undertake these tasks.

Performance will then be monitored by some variant of peer review. Although there will clearly always be a need in health services to examine unquantifiable determinants of performance, quantifiable information will have to form the basis for such review. Here the necessary technology does not yet exist, although the work on QALYs and avoidable mortality begins to show the way. As discussed above, a major problem is that the clinical budgeting philosophy, if implemented in a piecemeal fashion, is liable to result in distortions, as the attention of doctors and nurses is focused on activity that is measured by their performance indicators. The early trials of resource management should tell us whether incomplete systems lead to greater or fewer distortions than no system at all.

In summary, there is a substantial volume of management information now available at the strategic level, though with significant gaps, particularly so far as outcome data are concerned. At the operational level, of clinical team, there are some isolated developments, but in general the main emphasis has been on administrative matters rather than clinical management. Much of general practice remains untouched by the electronic revolution.

5. THE WHITE PAPER PROPOSALS

Most of the proposals in the White Paper have major implications for information flows in the NHS. As noted at the start of this paper, the two key areas are the introduction of self-governing hospitals, and of contracts for hospital services, and the introduction of practice budgets in some general practices. In addition the universal application of medical audit will require a major advance in information systems. The introduction of contracts is seen principally as a spur to competition, but has significant information implications. The other proposals are the result of applying the cybernetic model of managerial control described above.

5.1 Contracts

The introduction of contracts would dramatically alter the nature of the relationships between health authorities, general practice, and hospital and community services. Instead of the loosely hierarchical management structure currently in force, in which unit managers are responsible to the district, it is envisaged that district services will be delivered by means of a network of contracts between the buyers of services (district health authorities or general practices) and various providers, such as hospital trusts. The consequent competitive environment is intended to stimulate efficiency, and it is envisaged that accountability between buyers and providers will be achieved by the provisions of the contracts.

Within this framework, information serves a number of purposes:

- securing national accountability: ensuring the government's funds are being spent effectively;
- enabling the internal market to function efficiently, by ensuring that all parties can make informed decisions;
- enabling principals (the buyers of services) to secure control over their agents (the providers);
- ensuring that patients receive continuity of treatment from one episode of care to another.

These are now considered in turn.

(i) *The Government's requirements*

The Government will continue to need a large volume of information under the new arrangements. Much of this will be required to ensure that district health authorities are securing value for money from their contracts. The Audit Commission will clearly play a central objective in pursuing this objective, and in promulgating good practice (Tristem, 1989). There will in addition continue to be a need to collect and present information about the health status of the nation if the electorate is to be allowed to make an informed judgement about the performance of the Government. More mundane information requirements relate to epidemiological aspects of the nation's health. It is inconceivable that any market mechanism will be able to respond to all the trends in the nation's health, and the Government will clearly have a continuing role in identifying new problems and opportunities, particularly in areas such as health promotion and preventive medicine. The Government will also continue to require manpower information in order to carry out its responsibility for securing a satisfactory flow of trained personnel.

In addition the Government is likely to require information to check whether the market in particular areas is genuinely competitive. It is likely that in many parts of the country there will be a lack of real choice of potential providers. If the market is not competitive then regulation may be required, and detailed information will therefore be needed to determine the appropriate level of regulation. This suggests that the government may need to insist on quite detailed administrative data being required within the terms of contracts in case intervention should be needed.

(ii) *The market's requirements*

In order that buyers of health services can make informed choices they will require information about potential providers. This information will presumably take the form of prospectuses, which should contain reports on the past performance of the provider and plans for the future. Buyers will be particularly interested in the range of services provided, any potential capacity problems, and the quality of care provided. It is almost inevitable that waiting time statistics will play a crucial role in this area in the absence of any acceptable outcome measures.

A major consideration is that information possesses many of the characteristics of a public good. It is to a large extent nonrival—consumption by one party does not materially affect the ability of others to use the information—and it is also very difficult to exclude anyone from access to information once it has been made available. There is therefore no guarantee that providers will automatically provide the information required by buyers. Any analysis of the market in information therefore has to recognize that the provision of information in the less regulated environment envisaged in the White Paper may be far from efficient. It may be that, because freeriders, such as competitors, can use information without paying for it, there will be an underprovision. Or, conversely, because managers have an incentive to signal their performance to the outside world, there may be an overprovision.

There is therefore a compelling argument for standardization of information required for external reporting purposes. This will enable buyers to make meaningful comparisons of providers. It is evident from early work by the Department of Health (1990a) that the specifications will have to be quite detailed, and there will be the usual requirements for external audit of the information contained in prospectuses. The costs of making the internal market work are therefore likely to be considerable.

(iii) *Control of contracts*
Each contract will impose on buyers what are known as agency costs. These comprise the direct costs of monitoring the contract, and the indirect costs associated with devolving health care delivery to agents not directly under the control of health service management. These indirect costs take the form of a potential mismatch between the service sought by the health service (the principal) and the service delivered by the contractor (the agent). The most important instrument for securing control of agents, and therefore an important determinant of the monitoring costs, will be the information requirements of the contract. Health service management will have to balance the costs of requesting, auditing and processing extra information against the improvement in control it yields, and therefore ultimately against the improvement generated in terms of the health of the community.

The National Health Service already experiences agency costs, in the sense that, even within the organization, managers and clinicians have personal objectives that may not coincide with organizational objectives, and so their activity requires monitoring and control. In order to ensure that agency costs are kept in check, the NHS has hitherto relied to a large extent on a high level of commitment to the ideals of the NHS amongst its staff. In addition, under the present arrangements there is often a direct line of managerial control, whereby targets and guidelines can be agreed reasonably flexibly, and altered when necessary. If there is an information gap, it can usually be filled by direct enquiries between managers. Thus it might be surmised that hitherto agency costs in health care delivery have been relatively low. Presumably the government believes that the increased competition brought about by the White Paper proposals will yield benefits that outweigh the increased agency costs that are likely to arise as a result of the new arrangements.

The contract system will be very much more formal than the current management system. Contracts will have to specify the patient groups to be covered, perhaps relatively straightforward in many surgical specialties, but far more complex when applied to specialties such as general medicine. For example, if the contract is based on patients (rather than episodes of care) it will be necessary to set up systems which trace individual patients through the system, and which handle administrative complications such as readmissions.

Because of the need amongst buyers to secure financial control, there will be a need for frequent reports from providers to buyers, giving details of completed episodes of care and those still in progress. This latter group is likely to be quite large and, from an information perspective, complex to manage. For example, it may not be clear under which contract a particular admission is to be reported until the end of the care episode. Yet in order to assess their liabilities buyers may require considerable interim information such as provisional diagnosis and contract code. This will mean that there will be a continual need to update patient records throughout a care episode, and not just when it is completed.

If health objectives are to be met, measures of quality will have to be incorporated into any contractual arrangement, covering patient satisfaction as well as outcome. While these considerations present difficulties in the acute sector, the problems become even more formidable in the non-acute sectors such as mental illness. It is therefore likely that the efficient level of information provision is likely to be high, because the costs of *not* incorporating good quality process and outcome data would appear to be large, in the sense that agents will not have enough incentive to pursue the community's objectives in health.

Information developments such as those described above might be highly desirable and stimulate efficient health care, even without the White Paper. However, with the introduction of contracts they will become essential, and the information requirements will have to be specified in advance, within the terms of the contract. Gaps in the information base may bring about gross inefficiencies, as they may distort the behaviour of agents. And such *ex ante* specification of information flows may preclude rapid response to new circumstances, such as changes in medical technology, or changes in the health characteristics of the population. The danger is that the writers of contracts may not have the expertise or incentive to specify an efficient level of information. For example, risk-averse health service managers may require contractors to provide large volumes of information, in excess of the efficient level, in order to cover all possible circumstances. Conversely, in order to secure low tender offers, it may be decided to request too little information.

The Department of Health has developed suggested minimum data sets for incorporation in contracts (Department of Health, 1990a) and this would appear to be a sensible interim solution. First it takes advantage of economies of scale in developing the terms of contracts. More importantly, it opens the way to the development of standard records which can be transmitted between organizations easily.

This is going to become increasingly important, particularly at a district level (Department of Health, 1990b). At present, a district needs only to record episodes of care taking place within its boundaries, and to convey these records to the regional health authority (or central government). Under a system of contracts, an authority will have a detailed interest in all episodes of health care involving a resident of the district, regardless of where those episodes take place. As a result, the volume and complexity of *flows* of information to buyers will increase enormously under the new arrangements, as the emphasis changes from the district's catchment to its resident population. This issue is likely to be particularly important in areas such as London with large cross-boundary flows. The implication is that development of the necessary information technology networks and systems must be a high priority.

This is an indication that the process of monitoring contracts will impose a direct cost on health authorities and general practice, in the sense that much management effort will be required to audit and process the information forthcoming from contractors. If health service management does not have the capacity to undertake this role, then it may be that a second best solution would be to reduce the information requirements, thereby reducing control over contractors, but also reducing monitoring costs.

Agency costs may be a crucial factor in determining how many contracts a health authority will award. A small number of large contracts will impose relatively low agency costs, compared with the costs associated with a large number of contracts for relatively small volumes of work. However the latter arrangement would stand a better chance of securing a given level of services for minimum contract costs, as it becomes possible to identify the lowest tenders for each of a large number of tasks. Therefore the problem for buyers is to find an optimal balance between agency costs and direct contract costs.

In summary, the new system of contracts is likely to increase substantially the level of agency costs in health care delivery. These costs comprise the costs of monitoring contracts, and the costs associated with loss of direct control over health care delivery. Information will be the principal tool for monitoring purposes. There appear to be substantial gains from national standardization of information requirements. However, the optimal level of information will depend greatly on the ability of health service managers to process the information. The range of issues raised in this section suggests a clear need for a series of trials to determine the costs and benefits of different contract arrangements.

(iv) *Medical records*

Most clinicians would agree that, for any health system to be effective, medical records should be made available for future episodes of care, regardless of the agency currently offering treatment. Yet there is no guarantee that contractors will automatically provide such information. The providing organization has an incentive to provide adequate medical records only if it can be sure of retaining a continuing need to care for the patient. And of course such certainty would be antipathetic to the principle of competition. It would seem therefore that an urgent issue raised by the White Paper is the means by which the integrity of patient records can be maintained.

Contracts should therefore specify the required nature and quality of records, which should become accessible to all potential providers after an episode of care. Again, in order to ensure consistency regardless of the provider, a set of national standards must be developed. These standards need to encompass not only the minimum content and quality of records, but also the media on which they are stored. Increasingly the need for potentially many different organizations to share a medical record, and the increasing use made of electronic records, implies an urgent requirement for the development of information technology standards. In many ways this issue represents one of the most challenging aspects of the proposed new arrangements. Initial examination of the problem has emphasized the need to retain flexible solutions, given the rapid developments in technology (Department of Health, 1990c).

5.2 General practice budgets

The use of general practice budgets would be a dramatic departure for the NHS. Hitherto the family practitioner budgets have not been subject to cash limits. As discussed above, any budgeting system will require information on the relative expenditure needs of different general practices, on the costs of services, on patient outcomes, and on the processes used. Many of the issues raised under the contracts section above will be relevant to general practice budget holders. This section therefore examines only those problems specific to general practice.

The setting of budgets would require detailed information not only on patient numbers (which are notoriously unreliable) but also on their characteristics. There will be no incentive for general practitioners to accept high dependency patients if they generate only a standard capitation fee. If general practitioners are to be persuaded to care for 'at risk' groups, it may become necessary for an actuarially determined capitation to be associated with each patient, reflecting their expected demands on health services. In spite of the obvious practical difficulties of implementing such a scheme, insurance companies operate such systems, so there seems no theoretical reason why general practice should not be able to do so.

The introduction of budgets would of course require formal pricing of all services used by general practice. Each practice would require information on the use of resources, and financial planning models to monitor performance against budgets. Again, such systems are available, although their implementation in general practice would impose considerable costs, particularly in terms of requirements for additional managerial expertise. It is important to bear in mind, however, that very many of the costs incurred by patients are beyond the control of the general practitioner. For example, how should a practice quantify the liability incurred by referring to a consultant a patient with vague medical symptoms? It may be that, as a patient progresses through the hospital system, general practices will require continual feedback in order to monitor costs. There is no guarantee that such a flow of information would have any benefits in terms of patient care.

It will become necessary to monitor the quality of care in general practice in order to ensure that cost containment is balanced in an efficient manner with outcome in terms of health. The White Paper proposals are based crucially on the universal application of clinical audit. It is difficult to dispute the desirability of moving towards some form of peer review as a fundamental means of enhancing accountability in the medical profession. However, the measures will have to be supported by good quality outcome data if they are to influence the profession, and, as noted before, it is going to be some time before such data become universally acceptable. In any case, assessment of outcome will have to be undertaken in a very subtle way if aspects of care such as preventive medicine are to be given adequate priority.

It will also be important to ensure that the other potentially adverse effects of budgeting systems noted above are balanced against any benefits that might arise. In particular, although patient numbers and characteristics will play some part, previous levels of expenditure will inevitably be a major influence on budgets. Such a system would contain many of the perverse incentives associated with centrally planned organizations alluded to above, such as maintaining high expenditure in one year as one means of protecting budgets for future years.

A further mundane but very important consideration relates to the organizational structure of general practice. The bodies responsible for administering general practice will become the family practitioner service authorities (formerly family practitioner committees). In general the areas administered by these bodies do not have the same boundaries as health districts. There will therefore be a considerable complexity in the flow of information from providers of services to a large number of general practice budget holders via family practitioner service authorities. This same information will also have to be directed to the relevant district health authorities (so that they can monitor health care in their areas).

This suggests that regional health authorities, which are self-contained in terms of both districts and family practitioner authorities, may have to play a major role as clearing houses for information exchange. In this role, they would receive details of episodes of care from a large number of providers of care both inside and outside the region. Individual records (or suitable extracts) would then be directed to central government and to the appropriate districts, family practitioner service authorities, and general practices. The processing of information will clearly be very complex compared with the current system of a simple progression of data from originator to a single district to a single region, and will put a considerable strain on the data processing capabilities of the health services.

The key question is whether any efficiency benefits brought about by cash limits for general practitioner and competition amongst providers will outweigh the costs of implementing such systems. The efficient level of detail incorporated into the budgeting systems is determined again by the minimization of agency costs. A detailed system will impose considerable managerial costs, but may secure a relatively efficient use of resources. A more rough and ready system might not secure such an equitable or efficient pattern of health care, but will have compensations in the form of reduced managerial costs. As with contracts, a series of trials would seem to be the only way of determining the efficient level of detail for budgeting systems. In evaluating such trials, it will be important to bear in mind that practices which participate may be particularly highly motivated, and have access to managerial expertise of a much higher order than that available to the typical general practice. Care should therefore be taken in inferring the appropriate budgeting system for universal application.

5.3 Medical audit

Hitherto the NHS has attempted to secure an efficient level of health care from clinicians by relying on their adherence to an implicit code of conduct which concentrates on the clinician's responsibility to the individual patient. Rightly or wrongly, it has always been believed that any closer monitoring of clinical practice would impose costs, such as increased information requirements and the possible alienation of the medical profession, and that such costs would outweigh any potential benefits in the form of increased efficiency. However, the revolution in information technology has engineered a potentially huge reduction in the cost of information. An important objection to the closer managerial control of clinicians is therefore becoming less important.

However, as noted above, although the technology to store and transmit large volumes of information is now becoming available, the accounting systems to measure clinical behaviour are less advanced. It is vital that the opportunities opened up by the availability of information technology should not obscure the urgent need to search for satisfactory measures of clinical need, costs, outcome, and clinical process. It is likely that many of the data requirements of peer review will be relatively low cost by-products of financial control systems, such as those under trial in the resource management initiative. However, the interpretation of such data, and the process of peer review are likely to impose considerable costs.

Particularly careful attention should be focused on the system of incentives inherent in the review process. If clinicians perceive no rewards for participating in the process then it may become nothing more than a costly and demoralizing burden on the NHS. If the rewards are formulated poorly then the review system may provoke undesired side effects. For example, clinicians must inevitably control much of the data on which their performance review will be based. The incentives for distorting such data are therefore considerable, and some system of independent audit may be required. All the other potential pitfalls of performance review processes noted above should also be guarded against. In particular, if too much emphasis is placed on short term, quantifiable aspects of health care, then long-term, unquantifiable aspects may suffer.

The possible rewards that clinicians may seek for good performance may be increased budgets, improved facilities, enhanced remuneration, and more time to pursue activities, such as research, not related to direct patient care. Sanctions for poor performance might be formulated as the reverse of these. However, the net effect of any incentive scheme is likely to be increased expenditure. Any scheme will introduce an element of risk into the conditions of employment for clinicians, and all the evidence is that employees require increased expected returns in compensation for increased risk. As a result, any meaningful review process will impose costs in terms of incentives, as well as information costs and the direct managerial costs of running the scheme. These costs must be balanced against any improvements in the effectiveness of clinical activity brought about by the implementation of peer review.

6. THE WAY FORWARD

This chapter has concentrated on the problems involved in making effective use of information in the NHS, and the additional difficulties that would be introduced if the White Paper proposals are implemented. Improved information systems have been made possible by the revolution in information technology, and would offer many benefits in terms of the health of patients. Even without the White Paper, the health services would be undertaking a major review of the role of information, and how they might make best use of it.

Yet eminent economists have grappled for decades with the problems of modelling information as an economic commodity (Arrow, 1984), and have so far failed to failed to find a convincing solution, so it is not surprising that it appears difficult to give any quantitative guidance as to the optimal level of investment in information. Nevertheless, all the evidence from the private sector suggests that, notwithstanding all the caveats outlined above, the very best organizations invest heavily in information, and promote its dissemination and use throughout the organization. The key questions for the NHS are:

what is the cost of the information?
how much information should be sought?
what specific information should be recorded?
by what means should the information be disseminated?
how is the information to be used?

Only by answering these questions is it possible to determine the efficient level of information produced by the health services. The provision of information is in direct competition with personnel, hospitals, drugs, and all the other resources which yield more immediate benefits for patients. As a result, it is imperative that the use of information is subject to the same criterion of cost-effectiveness as the use of these more conventional resources. Recommendations by the NHS Information Management Group (1988) at least show a recognition of this problem.

In examining the White Paper proposals, the key role played by information in securing government objectives has been highlighted. The setting of budgets will require accurate data on case mix and resource requirements, even though work on diagnosis-related groups is a long way from being ready for universal implementation. NHS resources will have to be costed, a task that has not hitherto met with unambiguous success. The need for financial control will necessitate rapid and accurate billing of services used. This is perfectly feasible, but will impose considerable administrative costs in terms of data processing and the volume of information flows. Outcome will have to be audited, although the technology for doing so is not yet in place. If performance review is to yield real improvements in effectiveness it will be necessary to provide information on clinical processes.

The existing information infrastructure of the NHS is inadequate to support such a burden. As a result, investment in computer systems, support staff and management development will be required. There must be some doubt as to whether the resources exist within, or indeed outside, the NHS to secure the required changes in the envisaged time scale. And even if they do, there are large areas where adequate accounting systems do not yet exist. Clearly the rapid development of such systems is highly desirable, although the fact that they have not been developed satisfactorily to date suggests that many aspects of health care may be resistant to the sorts of accounting models used in business and commerce.

Throughout the discussion it has been stressed that only when results are available from well-designed trials will it be possible to answer the questions listed above. Such trials should examine the implications for health care of different types of contract arrangements, of different budgeting systems for general practice, and of different approaches to peer review. To implement any of these key proposals without some assessment of alternative types of arrangement would appear to be reckless, running the risk of jeopardizing current levels of effectiveness. Moreover, it is important that, in evaluating trials, care is taken to allow for the possibility that those participating in the trials might attract a higher level of managerial commitment and expertise than will be available in the NHS as a whole when the preferred systems are implemented universally.

Nevertheless, assuming that the proposals will be implemented, this chapter has attempted to spell out some of the problems that may beset them, and to indicate how their effects might be mitigated. In addition, it is possible to point to a number of key areas where further clarification from the Government is a priority. The first concerns the organizational structure which the information is intended to serve. If the purpose of much information is to attain accountability, then it is essential to specify the model of accountability on which the proposals are based. The underlying model appears to based on that of consumer and producer. Yet the ultimate consumer—the patient—plays very little part in the proposals, and the role of community health councils is difficult to determine. If it is assumed that general practitioners are acting on behalf of patients, then by what mechanism can patients hold general practice to account? Only when the model of accountability has been set out explicitly will it be possible to determine the information systems needed to achieve accountability.

The second crucial issue is the role of the centre in promoting information systems. To date, although the Korner initiative has specified basic datasets, and the Corporate Data Administration is attempting to develop a common data model, the NHS has rarely used its enormous purchasing power and accumulated experience to develop acceptable standard systems for universal use. To be sure, local discretion is an important feature of the health service. But, so far as information systems are concerned, the economies of scale derived from using the best aspects of existing local systems must be a powerful reason for specifying standard systems. The White Paper proposals would suggest that standardization of both computing systems and accounting systems will become increasingly important. For example, if patients might be treated at a variety of sites, their medical records should be compatible with each site's information systems. And as managers and general practice seek to identify the relative merits of alternative hospitals they will require performance data which they are confident offer strict comparability.

Finally, the widespread installation of information systems in the NHS will require a revolution in the information processing capabilities of clinicians, nurses, managers, and other personnel. A fundamental change in the 'undermanaged' philosophy of the NHS will be required, involving a commitment to training and management development not previously seen. Inevitably this will involve the employment of more staff in key disciplines such as personnel and training, the allocation of more staff time for management development, and a general diversion of resources from direct patient care. The originators of data—most importantly clinicians and medical records clerks—will have to be convinced that accurate information is a valuable resource, which is crucially devalued if it is not accurate and timely. As the NHS Training Authority (1989) suggests, it is inconceivable that these changes can be brought about without a significant increase in the total NHS budget.

References

Anslow, B. (1989). *IRIS: a developing system for the NHS*, Public Finance and Accountancy, 3 November 1989, 9–11

Arrow, K.J. (1984). *The economics of information*, Blackwell, Oxford

Ashford, J.R., M.S. Butts and T.C. Bailey (1981). Is there still a place for independent research into issues of public policy in England and Wales in the 1980s? *Journal of the Operational Research Society*, 32, 851–864

Bardsley M., Coles J. and Jenkins L. (eds.) (1987). *DRGs and health care: the management of case mix*, King Edward's Hospital Fund, London

Beer, S. (1966). *Decision and control*, Wiley, Chichester

Birman, I. (1978). From the achieved level. *Soviet Studies*, 30, 153–172

Bowen, B. and Payling, L. (1987). Expert systems for performance review. *Journal of the Operational Research Society*, 38, 929–934

Buxton, M. T. Packard, T. and Keen, J. (1989). *Resource management: process and progress*, Health Economics Research Group, Brunel University, Uxbridge

Department of Health (DoH) (1989). *Working for Patients*, Cm. 555, HMSO, London

Department of Health (DoH) (1990a). *Framework for information systems: information*, Department of Health, London

Department of Health (DoH) (1990b). *Framework for information systems: information. Annex 13: District information requirements*, Department of Health, London

Department of Health (DoH) (1990c). *Framework for information systems: IT*, Department of Health, London

Department of Health and Social Security (DHSS) (1985). *Performance indicators for the NHS*. Guidance for users, DHSS, London

Fischer, D (1981). On the optimisation of hospitals. In Boldy, D. (ed.), *Operational research applied to health services*, Croom Helm, London

Gudex, C. and Kind P. (1988). *The QALY Toolkit*. Discussion Paper 38, Centre for Health Economics, University of York

Keren, M. (1972). On the tautness of plans. *Review of Economic Studies*, 39, 469–486

Maciariello, J. A. (1984). *Management control systems*, Prentice/Hall, Englewood Cliffs

Mays, N. and G. Bevan (1987). *Resource allocation in the Health Service*, Occasional Papers on Social Administration, 81, Bedford Square Press, London

Molteno, B. and P. Bishop (1989). What CBS means for IT. *British Journal of Healthcare Computing*, 5(1), 40–43

NHS Information Management Group (1988). *Method for identifying the costs and benefits of computer systems used in health care*, National Health Service, London

NHS Management Inquiry (1983). *Report*, DHSS, London

NHS Management Board (1986). *A national strategic framework for information management in the hospital and community health services*, National Health Service, London

NHS Training Authority (1989). *The extension of resource management: an audit for action*, NHS Training Authority, Bristol

Norman, S., Quinn, H. and Malin, H. (1988). *The resource management initiative and ward nursing information systems*, Department of Health, London

Nove, A. (1976). *The Soviet Economic System*, second edition, Allen and Unwin, London

Peters, T. J. and Waterman, R.H. (1982). *In search of excellence. Lessons from America's best run companies*, Harper and Row, New York

Resource Allocation Working Party (RAWP) (1976). *Sharing resources for health in England*, HMSO, London

Rippington, T. (1988). The National Health Service—an annual report. In Jackson, P. and Terry, F. (eds.), *Public Domain 1988*, Public Finance Foundation, London

Smith, P. (1990). The use of performance indicators in the public sector. *Journal of the Royal Statistical Society*, Series A, 153, 53–72

Steering Group on Health Services Information (1982). *First report*, Department of Health and Social Security, London

Stewart, J. (1984). The role of information in public accountability. In Hopwood, A. and Tomkins, C. (eds.), *Issues in public sector accountability*, Philip Allen, Oxford

Tristem, R. (1989). Auditing the health service. *Public Finance and Accountancy*, 3 November, 17–18

Weitzman, M. (1976). The new Soviet incentive scheme. *Bell Journal of Economics and Management Science*, 7, 251–257

CHAPTER 5

Managing Capital Resources in the NHS

David Mayston

1. INTRODUCTION

This chapter analyses a number of important issues related to improving the management of capital resources in the NHS and suggests a way of resolving many of the underlying difficulties. The analysis looks at these difficulties both in the context of the pre-Review position of the NHS and in the context of the questions that remain for the management of capital resources after the NHS Review.

Capital is important in the NHS for the following reasons:

a. The provision of new capital directly affects the extent of investment in new hospital buildings, new medical equipment and the fulfilment of associated service planning targets.
b. Capital investment is itself in limited supply, and has decreased in real terms (that is, compared to the GDP deflator for gross domestic fixed capital formation) over the government sector as a whole since 1977, as in Figure 5.1. Capital spending by the Government on the NHS in real terms (as measured against the same GDP deflator) has slightly increased over the same period, as in Figure 5.2.
c. Land sales, as in Figures 5.3 and 5.4, have become an increasingly important source of finance for NHS capital expenditure, though one which in the future may become less easily sustainable, as the programme of closure of long-stay institutions draws nearer to completion and property prices have ceased to rise in many areas.
d. Whilst NHS net revenue expenditure is planned to be some 17.8 times that of capital expenditure in 1990–91 (HM Treasury, 1990), the improved use of capital resources, and the revenue expenditure associated with operating the capital assets, is likely to hold the key to significant future revenue savings (National Audit Office (NAO),

1988). Further cost improvements from other existing sources, such as competitive tendering, in contrast may become more difficult to achieve as much of their initial potential is already realised.

e. The existing NHS capital stock has many associated replacement and maintenance problems, as discussed in more detail later in this chapter.

f. There is evidence of inefficient management of existing and new capital in the NHS, as in the reports by Ceri Davies (1983), the Association of Health Service Treasurers (1985) and the NAO (1987, 1988).

g. NHS capital assets would form a key part of any future privatisation of the NHS.

Figure 5.1: Total government gross domestic fixed capital formation at constant 1987 prices

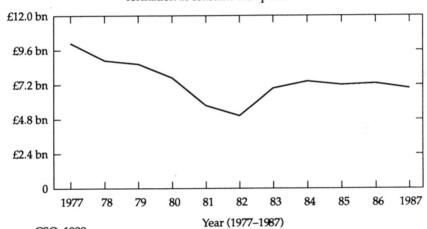

Source: CSO, 1988

Figure 5.2: Gross fixed capital formation in health by central government at constant 1987 prices

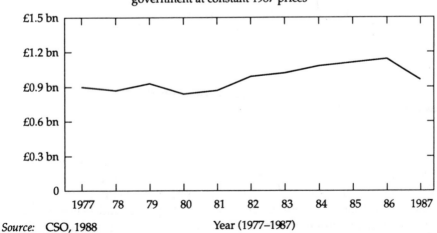

Source: CSO, 1988

Figure 5.3: Sale of proceeds of surplus NHS property

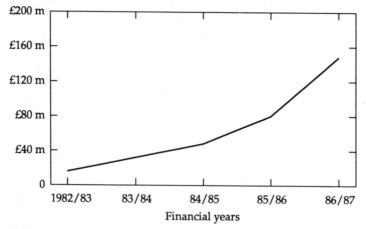

Source: NAO, 1988

Figure 5.4: NHS property disposals in England in acres

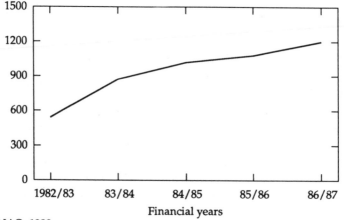

Source: NAO, 1988

2. SEPARATING THE ISSUES

Whilst capital is important for the NHS, one needs to be aware that any attempt at improving the management of, and accounting arrangements for, capital resources in the NHS touches on several problem areas that have been the source of continuing difficulties in the public and private sectors. The first of these problem areas is that of inflation accounting, with still no agreed system of inflation accounting currently in operation in the private sector in the UK, following the demise of the accounting standard SSAP 16 on current cost accounting. The importance of adequately accounting for inflation is, if anything, more significant in the NHS where there are many long-lived assets which were acquired before the rapid rise in prices of the 1970s.

Secondly, any attempt at charging for capital assets, in the way proposed by the NHS White Paper, raises questions of how to value in some comparable way the many individual items of capital equipment and other capital assets that exist in the NHS. The theoretical issue of whether or not one can measure against a common yardstick heterogeneous items of capital equipment has itself been the subject of one of the most heated debates in the economics literature (Harcourt, 1972; Bliss, 1975). However the associated valuation question is also of some immediate practical relevance once one imposes a capital charge based upon a valuation of different hospitals in different locations, such as central London and northern Scotland, with imperfect substitutability between the two in the provision of services.

Thirdly, even in the private sector there is some lack of clarity about the role and economic meaning of a depreciation charge, as discussed in Nobes (1984), with some academics advocating the adoption of cash-flow accounting in the private sector rather than conventional depreciation accounting (for example, Lee, 1972).

A further major problem area on which improving NHS capital resource management touches is that associated with the imposition of public expenditure controls. Health care is a sector in which cost containment has proved to be a major problem, both for public and private health care systems, with the NHS itself accounting for a substantial part of total UK public expenditure. Yet, as the recent UK experience of local authorities with capital controls demonstrates (Audit Commission, 1985), the existing public expenditure control systems based upon cash limits have given rise to major inefficiencies in the management of public capital resources.

In order to circumvent these controls on capital spending, many local authorities have used their semi-autonomous status to enter into unconventional financing arrangements, such as 'deferred purchase' or 'interest swap' agreements with commercial banks. Whilst the accounting standard SSAP 21 has attempted to counteract the similar problem of off-balance sheet financing in the private sector, the lack of adequate capital accounting in large parts of the public sector has contributed towards the build-up of very large financial liabilities and financial difficulties for local authorities, such as the London Borough of Hammersmith and Fulham.

More directly, capital charges can themselves risk the danger of establishing perverse incentives, such as the incentive under some industrial rating systems to remove factory roofs in order to reduce the capital charge that the rating system implies. In addition one needs to recognise that at least part of the problem of achieving an efficient management of NHS capital resources to date has been the political nature of many NHS investment decisions. In particular there has tended to be a new build bias resulting from the greater political esteem and local patronage associated with opening new hospitals compared to sacrificing revenue resources for the improved maintenance and renovation of existing buildings.

If the NHS is to avoid becoming enmeshed in the above problem areas, any new system for improving capital resource management in the NHS must be well designed and recognise the above complexities. Well-designed systems can then become user-friendly and simple to operate, even though they may be sophisticated in original design. In contrast, less well-designed systems may provide to be difficult to operate and can involve crossed wires that ultimately generate more heat than light.

In order to avoid such crossed wires, there is a need to separate a number of different, though related, issues that are involved in improving the management of capital resources in the NHS. These are the following:

a. the maintenance of control over health care costs and over total public expenditure;

b. the provision of incentives for the efficient management of capital resources in the NHS;

c. the monitoring of whether or not value for money is being achieved from capital resources invested in the NHS;

d. the costing of NHS services and the provision of information relevant to pricing the delivery of services where these are separately contracted for;

e. planning for the replacement and maintenance of existing NHS assets.

We will examine each of these issues, first in the context of the pre-Review situation of the NHS and then taking account of the recent changes proposed by the NHS Review.

3 PUBLIC EXPENDITURE CONTROL

As noted above, one of the major problems facing any modern health care system is that of avoiding *cost escalation* and achieving control over total expenditure. This has been achieved in recent years in the UK by the use of *cash limits* on the Hospital and Community Health Services (HCHS) budget and its component parts. Cash limits have effectively been extended under the NHS Review in part also to the Family Practitioner Services (FPS) budget through its proposals for family doctor budgets for larger practices and for 'indicative' drugs budgets for GPs generally. This latter extension of cash limits would be in line with the recent establishment of a cash limited Social Fund on the social security side of the former DHSS, in place of earlier demand-led entitlements and benefits. The imposition of cash limits in these new directions clearly raises important issues in their own right that are beyond the scope of this chapter.

It is notable here, however, that the previous system of cash limits for the HCHS has given rise to major problems for the efficient management of capital resources. Cash control as practiced to date is essentially an annual phenomenon associated with *annual* budgets, *annual* cash limits, and *annual* public expenditure plans for particular financial years. Capital, on the other hand, is concerned with the deployment of resources over longer periods of time cutting across different financial years.

Even the construction phase of a capital project, perhaps delayed by adverse weather conditions in the early Spring months, can run into problems when it meets cash limits that are set by reference to a financial year that ends on 31st March. To avoid this problem requires sufficient carry-forward arrangements to facilitate a delay of payment to the contractor until the work is completed. To date these carry-forward arrangements in the NHS have been rather limited (Jones and Prowle, 1987) in order to maintain control over annual public expenditure. However this presents NHS treasurers with the rather artificial task of ensuring cash expenditure takes place one side of the dividing line rather than the other. This leads also to the 'typewriters in March' syndrome whereby unused balances are off-loaded into less essential capital assets before the financial year-end.

In addition, the concentration upon cash-flow, rather than accruals, accounting, has in recent years led many authorities to stay within annual cash limits despite rapidly rising costs and annual expenditure by simply deferring cash payment until the following financial year (HFMA, 1987). In contrast, standard commercial accounting under the 'fundamental' accounting standard SSAP2, whereby expenditure is matched with the accounting period which benefits from that expenditure, rather than simply recorded in the period in which cash expenditure takes place, would reveal the full extent of the expenditure over-run by the authority, given its existing income.

The conflict between the efficient management of capital resources and aggregate public expenditure control is heightened by the relatively short time horizons within which adjustments in macro-economic management can occur, with annual (and at times more frequent) variations in public expenditure cash limits being in many past years a major policy tool for such macro-economic management. Reductions in annual capital expenditure budgets then have the advantage, as a weapon of macro-economic management, of producing a relatively large change in aggregate demand, as 'lumpy' projects are cancelled or deferred, without many of the immediate political disadvantages that cuts in revenue expenditure would bring.

However, the adverse impact of such variations on the efficient management of capital resources of such variations, particularly when these are made at short notice, is exemplified by the experience of capital expenditure controls in local authorities. Thus the Audit Commission has concluded that the existing systems have 'contributed to wasteful investment by a combination of delays to worthwhile projects, pressure to spend before the year end, failure to plan ahead and abrupt curbs in programmes with an associated loss of scale economies' (Audit Commission, 1985).

Fortunately, capital investment in the NHS has remained relatively stable compared to some other parts of the public sector, as Figure 5.2 illustrates. Lack of sudden variations in permitted capital investment remains one important condition for securing maximum value for money from the available capital resources. Given the large number of changes in interest rates which have occurred in recent years, increasing the proportion of private sector investment in the health sector would itself not necessarily achieve this condition. In addition transferring more capital expenditure decisions from the public sector to the private sector has the effect of placing even more reliance upon interest rates as a principal tool of macro-economic policy.   Increases in interest rates to meet short-term macro-economic difficulties may themselves cause long-term problems for the growth of the capital stock in the private sector.

The existing cash-based nature of public expenditure control, however, has posed particular problems for the efficient management of capital resources in the NHS also because of the 'lumpy' nature of capital investment. The available capital funds are clearly insufficient to finance a new District General Hospital (DGH) in each District Health Authority (DHA) each year and so cannot in total be efficiently devolved in cash form down to the district level each year. In addition, an important feature of the existing public expenditure control framework is the restriction on individual health authorities carrying over any substantial cash balance from one financial year to another.

The result has been that each Regional Health Authority (RHA) has tended to retain a regional 'pot of gold' of capital funds for which individual DHAs have bid to obtain finance as a 'free good' for their capital schemes. This in turn has lead to a tendency for 'overbidding' by individual districts intent on free regional capital, together with a compounding of the elements of political patronage and uncertainty in the receipt of capital funds at the district level. This is well illustrated by the following quotation from Mrs Korner based on her experience as a DHA Chairman:

> 'I and my colleagues learnt that, when it came to investment, there were two kinds of money—"our" money and "their" money. Our money came from internal sources—to tease this money out of revenue budget was difficult, requires foresight, planning, co-operation of staff and fine judgement.   "Their" money,   i.e. regional capital, was totally unpredictable in its timing and size, and its allocation seemed to many to depend on luck, on the marginality of the constituency, on the possibility and actuality of scandal and on the personal influence of the

chairman. In an attempt to attract some of this [free regional] money we...gambled for all or nothing, the schemes were extravagant in conception and often in revenue consequences.' (AHST, 1985).

The problems produced for the efficient management of NHS capital resources by such a system include the following:

a. DHAs have an incentive to pursue projects, such as energy-saving schemes, that are revenue-saving for the district but which are capital demanding, using up 'free' regional capital;

b. RHAs have an incentive to build cheaper buildings that save regional capital but which may result in greater revenue expenditure of operating and maintaining the buildings in the longer-term;

c. DHAs have an incentive to go for 'new build' solutions financed out of regional capital funds, rather than devote district revenue resources to maintaining and repairing existing buildings, whose quality is then allowed to deteriorate in order to present a stronger case to the RHA for additional regional capital;

d. the RHA Chairman may make capital decisions on a short-run political basis or attempt to maintain equity between different districts by promising each one a new District General Hospital (DGH) or new CAT scanner, leading to excess capacity across the region and an over-committed capital programme for many years to come;

e. DHAs have an incentive to treat the existing NHS estate as a 'free good' and under-utilise existing assets, such as floor space or operating theatres, when given the opportunity of 'free' new capital;

f. similarly the DHA, without special provisions, may have little incentive to seek additional finance from other sources, such as land sales, that may either revert to the RHA or weaken the district's case for additional regional capital funding. The extent of surplus land and property holdings in the NHS was examined in the Ceri Davies report (1983);

g. the uncertainty associated with the outcome of the traditional 'bidding' system may result in DHAs accepting small 'penny packet' schemes, as capital is shared out in physical terms in a given financial year amongst districts, rather than risk waiting for a more comprehensive longer-term solution that may not ultimately be financed by the RHA. Such 'make-do' schemes may then have the effect of 'maximising the surface area for a given volume' of buildings with accompanying energy-using and other inefficiencies;

h. the cash-based 'free-good' aspect of capital is reflected also in a lack of capital accounting in order to make local managers systematically aware of the capital costs which have been incurred in order to provide the assets that are available to the district;

i. without adequate accounting for the state of the capital stock, managers on three-year contracts may adopt a short-term perspective and divert expenditure away from maintenance and towards forms of expenditure with a more immediate pay-off.

The result of the above system is that neither DHAs nor the RHA have any great incentive to seek the minimisation of the total discounted life-cycle costs of service provision, including both revenue and capital costs, or to take into consideration the opportunity costs of retaining existing assets, such as land.

The implementation of option appraisal techniques (DHSS, 1987) and Approval in Principle (AIP) procedures for approval of major schemes by HM Treasury have more recently provided some brake on the above difficulties. However the same perverse incentives still generate strong pressures on DHAs to treat option appraisal exercises as chiefly *ex post* rationalisations of decisions sought for other reasons, or to fail to explore, or reveal information on, other options than those put forward for 'free' regional capital.

In addition, DHAs are often now permitted to retain some portion of the land sales income originating from their own district. However, without substantial modifications to the above traditional 'bidding' system, there may remain a disincentive to release such land from the fear of future accompanying offsetting reductions in regional capital funding as a result of such land sales income.

Given the major cost-containment and public expenditure control advantages of cash limits, the next question is whether there is a means of overcoming the above perverse incentives that are militating against the efficient management of capital resources in the NHS, whilst remaining within such public expenditure control. It is this question to which we turn in the next section.

4. CAPITAL CREDITS

We have noted above the strong cash-based nature of public expenditure control for reasons chiefly of macro-economic management in controlling aggregate demand in the economy. In order to secure improvements in micro-economic resource management, it is necessary to distinguish between several fundamental properties of money in order to devise a form of 'near money' that can facilitate such improvements.

The two most important properties of money here are firstly its use as *a store of value* and secondly its use as *a means of exchange*. The existing public expenditure control system restricts annual capital income through a regional cash limit that must be spent in the particular financial year, with limited carry-forward facilities. In addition it prevents individual health authorities from holding any significant cash balances from one financial year to another. In doing so, the system not only limits the use of money as a means of exchange, for purposes of public expenditure control, but also has the effect of preventing its effective use as a store of value for individual health authorities.

The result is to interfere with a natural economic function, that of *saving* over time. In particular, individual health authorities become forced to provide for the future through the medium of physical assets rather than financial assets, even though the latter could provide the opportunity for more flexibility to defer decisions on their final use and scope for accumulating them into a capital scheme of optimal size, or for viring them into revenue rather than capital expenditure.

The restriction on the use of money as a store of value for individual health authorities has some relevance to public expenditure control, in that the build-up of future entitlements to spend by health authorities can complicate such control. However, it is important to note that public expenditure control is concerned with *aggregate* expenditure, with no attempt at local macro-economic management at the regional, let alone the district, level. It is then possible to have zero overall outstanding liability for future spending across all authorities taken together, whilst still permitting positive balances for some district health authorities and negative balances for the others within the region.

Such indeed is the result of adopting the system advocated in this chapter. Under this system each RHA would become a 'banker' for individual district 'capital entitlement accounts' (CEAs) that are added to each year by the region crediting each district CEA with a share of the total regional capital income. Such a share is in the form of a 'near money' or capital credit that does act as a store of value (or of 'brownie points') for the individual DHA.

When the DHA receives approval to undertake capital expenditure in the district from the RHA, the DHA is charged out of its CEA balance, which would become negative for the individual DHA when the capital charges for the DHA to date exceed its accumulated capital credit income. The charge here is a real charge in the sense that more capital expenditure at any one time by the district causes its net entitlement to future capital expenditure to be reduced.

Such a real charge is, however, compatible with the use of a form of near money, or capital credit, which acts as a store of value for the DHA. This can then be distinguished from cash that is completely liquid and which would present potential problems for public expenditure control if held in balances in an unrestricted way for DHAs.

Under this system, the RHA would have the responsibility to manage the regional capital programme of approved capital schemes in the region within its regional cash limit on total capital expenditure. This would include in particular 'lumpy' large projects, such as new DGHs, with the cash management for smaller schemes delegated to the district level if desired under delegated district cash limits for such minor schemes, and the RHA providing regional brokerage facilities to ease the annuality problem of cash management between financial years.

Again the DHA would be charged out of its capital credit balance whenever capital expenditure was incurred on the DHA's behalf by the Region within the regional cash limit on capital expenditure. Because a capital credit only takes on the additional function of money as a 'medium of exchange' when it receives cash authorisation for its expenditure by the RHA within the regional cash limit, there is no danger of any loss of control of total regional capital expenditure. In addition, by distinguishing between the DHA's capital credit balance in a long-term Capital Entitlement Account (CEA) that can be built up and run down over time by the district, and cash-flow management by the RHA, one can achieve both the natural economic function of saving by individual DHAs in financial terms and public expenditure control at the Regional level.

The share of the total regional capital received by a district each year as a new capital credit into its CEA would be determined either on a population-weighted 'fair share' basis, adjusted for cross-boundary flows, or on the basis of the number of patients treated within the district. When this is combined with the above charging system, one can then achieve micro-economic efficiency and equity at the district level, at the same time as macro-economic control of public expenditure. Moreover, because the building up and running down of capital credit balances by individual DHAs involves some saving and others effectively borrowing through the medium of the RHA acting as the banker for these accounts, one has established an internal capital market that can promote greater efficiency in the use of capital resources within the NHS without any new additional cash needed 'up-front' to operate the system.

The achievement of equity between districts can be attained through the use of a RAWP or similar style formula to allocate the total available annual capital budget for the region between the individual districts. Such a formula can take into account trends over time in service priorities and in each district's target population in each specialty area. In addition, it can be extended to include an adjustment for the existing endowment and condition of capital stock in each individual district, as in Mayston (1990). Again by distinguishing between capital credits and cash, one can ensure equity and stability in the relative distribution of capital credit income each year into individual district CEAs, at the same time as permitting uneven and 'lumpy' receipts in any given year of the amount of physical capital any one district receives.

The total sum of capital credits allocated each year by the region into individual district CEAs is required to equal the total regional capital cash limit, which in turn equals the total regional capital expenditure. As a result, the total liabilities, or entitlements to spend, created across the region as a whole are balanced by the total assets created, with therefore no regional build-up of excess liability, or net entitlement to future public expenditure outside of the existing system of public expenditure control.

The simplest system of capital charging against the accumulated district CEA balances is that of a 100 per cent deduction of the district's capital expenditure in the same year as the expenditure is actually incurred. This system has the advantage of not requiring any detailed information on expected individual asset lives. A time cost of capital can still be built in by charging interest on negative balances of capital credits in a DHA's CEA and paying interest at the same rate on positive balances. Because of the lack of any net liability across the region as a whole, the total interest paid out by the RHA would each year equal the total interest received from DHAs with negative balances, so that there is no net cash-flow consequence across the region as a whole.

The DHA then has an incentive to consider whether or not the capital expenditure could be deferred, and to trade-off this capital expenditure against the additional revenue income that the interest plus principal would generate if the capital expenditure were not undertaken. The inclusion of such a capital charge and interest element would thus introduce a 'time value of money' that would provide an incentive for the DHA to itself carry out unbiased option appraisal and life-cycle costing exercises in order to find the most efficient and effective use of its capital resources, as reflected in its CEA balance. When this interest rate is set equal in real terms to the recommended Treasury discount rate for option appraisal exercises, the incentives provided by this capital charging system are aligned with the recommendations that would follow from implementing the option appraisal procedures, including the incentive to explore all relevant options.

Thus, even with the relatively simple system of 100 per cent first year charge, each DHA has a strong incentive to find the most efficient use for its scarce capital resources. Given also sufficient virement between capital and revenue income, this implies also overall efficiency in the use of each DHA's scarce resources (Mayston, 1990).

A slightly more complicated system is to charge capital expenditure against the CEA balance equally over the expected useful life of each asset. Without the inclusion of an interest element, this becomes equivalent to a straight-line depreciation charge. With the inclusion of an interest element, it becomes equivalent to an annuity depreciation or leasing charge, that will repay the original principal, or the purchase price of the asset, including a constant percentage financing charge, by an equal annual contribution over the life of the asset. It is then based upon the same principle as an ordinary domestic repayment mortgage.

There are two ways of dividing the total constant annual capital charge that results from a given item of capital expenditure. The first, as in Figure 5.5, involves interest being charged at a constant annual rate on the outstanding capital. As time progresses more capital is repaid and the total interest element within the constant annual charge reduces, so that a larger capital repayment is made each year.

Figure 5.5: Annuity depreciation

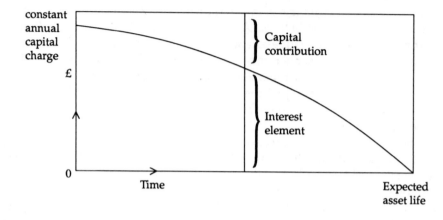

The second method is to keep the capital contribution element constant over the life of the asset, at the same rate that would be implied by straight-line depreciation. The interest element is then also constant and may be shown to equal the interest due on the average amount of capital, in present value terms, that is outstanding over the life of the asset under this constant capital repayment method. This method is illustrated in Figure 5.6.

Figure 5.6: Straight-line depreciation

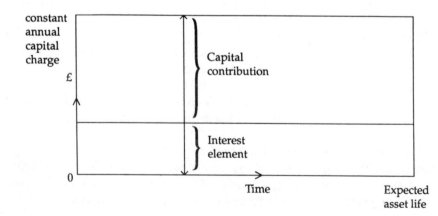

5. THE RELEVANCE OF ACCRUALS ACCOUNTING

The above capital credit system can readily generate financial statements for the DHA that satisfy relevant accounting standards.   These financial statements are in the form of a Statement of Income and Costs and a Balance Sheet which incorporate capital accounting satisfying the relevant accounting standards SSAP2, SSAP4, SSAP12, and SSAP21 (ICAEW, 1988).   These financial statements are illustrated in Table 5.1 using the method illustrated in Figure 5.5.

Table 5.1: Statement of Income and Costs

| | £m at constant March 19X2 prices | | | | |
Financial Year:	19X1/2	19X2/3	19X3/4	19X4/5	19X5/6
INCOME:					
Revenue Allocation	61.000	61.500	62.000	62.500	63.000
Income from Fees etc	2.500	2.500	2.500	2.500	2.500
CEA Income	3.000	3.000	3.000	3.000	3.000
CEA Interest	0.000	0.209	0.429	0.660	0.903
Total Income	66.500	67.209	67.929	68.660	69.403
COSTS OF SERVICE:					
Revenue Expenditure	60.000	60.500	61.000	61.500	62.000
Capital Contribution	1.810	1.901	1.996	2.095	2.200
Interest	0.500	0.409	0.314	0.215	0.110
Total Capital Cost	2.310	2.310	2.310	2.310	2.310
Total Annual Cost	62.310	62.810	63.310	63.810	64.310
Credit Credits Retained	4.190	4.399	4.619	4.850	5.093

| BALANCE SHEET | £m at constant March 19X2 prices | | | | |
at 31st March	19X2	19X3	19X4	19X5	19X6
ASSETS					
Fixed Assets					
at Cost	10.000	10.000	10.000	10.000	10.000
Cumulative Depreciation	1.810	3.711	5.706	7.801	10.000
Net Book Value	8.190	6.289	4.294	2.199	0.000
CEA Balance	4.190	8.589	13.209	18.059	23.152
	12.380	14.879	17.503	20.258	23.152
CAPITAL AND RESERVES					
Capital Entitlement Account	4.190	8.589	13.209	18.059	23.152
Outstanding Obligations	8.190	6.289	4.294	2.199	0.000
	12.380	14.879	17.503	20.258	23.152

In the example, the DHA has increasing real income from its revenue allocation from £61 million in the financial year 19X1/2 rising to £63 million in the financial year 19X5/6, with income from fees etc. of £2.5 million per year. In addition it receives capital credit income into its Capital Entitlement Account of £3 million per year as its equitable share of the total regional capital budget, together with interest at five per cent in real terms on its accumulated CEA Balance in the Balance Sheet. Thus in 19X2/3 it receives interest of five per cent at constant prices on the £4.190 million accumulated CEA Balance at 31st March 19X2, that is, £0.209 million.

In addition to Revenue Expenditure rising from £60 million in 19X1/2 to £62 million in 19X5/6, the DHA is also subject to a capital charge against its accumulated CEA Balance. The example shown in Table 5.1 involves the acquisition of a capital asset costing £10 million at the start of the financial year 19X1/2, with an expected useful life of five years. Under an interest rate of five per cent in real terms, this generates a total constant annual lease or mortgage charge of £2.310 million per annum. As in the Statement of Income and Costs in Table 5.1, and Figure 5.5, this is made up of two parts. The first of these is an interest element which declines over time from an initial value of five per cent of £10 million, that is £0.5 million, as the net book value declining to zero over the five year period as more and more capital is repaid. The second is the annual capital contribution, which adds to the cumulative write-off or depreciation in the balance sheet, and which increases over time in Table 5.1 and Figure 5.5 to offset the falling interest element.

By spreading out the total capital costs evenly over the expected useful life of the asset, one is satisfying the fundamental accruals concept of SSAP2 and SSAP12 on Accounting for Depreciation, which seek to match the capital costs of an asset with the periods of time 'expected to benefit from its use'. In addition by adopting the method of Figure 5.5, with the accounting treatment of Outstanding Obligations as in Table 5.1, one is satisfying also SSAP 21 on Accounting for Leases and Hire Purchase Contracts.

The treatment of existing assets would involve offsetting the asset valuation in the Balance Sheet with an initial credit balance or '100 per cent government grant' in the reserves. This initial balance is then reduced each year by the extent of an annual capital credit transferred as an income item in the Statement of Income and Costs so as to offset exactly the capital contribution element of the annual depreciation charge in the cost entries. Such a treatment is then in conformity with method b of SSAP 4 recommended by ED 43, which involves treating 'the amount of the grant as a deferred credit which is credited to profit and loss account by instalments over the expected lives of the related assets'.

As noted above, it is possible to price capital, with its resultant incentive effects, to the recipient district simply by a 100 per cent charge in the first year. Spreading out the capital charge over the expected useful life of each asset then has the following economic rationale. First, it gives an indication of the *average capital cost per period of expected use* that has been incurred to provide the annual services of the district. Secondly, it provides a reminder of these capital costs in the current year's Statement of Income and Costs, so that an assessment can be formed of whether or not *value for money* is currently being obtained from the assets. These two factors are relevant to monitoring the efficiency of a DHA or unit and to assessing whether equity is being, preserved in the distribution of capital resources between DHAs or units providing similar services.

It becomes important to clarify the purpose of spreading out the accounting charge (as distinct from any cash financing of the asset) over the expected useful life of the asset, particularly when it comes to making allowance for inflation in the financial statements. The charge here relates to the capital resources which have been invested to provide the asset in question. A measure of these real resources in terms of the present price level is provided by a simple single-index adjustment to the present price level so that all previous figures are converted to constant purchasing power terms. This itself is much simpler to compute for assets whose purchase price is known than a system of current cost accounting (CCA), which under the now withdrawn current cost accounting standard SSAP 16 would require the following complicated procedures:

i. the application of different specific indices for the many different types of health service assets;
ii. an adjustment for differences in 'service potential' between each existing asset and a corresponding 'modern equivalent asset';
iii. an adjustment for differences in operating costs between each existing asset and a corresponding 'modern equivalent asset';
iv. an adjustment for differences in the expected useful life of each existing asset and a corresponding 'modern equivalent asset'.

Since the NHS produces a very large range of differentiated outputs from a great variety of specialised equipment and other assets, many of which are subject to substantial technological change, with the nature of many specialisms changing significantly over time, the ability to identify a 'modern equivalent asset' and compare 'service potentials' can prove to be a complex and potentially impossible task.

The use of replacement cost as the 'current' cost tends to imply that assets physically depreciate through use, whereas many NHS assets physically deteriorate and/or become obsolescent through the passage of time. In addition, when assets are not to be replaced, the 'value to the business' concept of SSAP 16 requires the computation of the 'recoverable amount', which requires a comparison between an estimate of the net realisable value of the asset and 'the amount recoverable from its further use'.

Aside from the problems of estimating the net realisable value of many NHS assets, there is the conceptual problem of measuring 'the amount recoverable from its further use' when the main activities of the NHS are not based upon fees per service. Yet this is the amount which must be measured under current cost accounting, particularly where the asset is to be retained but not replaced. In addition, the calculation of whether an asset would currently be replaced becomes complicated by the existence of cash limits, which would prevent more than a limited number of assets being replaced at any one time.

The above problems are avoided if one makes use of a single general index adjustment to constant purchasing power accounting. For existing assets that were acquired some years ago, this encounters the difficulty that records are often not available in the public sector for assets acquired in the past. A one-off revaluation of such assets to depreciated replacement cost then becomes relevant, linked in then to an annual single-index adjustment thereafter.

The average annual capital cost indicated by the above financial statements can be used as a performance indicator to monitor whether or not value for money is being obtained from the relevant assets. The greater the utilisation of these assets and the lower the capital cost incurred to provide them, the lower will be the average capital cost per unit of service delivered, as indicated by the annual depreciation charge divided by the through-put of cases treated. However, for many NHS assets there may arise the problem of multiple use of any given asset, with then a problem of allocating the annual depreciation charge across these different users of the same asset.

6. INCENTIVES

A system of capital charging can provide incentives for greater efficiency in the use of new capital resources, and for the attainment of greater value for money from those existing capital assets that are retained. However, account needs to be taken of the fact that the original capital cost of many NHS assets is now a sunk cost which will not vary however much the asset is subsequently used. This sunk cost must in turn be distinguished from the opportunity cost of subsequently using the asset within the NHS.

This distinction is particularly important in view of the danger of a system of capital charging setting up perverse incentives (for example, to get rid of assets or demolish buildings) in order to avoid the capital charge, even though the net cost saved or revenue realised by the NHS as a whole may fall short of the operational benefit of continuing to retain the asset in the NHS. Such perverse incentives have been generated by existing capital charging systems in the form of industrial property rates that can encourage the removal of roofs from temporarily empty factories in order to avoid the rate or capital charge, even though there is a negative expected long-term benefit to the owner, aside from saving the rate charge, from removing the roof.

The opportunity cost of continuing to use the asset in its present use will, typically, be equal to the net realisable value (NRV) of the asset in question. If there are other potential users of the asset within the NHS, the NRV figure needs to be extended to the more general figure of the 'alternative value to the organisation' (AVTO) discussed in Mayston (1989). Even if this is simply the NRV, there arise a number of problems of actually estimating its value, particularly if one goes down to the level of detail of individual items of equipment, where well organised second-hand markets may not exist.

In the case of land, these problems include the need to assess the likelihood of planning permission being granted that permits a change of use and the commercial development of any land sold by the NHS. In addition there can be problems of valuation of NRV depending upon whether several assets are sold all at once or one at a time. In view of the difficulties of introducing a system of asset rents based upon opportunity cost valuations comprehensively across all NHS assets, there is a strong case for introducing any such system selectively for only those assets, such as surplus land, for which disposal or redeployment might be desirable.

However if such a selective asset rental system is to be effective in providing incentives to districts to make better use of existing assets, the asset rent should arguably be more than simply a notional rent as proposed in the Ceri Davies report (1983). It is then possible to incorporate a selective asset rental system that provides a financial incentive only to retain an asset when this is beneficial to the NHS within the above capital credit system in one of two following ways.

The first method is simply to allow the DHA to retain the proceeds of any disposal in its CEA account with the RHA. The sale proceeds provide cash in the year of disposal to the RHA, which it can use to augment its cash limit to increase the permitted capital expenditure programme across the region as a whole. Those DHAs that undertake this additional capital expenditure in the year of disposal are then essentially borrowing from the DHA that has made the disposal. The capital credit charges on their CEA accounts resulting from this capital expenditure then reduce their claims on future capital expenditure in the region. Thus the DHA that makes the disposal is able to realise this repayment in the form of additional capital expenditure equal to these disposal proceeds plus accumulated interest when it wishes to undertake this additional capital expenditure.

Any inequitable initial distribution across DHAs of disposable land and other assets can be adjusted for by reducing the annual capital credit income in a lump sum way of those DHAs heavily endowed with disposable assets, and increasing the annual capital credit income of those not so fortunately endowed.

The second method is to have an explicit annual asset rent imposed by the RHA on those district assets which the RHA considers may be surplus to operational needs. A *neutral* system of asset rents, as in Mayston (1989), would then offset this asset rent by an annual grant which the DHA may retain whether or not the asset is given up. If the DHA does give up possession of the asset, it no longer pays the asset rent to the RHA but keeps the grant, so that the net financial incentive to give up the asset rather than retain possession is equal to the asset rent. The asset rent is set equal to the above AVTO value, which causes the DHA to face the opportunity cost of the assets employed.

A *non-neutral* system would involve an offsetting annual grant of capital credit income for each DHA that was not necessarily equal to the asset rent, so that redistribution of capital endowments across DHAs is then feasible. However, since the grant is given whether or not the DHA retains possession of the asset, the net effect on its CEA balance of retaining, rather than not retaining, the asset is still the value of the asset rent. Since this is set equal to the above AVTO value, the DHA again faces the full opportunity cost of retaining the asset.

Such a system of explicit asset rents would be operated by the RHA through a regional asset management fund. The total level of all district grants out of the fund would be set equal to the total value of asset rents across all districts and all assets. When an asset is disposed of, the DHA would no longer have to pay the rent on the asset. The RHA would then have to realise the opportunity cost of the asset in order to finance this fall in income from district asset rents to the regional asset management fund. In order to keep the asset management fund solvent, the RHA thus has a strong incentive to set the asset rents at a realistic level in case it has to realise the opportunity cost value that it has set for each asset rent.

It is possible to incorporate an asset rental element alongside the capital charging system through the notion of a multi-part lease. This would involve the basic lease charge in the form of an annuity depreciation or mortgage charge that must be paid or accounted for however the asset is deployed. The second part would be a buy-back provision equal to the annual rent or lump sum that the DHA would receive if it gave up the asset.

The first method mentioned above has the advantage that it is simpler to operate and does not require in advance the computation of net realisable values for the setting of explicit asset rents. The second method requires a more elaborate system of asset values but places the carrot slightly closer under the nose of the DHA. If the main disposable asset is land, the net realisable values for the second method may be estimated by the District Valuer's survey which is now carried out periodically for NHS properties.

However, such values may change quite rapidly from year to year and will require a full investigation of the development potential of the land which the District Valuer may not have time to carry out at modest cost. The first method, on the other hand, provides an incentive for each DHA to investigate these development possibilities as closely as it considers desirable, without establishing an administratively complicated system of explicit market assessments and asset rents on a potentially large number of assets. For these reasons, there is much to recommend the first method.

7. REPLACEMENT AND MAINTENANCE

A further distinction that is important to make in the context of capital charging and the use of depreciation accounting in the NHS is that between accounting depreciation and provision for the *maintenance and replacement* of assets.   As emphasised in Baxter (1981) and Harvey and Keer (1983), accounting depreciation is not intended to provide a 'sinking fund' for the replacement of assets.

The only indirect way that a depreciation charge can have this effect is, typically, through the interaction between the depreciation charge in the computation in commercial accounting of profit and the requirements of Section 263 of the Companies Act 1985. These restrict dividends or similar distributions to shareholders to be made only out of 'accumulated realised profit less accumulated realised losses', where 'realised profit' under Paragraph 91 of Schedule 4 of the Companies Act is to be determined 'in accordance with principles generally accepted with respect to the determination for accounting purposes of realised profit at the time those accounts were prepared', that is inclusive of a deduction for depreciation.

The effect of including a depreciation charge is thus to retain more funds in the firm than might otherwise have been the case but only if the proposed level of dividends if paid would have lead to zero retained earnings. However, there is no guarantee even then that these funds are set aside for the replacement of the assets whose purchase gave rise to the depreciation charge, rather than invested in other tangible or intangible assets. Moreover, since the 'generally accepted accounting principles' for the computation of profits in a company's accounts currently involve historic cost depreciation, the indirect connection between the commercial depreciation charge and provision for the replacement of assets is further weakened. The historic cost of assets acquired many years ago may be quite different from the replacement cost of assets at the time that they will need replacement.

The connection between a depreciation charge and the replacement of assets becomes even weaker in the context of a cash-limited public service where health authorities in aggregate cannot save over time.   The total capital available to the service must then be adjusted to take account of replacement needs at the time that they fall due, if both new-build requirements and replacement needs are to be satisfied.   Only if the age distribution of assets in the NHS is uniform will a standard straight-line depreciation charge (even ignoring inflation and changes in relative prices) typically provide a good prediction of the annual cash-flow demands for replacement expenditure.

If one examines the age distribution of the floor area of NHS property in England, the available evidence shown in Figure 5.7 suggests that it is very non-uniformly distributed (NAO, 1988). Similarly the graphs in Figures 5.8 and 5.9 below of capital expenditure in real terms (deflated by the GDP deflator for fixed domestic capital formation) since the inception of the NHS

in 1948 reveal an uneven time pattern of past expenditure, both for total fixed
assets and for both Buildings and Works and Plant and Machinery. A similar
uneven time pattern to hospital capital formation is evident also before 1948
(Pinker, 1966; Feinstein and Pollard, 1988). This suggests that there may be a
significant bunching of future capital replacement needs, rather than their
being uniformly spread out over time, a point that is discussed in more
detail below.

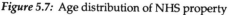

Figure 5.7: Age distribution of NHS property

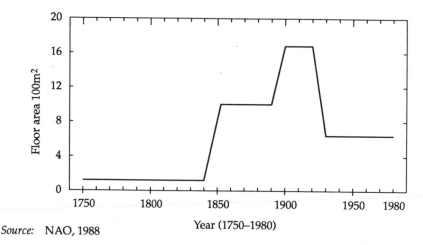

Source: NAO, 1988

Figure 5.8 shows the breakdown of total investment since 1948 in both
public and private sector health services by type of asset, and Figure 5.9 the
breakdown of this total between the public and private sectors. Figure 5.10
shows one significant trend implicit in Figure 5.9, that of a substantial rise
since 1974 in the proportion of total investment in health services carried out
by the private sector.

Figures 5.7–5.9 also reveal the need for more detailed examination of
future replacement and maintenance needs. Figure 5.7 shows that some 76
per cent of the floor area of NHS property in England in 1982 pre-dated the
formation of the NHS in 1948, and that some 53 per cent was pre–1919 in
origin. Some of these ageing buildings have been disposed of since 1982,
particularly under the programme of closure of long-stay mental institutions.
Many of the remaining buildings are still structurally sound, and perhaps of
much greater longevity than some more recent constructions, such as those
of the 1960s. However, this ageing stock cannot be expected to be of infinite
economic life, particularly taking into account energy and maintenance
costs. This conclusion is reinforced by the NEDO findings of some £1.7
billion backlog maintenance in the NHS, with the National Audit Office
(1988) confirming examples of up to 59 per cent of DHA property in Condition

D (that is, 'inoperable or unacceptable' condition, with 'major or costly repairs necessary') and up to 97 per cent in Condition C, requiring significant repairs to raise it to an acceptable standard.

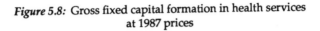

Figure 5.8: Gross fixed capital formation in health services at 1987 prices

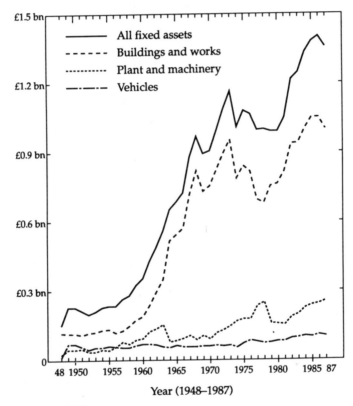

Year (1948–1987)

Sources: CSO, 1954–1988

In addition, however, Figure 5.9 reveals a substantial build-up during the 1960s in NHS capital expenditure since 1948 to a new higher level from approximately 1967 onwards. Many large items of plant, such as roofs, boilers and lifts, have an estimated economic life of 15–25 years (NBA, 1985), suggesting an 'echo effect' of this steady build-up to a newer higher level of this replacement needs for capital expenditure from the mid–1980's onwards.

Figure 5.9: Gross fixed capital formation in health services at 1987 prices

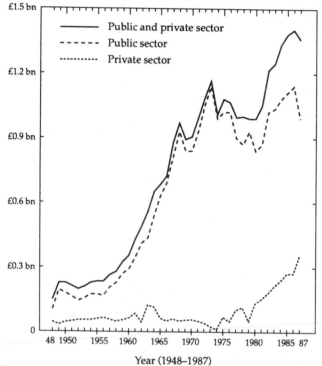

Sources: CSO, 1954–1988

Figure 5.10: Private share of investment in health services

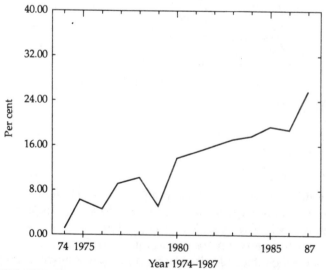

Source: CSO, 1975–1988

On top of this is the increasing rate of 'embodied technical progress' in health care systems, in more advanced technology medicine and computerised management information systems. These involve greater capital investment in equipment now subject to more rapid technological obsolescence than earlier generations of medical equipment, thereby accelerating the projected curve of future replacement needs.

Behind these general trends, however, there is a lack of detailed information for management and planning. As the Public Accounts Committee (1988) noted, the six surveys required by Health Circular (86) 13 in November 1986 for the provision of an Estate Data Base are still incomplete in many DHAs. These surveys include records of DHA property holdings, of their physical condition, functional suitability, space utilisation, energy performance and of their compliance with statutory standards. Without this data, effective long-term estate management in the NHS becomes difficult to achieve.

Such a lack of information on detailed replacement and maintenance needs, however, is only part of the incomplete nature of the existing system for planning investment in the NHS. Whilst Regional strategic plans have only relatively recently formed part of the NHS decision-making process, such plans have tended to follow the determination of the national aggregate level of capital investment in the NHS, rather than *vice versa*. This relative lack of attention to detailed future service planning and replacement needs in determining the NHS aggregate total of capital expenditure is reinforced by the relative neglect of capital in macro-economic planning. In particular, it is notable that the Treasury's macro-economic model (HM Treasury, 1987) takes no account of the condition or extent of the capital stock, either in the public and private sectors, as a determinant of the potential future output of goods and services, or as a determinant of the need for future expenditure to make good any present expenditure short-falls. This is not an ideal basis for either macro- or micro-economic policy formation if capital resources are to be efficiently deployed in the long term.

8. INTERIM CONCLUSIONS

The above discussion has emphasised that, even within the pre-Review framework of the NHS, it is possible to devise a system for the improved management of capital resources in the NHS that has the following important advantages:

i. it encourages the more efficient use of new and existing capital resources, whilst containing total costs within cash limits;
ii. it provides incentives for option appraisals to be carried out by DHAs in a realistic way to minimise the total cost of achieving a given service delivery target;

iii. it provides incentives for revenue and capital expenditure to be optimised towards minimising the total life-cycle cost of service delivery;

iv. it assists in the Griffiths' reforms of devolving more resources and decision-making to district general managers by giving them greater control over the development of capital resources in the district and more involvement in the long-term development of the district. This in particular contrasts with the traditional 'bidding' system for capital projects, where the regional capital programme becomes overcommitted into the distant future with major schemes that are the result mainly of political patronage, but which leave individual district general managers with little managerial or resource flexibility;

v. it helps to overcome the 'new-build' bias of political decision-making on capital investment in the NHS and to stimulate the search for solutions, such as the improved maintenance of existing assets, which minimise the total cost of service provision;

vi. it encourages the pooling and sharing of capital facilities across DHAs through seeking an equitable distribution of capital entitlements in more liquid form, rather than in the form of equal amounts of physical assets, such as new DGHs or CAT scanners, which are then under-utilised;

vii. it can facilitate longer-term service planning against the background of greater knowledge by the district of its likely share of total regional capital resources than under a traditional 'bidding' system where success in the bidding process is more uncertain;

viii. it encourages existing capital assets to be no longer viewed as a 'free good' but rather to be deployed as a key resource in service delivery in order to minimise the demand on new capital resources;

ix. it encourages the disposal of surplus assets at the optimal time for the district and the rationalisation of the existing estate to a size that can be adequately maintained, with the sale proceeds reinvested by the district over time in new or up-graded existing facilities using the banking facilities provided by the RHA;

x. it generates improved capital accounts for the DHA which can be used to monitor whether value for money is being achieved from capital expenditure within the district, and make local managers aware of the total average costs, including capital costs, which have been incurred to provide services;

xi. it generates improved performance indicators that take into account capital costs in estimating the total cost per unit of service delivered;

xii. it encourages the development of an internal market in the NHS, as proposed by Enthoven (1985), by giving each DHA greater autonomy and incentive to attract patients outside the district, and by establishing an internal capital market, with the RHA acting as 'banker' for the receipt and transfer of credits between districts within overall cash limits.

The capital credit system thus represents an evolutionary approach, building upon existing initiatives in the NHS and extending them in the direction of an internal market and greater economic efficiency. Such a system can, moreover, maintain cost control within cash limits and the existing system of public expenditure control. However, there remains the need to set these cash limits in total at amounts appropriate for financing the desired level of service to patients. In addition, if local managers are to manage their capital resources efficiently over time, there is a need to ensure sufficient predictability of these amounts, and sufficient flexibility of their use between neighbouring financial years.

9. THE NHS REVIEW PROPOSALS

In previous sections the problems of capital resource management within the pre-Review situation of the NHS have been examined and a possible solution to these problems suggested. This section examines the proposals of the NHS Review White Paper, *Working for Patients,* and its accompanying Working Papers, in terms of their likely impact on the management of capital resources in the NHS.

Perhaps the most far-reaching proposal of the Review in this regard is for the formation of 'opted-out' self-governing hospitals. This in particular raises many questions for the link between regional and district service planning and the provision of hospital and other capital resources to meet service needs.

Key features of many capital resources, such as hospital facilities, are their geographical fixity, and both the time lag and high cost involved if new facilities close by must be constructed to substitute for existing facilities no longer being available. In areas where there are many hospitals within reasonable travelling distance with spare capacity, a district general manager may readily be able to negotiate contracts with self-governing hospitals under competitive conditions.

However, in areas where this condition does not hold, the 'opting out' of an existing DGH can cause major problems of assured supply to NHS patients within reasonable travelling distance. Such a tendency will be considerably increased if private patients prove more profitable to the self-governing hospital than those financed by the NHS district. To overcome these problems would require:

a. the establishment of long-term contracts with assured supply between self-governing hospitals and DHAs, and/or

b. an extension of the list of 'core' services in para. 4.15 of the White Paper to include all services which need to be supplied locally, together with an obligation upon the local self-governing hospital to supply these services at reasonable cost.

A second related direction in which the opting out of hospitals can introduce complications is that of estate rationalisation. One solution to the problem of a large ageing capital stock with poor condition buildings and high maintenance needs is to rationalise on more intensively used modern facilities, such as those provided by a new or recently built DGH. However, if this 'flagship' DGH then sails off into a more distant relationship with the DHA under 'self-governing' status, the DHA may be left in the position of having no local hospital on which it can rely for many services. Again this might only be rectified through imposing condition a or b above, or alternatively:

c. that no hospital with a significant 'local monopoly' position can become self-governing unless conditions a or b are imposed.

The Review White Paper does contain some provisions in this direction in its statement that: 'The Secretary of State will need specific powers for use in reserve to prevent any NHS Hospital Trust with anything near to a local monopoly of service provision from exploiting its position, for example by charging unreasonable high prices for its services' (paragraph 3.9). However, the White Paper (paragraph 3.6) also proposes freedom for self-governing NHS Hospital Trusts to earn revenue from private patients. The imposition of price control on contracts for NHS patients, without any additional obligation to treat these patients outside the limited 'core services', could then risk a diversion of contracts that the NHS Hospital Trust enters into, away from the NHS and towards the private sector.

The ability of hospitals to opt out of DHA control poses a second potential problem for estate rationalisation in that those hospitals faced with closure or merger may seek to opt out in order to avoid this fate. This situation would then parallel that in the education sector where the Audit Commission (1984) identified 500,000 surplus places in secondary schools and advocated a more systematic approach by local authorities to the rationalisation of surplus places. The later introduction under the 1988 Education Reform Act of the ability of secondary schools to opt out of local education authority control then encouraged schools threatened with closure under the planned rationalisation programme to continue in existence through the opting out provisions of the new Act.

In the NHS Review White Paper, there is fortunately the condition stated that 'The Secretary of State will need to satisfy himself that self-governing status is not simply being sought as an alternative to an unpalatable but necessary closure'. The same paragraph (3.17) also states that 'The NHS must not be obliged to retain hospitals which are redundant to its needs'. Yet there is a danger that the DHA will decide to retain facilities under its own control that it would otherwise have disposed of, in order to maintain at least some guaranteed source of supply, if a DHA does face the threat of its flagship DGH opting out.

It may be the case that self-governing hospitals will seek to make more intensive use of the land and space that they control and more readily dispose of assets considered surplus to needs. The White Paper contains the particular proposal that each associated NHS Hospital Trust 'will be free to dispose of its assets, subject only to a reserve power for the Secretary of State to intervene if a disposal would be against the public interest' (DoH, 1989, p.26). Given the windfall nature of the gains to the more fortunate hospitals with surplus land that would otherwise result from this proposal, it becomes particularly important to ensure that there is adequate allowance for this factor in the funding arrangements.

There is evidence, as in the National Audit Office report on Estate Management in the NHS, that there may be substantial scope for the improved use of existing space in NHS hospitals, with estimates of the revenue savings attainable from the improved utilisation of the existing NHS estate in England of up to £500 million a year (NAO, 1988). In addition, the improved use of existing facilities may reduce the need for expensive new assets to be acquired, which a political bias towards new build solutions might otherwise encourage.

The greater autonomy of NHS Hospital Trusts than under DHA and RHA control may indeed encourage such a greater utilisation of existing space. Similarly, the proposed introduction of funding for both self-governing and other NHS hospitals on the basis of the number of patients treated in different categories may help to improve the utilisation of related assets, such as operating theatres. Another recent study by the NAO (1987) found that in the DHAs examined only some 50–60 per cent of the available operating theatre time was actually utilised, even within a standard working weekday.

Part of such under-utilisation may reflect poor management, which might be overcome by systems for the improved scheduling of operations and staff and their coordination with bed admissions, as have been developed at Trent RHA and Bath DHA. Basing the revenue of hospitals more on the number of cases treated under the new contracting arrangements is likely in itself to encourage the greater utilisation of the existing capital facilities.

However the remainder of the under-utilisation of existing capacity may reflect revenue pressures to limit the number of operations taking place in different specialties. As stressed in Chapter 3, substantial increases in output from existing capital facilities may then be possible, so long as sufficient additional revenue funding is made available to cover the marginal costs involved.

In a simple economic world, the process of competitive bidding for DHA contracts would guarantee the achievement of supply at minimum average cost, inclusive of capital cost, as in an elementary text-book analysis (see, for example, Samuelson and Nordhaus, 1989). However, the real world involves a number of important additional complexities that need to be taken into account.

The first is that hospitals differ in their geographical locations, with consumers in general not indifferent between these different locations. There is then a risk that excess capacity will prevail under such monopolistic competition between competing hospitals, as the standard analysis of monopolistic competition implies (Henderson and Quandt, 1980). Under such excess capacity, average costs will be above the minimum possible.

Secondly, improved utilisation under falling average costs will tend to reinforce the local monopoly position of some hospitals, reducing the ability of the purchasing DHA to obtain competitive prices in the future, unless it signs long-term contracts with the more efficient provider hospitals. There is also a risk that some hospitals will resort to predatory pricing to drive out rival suppliers, in order to establish local monopoly positions that can later be exploited. As noted above, the Review White Paper proposes reserve powers to prevent counteract such excessive prices.

Thirdly, since hospitals are typically producing multiple outputs, there may well arise 'economies of scope', such that the total cost of two activities combined is less than undertaking them separately in different hospitals. This may indeed occur if it is cheaper to provide accident and emergency cover alongside other acute services, so that specialists are readily at hand to treat emergency cases as well as other acute cases.

Seeking the lowest cost bid on each individual service would then be akin to making the market for health services 'contestable'. However, contestable markets involve the problem that even an efficient supplier may not be able to find a 'sustainable' set of prices that ensure its financial viability, even when it is the minimum cost supplier for a given range of services (see Baumol, Panzar and Willig, 1982). Such sustainability is required if the hospital is to be able to set prices in its bid for DHA contracts that prevent a competitor from creaming off parts of its output and thereby leaving the hospital with remaining parts of its service that it must run at a higher average cost than otherwise, with the risk of financial insolvency.

Once inter-temporal considerations are included within the analysis of contestable markets for DHA contracts, such 'unsustainability can come closer to being the rule rather than the exception' such that 'the domain of the invisible hand can be far more limited than intuition may have lead us to suspect. Often there may be no sustainable solutions and the market mechanism may well produce an intertemporal allocation of resources that is patently inefficient' (Baumol *et al.*, 1982, pp.405–6).

Moreover such problems are likely to be greater where demand is growing over time and/or where there is a positive rate of physical deterioration or technological obsolescence of the capital stock (op.cit., p.421), a condition which appears to apply to health care in the UK. Lack of a sustainable price vector may then result in both 'vulnerability of an industry to forms of entry that raise total production costs, as when entry reduces the economies of scale and scope the industry might otherwise offer' and the '"disorderly" evolution of industry, that is, a time path of evolution of industry structure and utilisation of capital that can be said to be inconsistent with intertemporal efficiency in resource allocation' (op.cit., pp.348–9). In both cases these call into doubt whether greater contestability of DHA contracts and the market for patient services will necessarily lead to more efficient investment and capital utilisation for new and existing capital resources.

A greater market orientation may, however, encourage a greater level of investment in the provision of health care facilities in the face of growing demand than would be provided by a system where the Treasury imposes strict cash limits upon capital and revenue expenditure in the NHS. However, the existing cash limits for total DHA expenditure, including capital, are not abolished by the NHS Review which also proposes an overall annual financing limit for each individual self-governing hospital on borrowing from the Government and the private sector.

Much will then depend upon the size of these limits, but if they are no greater in total than at present, greater investment in NHS provision is not assured. Greater investment in health care provision may be generated through a shift of patients out of the NHS into private insurance, as self-governing hospitals find private patients more profitable and quality of service to NHS patients declines under cost pressures rising faster than the likely increase in NHS cash limits.

The proposed imposition of annual financing limits on individual self-governing hospitals may then provide a brake on this process in so far as it involves the expansion of existing NHS hospitals. In addition it risks generating a new form of bureaucratic regulation of the self-governing hospitals to determine these annual financing limits on their total borrowing and associated investment, whilst lacking the service planning advantages of the existing DHA control over unit investment plans.

Rather than imposing annual financing limits at the level of individual self-governing hospitals, there is then a case for an internal market in annual capital expenditure authorisations within a nationally determined total. Such authorisations would have to be bid for by individual self-governing hospitals paying a favourable premium payment in later years into the fund.

Such an internal market would in principle allocate the available total cash-limited capital expenditure efficiently amongst those with the highest willingness to pay. So long as individual DHA and GP budgets have been set at an optimal level, this may also ensure an equitable allocation of capital resources. However, devolving capital expenditure decisions down to the unit level raises the problem of a lack of simultaneity and co-ordination in such decentralised decision-making. The optimal investment strategy for one self-governing hospital depends upon the investment plans of other hospitals offering, or potentially offering, similar services.

Without co-ordination within district and regional strategic service plans, or well-functioning futures markets, or the correct anticipation of future prices and levels of supply, market processes can lead to inefficient decisions, as standard cobweb models demonstrate (Gravelle and Rees, 1981, pp.277–286), particularly where capital investment involves indivisibilities and sunk costs. The means of ameliorating these difficulties may again be through the district negotiating long-term contracts with assured supply with individual hospitals, so that inter-temporal capacity, supply and service planning considerations can be adequately matched together.

Such long-term contracts would go some way towards resolving the potential conflict inherent in the current proposals of the NHS Review White Paper. This asserts that 'Funds for capital investment will continue to be financed by the Exchequer, and, except for NHS Hospital Trusts, will be allocated by RHAs from within an overall capital programme. There will therefore continue to be strategic oversight of capital planning..'. The exclusion of the self-governing NHS Hospital Trusts from the regional capital programme would make regional strategic planning difficult whenever self-governing status is given to key local hospitals, unless such hospitals can be incorporated into regional strategic service planning through long-term contracts for the supply of specific services within the region.

Devolving investment decisions down to individual self-governing units may also involve each unit bearing more total financial risk, including specific risks, than if risk had been spread more widely at the district or regional level. This may then encourage it to be less willing to invest in projects, if there is uncertainty in the financial return, and tends to raise the probability of financial insolvency of the unit, particularly where it fails to carry out realistic investment appraisals.

Given the binding nature of cash limits on capital expenditure across the NHS as a whole, and the expected desire of some self-governing hospitals to increase their level of investment, there may well be pressure on their management to raise outside finance in ways that maximise the funds initially available for expansion. Such a situation would then parallel that of some local authorities which have sought to overcome the binding nature of capital expenditure controls in recent years through unconventional financing arrangements, such as deferred purchase arrangements and interest rate swap agreements. These tend to involve increasing the cash currently available for investment either at the expense of exceptionally large later repayments or a high degree of risk through the inclusion of put or call option elements. Fortunately unconventional financing arrangement are now the subject of restriction in the NHS.

Increasing the mixture of public and private finance also raises interesting questions on the borderline between the public and private sectors as to the optimal mix of these sources of finance, in order to minimise the weighted average cost of capital (WACC) or to achieve other goals. Raising finance from the private sector tends to involve a higher implicit rate of interest than that which would be paid on an equivalent loan financed through the Public Sector Borrowing Requirement (PSBR).

Such a cheaper form of additional finance is, however, prevented at the margin through the binding nature of the existing cash limits on NHS capital expenditure. Where these are imposed for reasons of macro-economic management, it is unclear that an expansion in the use of lower cost public borrowing would necessarily have any more adverse macro-economic impact than opening up public investment opportunities to more expensive private finance. Increasing the extent of private financing of NHS projects would then be for reasons of increasing the extent of private involvement *per se*, rather than for reasons of macro-economic management or for minimising the weighted average cost of capital.

Self-governing hospitals will face continued restrictions upon their total borrowing from the Government and the private sector. It is likely that they will then seek to make greater use of any surplus land left to them by their parent DHA on achieving self-governing status, in order to generate additional finance. If the gains to different hospitals from the disposal of land are not to be simply on a random windfall basis, the capital charges to the relevant hospitals will need to reflect the value of the land they have available for disposal, including its development potential. This makes it particularly important that site valuations be carried out on an appropriate basis. In addition it touches upon the system of capital charges proposed under the NHS Review, examined in the next section.

10. THE PROPOSED SYSTEM OF CAPITAL CHARGES

It is argued in Sections 4 to 8 that it is possible to design a system of improved capital accounting and incentives for improved asset management in the NHS, whilst staying within cash limits and aggregate expenditure control. To do so involves distinguishing cash from a form of 'near money' or capital credit that was held in the district's long-term Capital Entitlement Account (CEA). This 'near money' acts as a store of value for the DHA, but not directly as a means of exchange unless accompanied in any given year by cash authorisation by the RHA within the regional cash limit. Such a distinction makes possible a system of capital charges for capital expenditure against a district's CEA either through a 100 per cent first year charge or through a lease charge that follows the principles of accruals accounting. In doing so it maintains cash expenditure each year within cash limits and ensures no build-up of net long-term liabilities across the system as a whole.

The system of capital charging proposed in the Review White Paper (DoH, 1989) and in the subsequent Working Papers 5 and 9, differs from the above system in several important respects. The first is that the system proposed by the White Paper seeks to impose a cash charge. However, we have noted above the difficulties which arise because of the cash-based nature of the earlier system of managing capital resources and the need to move beyond this in order to resolve some of the underlying problems of capital resource management in the NHS.

In particular there is a need to give districts inter-temporal budgets that they can manage efficiently over time, and out of which actual capital expenditure is charged against the outstanding balance. A cash system of charges would achieve this so long as DHAs are allowed to hold significant cash balances over time. To do so, however, would encounter problems of public expenditure control within cash limits. The problems can be overcome using a capital credit system, but not by a cash system, unless one 'neutralises' the full liquidity of the cash involved.

It is important to note here that a cash charge and a real charge are not synonymous terms. As in the case of a building society or credit card account, a charge that eats into the available remaining credit in the account or adds to the outstanding debt is just as much a real charge as one that is in simple cash terms. The introduction of a 'long transitional period' (Working Paper 9) before the cash charge of the Review becomes operational, moreover, means that it is less of a real charge than a capital credit charge that could be introduced without such a lag.

The second distinguishing feature of the post-Review system of capital charging is that it potentially eats into the amount of revenue that a district has to spend on patient services, rather than into its long-term entitlement to additional capital expenditure. For any district that has at present more than its population-weighted share of the value of its existing capital assets, the proposed capital charge would involve a reduction in the amount of cash it has for revenue expenditure below what it would at present receive. Particularly in the four Thames Regions, there will be districts and units that have asset valuations greater than their population-weighted shares simply because land values are greater closer to London. These districts and units will then tend to suffer most financially, unless one adjusts the notion of population-weighted shares to a more fair-shares basis that also takes into account standards of access and potential travel times of patients to hospitals.

The statement in the Review White Paper that 'there will be no reductions in funds available for patient services' resulting from the introduction of the proposed capital charging and funding system remains true in aggregate terms, but with some districts gaining in cash revenue terms at the expense of others. The financial impact of the proposed Review system on the losing districts is then much stronger than under a capital credit system. Under the system advocated earlier in this chapter, a district with a relatively large stock of existing assets would secure relatively less long-term entitlement to new capital expenditure in the district, on the grounds that the district already has a large existing endowment of capital.

The existing use value of the existing assets may then be an appropriate value of the existing stock in calculating this long-term entitlement to more capital. However, even here it may be more appropriate to work in physical units (such as the 'adjusted bed values' of the Wessex RHA capital planning system), where capital values of land and buildings differ across a region because of different land values as one moves closer to large centres of population.

Under the Review proposals for capital charges, there may be pressure to reduce the size of the existing stock in order to reduce the capital charges, even where the opportunity cost of continued occupation and the disposal value of the site are small. Once it may affect disposal decisions, it is arguable that it is on the basis of opportunity cost and net realisable value that the capital charge should be based.

There is then an important difference, recognised earlier in Section 6 above, between a system of charging or asset rents based upon opportunity cost, and a system of capital accounting that seeks to monitor whether value for money is being obtained from the capital that has been sunk into the assets and to optimise decisions on new capital expenditure. The numbers and values which are relevant to the first objective are then not necessarily relevant to the second objective.

A further feature of the Review system of capital charges is that it does not interact directly with the allocation of capital resources in the NHS. Working Paper 9 states simply: 'There will continue to be separate allocations for capital to Regions'. However, a large part of the scope for improved capital resource management in the NHS is through overcoming the new-build bias and diverting more resources to the greater utilisation, maintenance and replacement of existing assets. Without greater permitted virement between revenue and capital expenditure, the proposed capital charging system will not necessarily bring this about.

Nevertheless the proposed capital charging system will encourage districts and units to look more carefully at the acquisition of new capital assets, and carry out more realistic option appraisals. However, unless an additional equilibriating mechanism is introduced, there is no guarantee that the demand for new capital projects at the proposed six per cent real interest rate will necessarily equal the available total of new capital resources, or that the balance between capital and revenue expenditure will be optimised by the new system of capital charging.

11. PURCHASER AND PROVIDER ROLES

Central to the NHS Review is the development of distinct purchaser-provider roles. For capital resource allocation, the separation of the purchaser role of the DHA from the provider role of unit hospitals introduces a new layer in the ownership relationship. As seen earlier in this chapter, a large part of the problem to date in capital resource management in the NHS has arisen because of the difficulty of efficiently devolving capital resource management in cash terms down to district level on an annual basis, when many capital expenditure items, such as a new DGH, are 'lumpy' and total capital resources do not stretch to a new DGH each year for every district. Introducing a new layer of effective ownership of capital assets at the unit level then needs careful implementation if it is to avoid compounding this lumpiness problem.

The nexus of the purchaser-provider relationship is the proposed contract between the two. The inter-relationship between capital charging and capital funding within the context of the contracting process then holds the key to the management of capital resources within the post-Review NHS. The award of a contract by a purchaser to a provider will carry with it the funding for a specified number of patients in different care groups. Associated with this number of patients will be a capital funding element that may offset the capital charge that the provider will incur.

The contracting decision by the purchasing DHA provides it with the opportunity to take a hard look at its desired long-term sources of supply. In principle it can then select the least-cost long term sources of supply consistent with a given target quality of care, subject to the considerations discussed in Section 10 above.

For new capital investments to be worthwhile and financially viable, the purchasing district or districts will need to enter into contracts with the supplier of the new facilities that include a capital funding element sufficient to cover the capital charges that the new facilities generate. Particularly where the new facilities involve new service benefits rather than revenue savings, it is important that the purchasing districts have sufficient additional capital funding available to 'validate' the investment decision in this way. Because the 'capital funding' element of the capital charging system introduced by the Review is not the same thing as the amount of regional or district capital expenditure available in a given year, it is unclear from the present proposals that individual purchasing districts will be given in advance the capital funding they need to validate these investment decisions.

This is especially so as the amount of new 'capital funding' needed will depend on the expected length of useful life of the assets to be acquired by the new capital expenditure. However, at the start of the accounting period the district and units may not yet have decided which assets they will later acquire and hence not know the length of the relevant asset lives.

One way out of this difficulty would be to adopt a form of lease accounting, as in the accounting standard SSAP 21, for the investment. The purchasing district would then use its capital expenditure approval from the RHA to fund in cash terms the new investment, and act as the lessor of the asset to the providing unit. It would account for the corresponding finance lease in its balance sheet and income statement on a similar basis to a loan, in accordance with SSAP 21. The purchasing district would then enter into a contract with the providing unit that included sufficient offsetting funding to cover the lease payments, of capital repayments plus interest, of the providing unit. The purchasing DHA would be able to fund this out of its associated income statement from the receipts from the lease.

The provider unit would then act as the lessee of the new investment. It would show in its Statement of Income and Costs the capital contribution and interest of the annual lease payment, and in its Balance Sheet the fixed asset involved and the outstanding obligations under the lease, as in Table 5.1 above.

Such a system of lease accounting between purchasers and providers could, moreover, be dovetailed with our earlier suggested capital credit system between the RHA acting as bankers and the DHA acting here as the lessor and purchaser. The DHA's 'fair share' of the total regional capital would then be based in part on the resident population of the district. The contract between the purchasing DHA and the provider unit would then have the effect of passing on some of the associated capital credit income of the DHA to the providing unit on the basis of the number of patients treated under the contract, in order to offset the lease charge involved. The RHA as banker would have the responsibility of cash-flow management within regional cash limits, and of scheduling the cash authorisation of capital expenditure by individual DHAs accordingly.

The above lease accounting could, moreover, be extended to existing assets under long-term contracts. It would again provide the opportunity for an examination of the appropriate long-term sources of supply. Such lease contracts would then be distinct from the contracts with the unit's management, which would typically be on a shorter-term basis. When combined with a capital credit system between districts and regions, the charge for existing assets in the district would be reflected in a reduction in the district's entitlement to new capital credits below what it would otherwise have been. The value for money monitoring advantages of lease accounting between unit providers and district purchasers would then be combined with the capital resource management advantages of the capital credit system between district and regional health authorities.

12. COST COMPARISONS AND PRICING

A final important area on which capital accounting and capital charging touches is that of the comparison of costs between different hospitals, and the use of cost information in the pricing of contracts and other decisions. A number of difficulties can occur in this area, unless appropriate offsetting allowance is made for them.

The first is that any reduction in the value of assets because of their poor condition can imply that the corresponding hospital is a low cost source of supply. In order to remove the implied incentive to house patients in sub-standard Condition C or D buildings, the contract between purchaser and providers will need to include a specification of, or adjustment for, the quality of accommodation to be provided. Similarly the adjustment for the condition of the assets will need to ensure that it does not generate perverse incentives to fail to maintain assets at the optimal level.

Since the value of land will form part of the asset valuation on which an interest charge will be levied, those hospitals close to London and other major centres will appear as high cost hospitals. To some extent this will reflect the greater opportunity cost of locating in these positions compared to further away from such population centres. However, there is in most cases a greater service value to patients and their visitors in being located close to such centres than in more distant parts of the country. Again appropriate adjustments must be made for this factor in the specification of contracts and the making of cost comparisons between hospitals in different locations.

In addition, allowance will need to be made in the funding formula for different NHS Regions, such as the Thames Regions, to take into account their higher land cost in securing a given level of accessibility of hospitals to patients. Consideration will also need to be given here to the relative cost of providing a given level of accessibility to patients in areas of population sparcity, such as Northumberland, whenever this involves providing a greater number of smaller hospitals.

There is in general an important distinction that needs to be made between the accounting depreciation charge, and the economic marginal cost of using the asset rather than not using the asset. The accounting depreciation charge will typically reflect the past capital *already sunk* in the assets, updated to present price levels and averaged out over the expected useful life of the asset. The accounting depreciation charge can then be viewed as an estimate of the minimum annual benefit that must be obtained from the asset for it to justify its original capital investment. However this in general differs from the additional resource cost which is incurred if the asset is used rather than not used.

If there is spare capacity both before and after the additional use, then the capital cost involved may be zero, unless there is additional physical deterioration produced by the extra use, or the asset would otherwise be disposed of or re-deployed elsewhere. If there is not such spare capacity, then the replacement cost in order to extend existing capacity may also enter into the calculation. The Review White Paper fortunately shows some recognition of these problems in its provision in paragraph 4.20 for something akin to a two-part tariff form of contract. This involves an initial payment associated with a minimum intake of patients that contributes to fixed costs, and scope for additional patients to be treated at marginal cost. From the viewpoint of the capital charging system at least, fixed costs will presumably include the capital charge.

The difference between the annual depreciation charge associated with the accounting book value and an annual rent based upon the likely disposal proceeds becomes important when disposal of the asset is one of the possible outcomes of a contract and pricing discussion. Since the depreciation charge reflects basically a sunk cost, it will not necessarily be saved if the asset is subsequently disposed of as a result of these discussions. This difference can fortunately be taken into account by incorporating the expected value of the 'final adjustment' proposed in the Capital Charging Working Paper 9 into these discussions and associated option appraisals. This expected adjustment will reflect the expected difference between the net book value that would be outstanding at the time of disposal and the sale proceeds likely to be achieved.

In many instances, such as in the use of operating theatres, there may be multiple users of a given capital asset. There then arises the problem of cost allocation of the capital charge between these different users. From the viewpoint of pricing the individual specialty users, there is then a strong case for some approximation to peak-load pricing to take into account the correlation between their time of use and peak demand. In addition, from the viewpoint of internal accounting, there is a strong case for the use of contribution accounting to reflect the different contributions that different users make at these prices to the total depreciation charge, without any presumption that they should all be charged the same amount. Such varying prices are also relevant to cost comparisons across different hospitals, in that a hospital that can process cases at an off-peak time in terms of the total demand on the facility will have a lower economic cost *ceteris paribus* than one which processes these cases at peak times. Again, however, appropriate allowance will have to be made in the contract specification and payments for any lower convenience of service to the patient that this off-peak usage may imply.

13. CONCLUSIONS

As discussed in Sections 4 to 8 of this chapter, there is a system of improved capital accounting and the improved management of capital resources in the NHS that involves the RHA acting as a banker, with cash-flow management by the RHA distinguished from the management of capital entitlements and of individual projects by individual districts. Such a system would dovetail with many existing initiatives in the NHS, such as the development of general management under the Griffiths' reforms, and the build-up of improved management information under the Korner initiatives.

Moreover it would be compatible with the existing cash limit system for public expenditure control, whilst developing an internal capital market for the NHS. By providing incentives for the most effective use of capital resources to individual districts, it would promote maximum value for money of resources within the NHS, whilst still facilitating a second major objective of modern health care systems, that of the containment of total costs. This framework would also incorporate more automatic virement between revenue and capital expenditure at the district level in order to optimise the balance between the two.

The system proposed in the NHS Review White Paper and accompanying Working Papers differs significantly from the above system in a number of important respects discussed above. In particular the Review system does not provide any direct mechanism for improving the allocation of district revenue and capital resources over time or for optimising the balance between total revenue and capital expenditure. In doing so, it neglects two important sources of inefficiency in the pre-Review management of capital resources in the NHS.

There may then be scope for securing the advantages of a capital credit system between DHAs and RHAs, whilst implementing a system of capital charging based upon lease accounting between DHAs and individual units. The current development of asset registers would also assist in the provision of improved information for asset replacement and maintenance.

Whilst improved capital accounting and capital charging can potentially improve the management of the available capital resources in the NHS, much will depend also on the total level of funding of the NHS. In particular, the key problems of improved utilisation, maintenance and replacement of existing assets depend in part for their effective solution on increasing the total funding available in these directions. However, whichever level of funding is chosen, it will remain important to ensure that the system of capital accounting and charging adopted not only avoids a number of significant pitfalls, but also has positive economic and financial benefits in excess of its costs of implementation.

References

Assocation of Health Service Treasurers (AHST) (1985). *Managing Capital Assets in the National Health Service*, CIPFA, London

Audit Commission (1984). *Obtaining Better Value in Education: Aspects of Non-Teaching Costs in Secondary Schools*, HMSO, London

Audit Commission (1985). *Public Expenditure Controls in Local Government in England*, HMSO, London

Baumol, W.J., Panzar, J.C. and Willig, R.D. (1982). *Contestable Markets and the Theory of Industry Structure*, Harcourt Brace Javanovich, New York

Baxter, W.T. (1981). *Depreciation*, Sweet and Maxwell, London

Bliss, C.J. (1975). *Capital Theory and the Distribution of Income*, North-Holland, Amsterdam

Central Statistical Office (1954). *National Income and Expenditure 1946–1953*, HMSO, London, and later editions

Central Statistical Office (1988). *National Income and Expenditure*, HMSO, London

Davies, Ceri (1983). *Underused and Surplus Property in the National Health Service*, HMSO, London

Department of Health (DoH) (1989). *Working for Patients*, Cm. 555, HMSO, London

Department of Health (DoH) (1989). *Self-governing Hospitals*, NHS Review Working Paper 1, HMSO, London

Department of Health (DoH) (1989). *Capital Charges*, NHS Review Working Paper 5, HMSO, London

Department of Health (DoH) (1989). *Capital Charges : Funding Issues*, NHS Review Working Paper 9, HMSO, London

Department of Health and Social Security (DHSS) (1987). *Option Appraisal*, HMSO, London

Enthoven, Alain C. (1985). *Reflections on the Management of the National Health Service*, Occasional Papers 5, Nuffield Provincial Hospitals Trust, London

Feinstein, C.H. and Pollard, S. (1988). *Studies in Capital Formation in the United Kingdom*, Oxford University Press, Oxford

Gravelle, H. and Rees, R. (1981). *Microeconomics*, Longman, London

HM Treasury (1987). *HM Treasury Macroeconomic Model : Documentation*, HM Treasury, London

HM Treasury (1990). The Government's Expenditure Plans 1990–91 to 1992–93. Cm. 1013, Chapter 13: Department of Health, HMSO, London

Harcourt, G.C. (1972). *Some Cambridge Controversies in the Theory of Capital*, Cambridge University Press, Cambridge

Harvey, M.and Keer, F. (1983). *Financial Accounting Theory and Standards*, 2nd edn, Prentice-Hall, London

Healthcare Financial Management Association (HFMA) (1987). *Health Service Trends*, Volume II, CIPFA, London

Henderson, J.M. and Quandt, R.E. (1980). *Microeconomic Theory*, 3rd edn, McGraw-Hill, London

Institute of Chartered Accountants in England and Wales (ICAEW) (1988). *Accounting Standards 1988/9* ICAEW, London

Jones, T. and Prowle, M. (1987). *Health Service Finance*, 2nd edn, Certified Accountants Educational Trust, London

Lee, T.A. (1972). A Case for Cash Flow Accounting. *Journal of Business Finance*, vol. 4, No. 2

Mayston, D.J. (1989). Capital Asset Accounting in Local Authorities. In *Accountability and Management in Public Sector Accounting*, CIPFA, London

Mayston, D.J. (1990). *The Economics of Capital-Revenue Optimisation in the Public Provision of Health Care*, mimeo, forthcoming

National Audit Office (NAO) (1987). *Use of Operating Theatres in the National Health Service*, HC 143, HMSO, London

National Audit Office (NAO) (1988). *Estate Management in the National Health Service*, HC 405, HMSO, London

NBA Construction Consultants (1985). *Maintenance Cyles and Life Expectancies of Building Components and Materials: a guide to data and sources*, NBA, London

Nobes, C. (1984). *Depreciation Problems in the Context of Historic Cost Accounting*, University of Strathclyde, Glasgow

Pinker, R. (1966). *English Hospital Statistics 1861–1938*, Heinemann, London

Public Accounts Committee (1988). *Estate Management in the National Health Service*, HC 481, Session 1987–88, HMSO, London

Samuelson, P.A. and Nordhaus, W.D. (1989). *Economics*, 13th Edition, McGraw-Hill, Berks

CHAPTER 6

Ethics, Clinical Freedom and the Doctors' Role

Alan Williams

In her Foreword to the NHS White Paper *Working for Patients* (DoH, 1989) the Prime Minister offers us two forthright assurances. The first is that:

'The National Health Service will continue to be available to all, regardless of income, and to be financed mainly out of general taxation'.

and the second, that:

'The patient's needs will always be paramount'.

The first concern will be to assess precisely what those two assurances mean, and whether they can be relied on.

The first assurance is expanded somewhat in the report itself, where the following sentence is added.

'The principles which have guided [the NHS] for the last 40 years will continue to guide it into the twenty-first century'.

As everyone knows, the ideology which gave birth to the NHS was an egalitarian one. But the ideology of the present Government is a libertarian one. It therefore seems very odd that a Government which has prided itself on its unswerving pursuit of libertarian ideals and a Prime Minister who has avowed her intention to destroy socialism, should appear to be such a staunch defender and supporter of the only really socialist post-war institution to make a substantial impact on British society and to win the support of the vast majority of the citizenry. There must surely be a catch somewhere, or has the leopard really changed its spots?

Let us stand back from the White Paper and look more broadly at how different ideologies shape different health care systems. In 1971, an American writer, Avedis Donabedian, published an examination of basic values concerning social responsibility for personal health services, on which I have drawn heavily in the past (Williams, 1988a) and on which I shall now draw heavily again. Using a summary version of his framework (see Table 6.1) a distinction is drawn between the Libertarian and Egalitarian attitudes towards Personal Responsibility, Social Concern, Freedom, and Equality. I think it important that each of us should decide whereabouts we stand in this polarity and be honest and open about it, because our (perhaps unconscious) ideological position inevitably colours our views as to what makes one health care system (or one set of proposed reforms) 'better' than another. Generally speaking, I am of the Egalitarian persuasion, whereas the present Government is undoubtedly of the Libertarian persuasion.

In Table 6.1 the two key contrasts to which attention should be drawn concern our respective attitudes towards 'Freedom' and 'Equality'. To a *Libertarian*, Freedom is a supreme good in itself and centralised health planning and a large governmental role in health care financing are seen as an unwarranted abridgement of the freedom both of patients and of health care professionals, and private medicine is viewed as a bulwark against totalitarianism. As for Equality, to a Libertarian equality before the law is the key concept, with clear precedence being given to freedom over equality wherever the two conflict. I am sure those are views to which the Prime Minister would assent without hesitation or qualification. To an *Egalitarian*, on the other hand, Freedom is seen as the presence of real opportunities of choice, upon which economic factors are often a more severe constraint than legal ones. Government is not seen as an external threat to the freedom of the individual but as the means by which otherwise disadvantaged people enlarge their scope for choice. Equality is seen as the extension to the many of the freedoms otherwise enjoyed only by the few. Those are the views to which *I* would assent without hesitation or qualification. Where, Reader, do *you* stand?

As indicated in Table 6.2, the Libertarian ideology favours a health service in which individuals are regarded as the best judges of their own welfare, and priorities are determined by patients' willingness and ability to pay, whereas the Egalitarian ideology assumes that, when ill, people are frequently poor judges of their own welfare, so willingness and ability to pay are rejected in favour of *social* judgements about need being the basis of priority setting. Libertarians expect profit-seeking behaviour by the providers of health care to lead to the optimal outcome, whereas Egalitarians rely on professional ethics and dedication to public service. In the former setting, competition is the spur to efficiency, in the latter, it is managerial or peer review which is relied on to keep people up to scratch. In the market system, the objective is to satisfy the wishes of *those who are willing and able to pay*. In the public system the electorate has to decide the extent to which *the overall level of health enjoyed by the whole population* has been improved by what the system offers. Typically it is the poor who are the most disenchanted with the (libertarian) private systems because they are the ones who miss out and it is the rich who are most disenchanted with the (egalitarian) public systems unless they have ample scope for opting out, and are not taxed too highly to finance the public system (Culyer *et al.*, 1981).

Table 6.1: Attitudes typically associated with viewpoints A and B

	Viewpoint A (Libertarian)	Viewpoint B (Egalitarian)
Personal responsibility	Personal responsibility for achievement is very important, and this is weakened if people are offered unearned rewards. Moreover, such unearned rewards weaken the motive force that assures economic well-being, and in so doing they also undermine moral well-being, because of the intimate connection between moral well-being and the personal effort to achieve.	Personal incentives to achieve are desirable, but economic failure is not equated with moral depravity or social worthlessness.
Social Concern	Social Darwinism dictates a seemingly cruel indifference to the fate of those who cannot make the grade. A less extreme position is that charity, expressed and effected preferably under private auspices, is the proper vehicle, but it needs to be exercised under carefully prescribed conditions, for example, such that the potential recipient must first mobilise all his own resources and, when helped, must not be in as favourable a position as those who are self-supporting (the principle of 'lesser eligibility').	Private charitable action is not rejected but is seen as potentially dangerous morally (because it is often demeaning to the recipient and corrupting to the donor) and usually inequitable. It seems preferable to establish social mechanisms that create and sustain self-sufficiency and that are accessible according to precise rules concerning entitlement that are applied equitably and explicitly sanctioned by society at large.
Freedom	Freedom is to be sought as a supreme good in itself. Compulsion attenuates both personal responsibility and individualistic and voluntary expressions of social concern. Centralised health planning and a large governmental role in health care financing are seen as an unwarranted abridgement of the freedom of clients as well as of health professionals, and private medicine is thereby viewed as a bulwark against totalitarianism.	Freedom is seen as the presence of real opportunities of choice; although economic constraints are less openly coercive than political constraints, they are nonetheless real, and often the effective limits on choice. Freedom is not indivisible but may be sacrificed in one respect in order to obtain greater freedom in some other. Government is not an external threat to individuals in the society but is the means by which individuals achieve greater scope for action (that is, greater real freedom).
Equality	Equality before the law is the key concept, with clear precedence being given to freedom over equality wherever the two conflict.	Since the only moral justification for using personal achievement as the basis for distributing rewards is that everyone has equal opportunities for such achievement, then the main emphasis is on equality of opportunity; where this cannot be assured the moral worth of achievement is thereby undermined. Equality is seen as an extension to the many of the freedom actually enjoyed by only the few.

Table 6.2: Idealised Health Care Systems

		Private	Public
Demand	1	Individuals are the best judges of their own welfare.	When ill, individuals are frequently imperfect judges of their own welfare.
	2	Priorities determined by own willingness and ability to pay.	Priorities determined by social judgements about need.
	3	Erratic and potentially catastrophic nature of demand mediated by private insurance.	Erratic and potentially catastrophic nature of demand made irrelevant by provision of free services.
	4	Matters of equity to be dealt with elsewhere (e.g. in the tax and social security systems).	Since the distribution of income and wealth unlikely to be equitable in relation to the need for health care, the system must be insulated from its influence.
Supply	1	Profit is the proper and effective way to motivate suppliers to respond to the needs of demanders.	Professional ethics and dedication to public service are the appropriate motivation, focusing on success in curing or caring.
	2	Priorities determined by people's willingness and ability to pay and by the costs of meeting their wishes at the margin.	Priorities determined by where the greatest improvements in caring or curing can be effected at the margin.
	3	Suppliers have strong incentive to adopt least-cost methods of provision.	Predetermined limit on available resources generates a strong incentive for suppliers to adopt least-cost methods of provision.
Adjustment mechanism	1	Many competing suppliers ensure that offer prices are kept low, and reflect costs.	Central review of activities generates efficiency audit of service provision and management pressures keep the system cost-effective.
	2	Well-informed consumers are able to seek out the most cost-effective form of treatment for themselves.	Well-informed clinicians are able to prescribe the most cost-effective form of treatment for each patient.
	3	If, at the price that clears the market medical practice is profitable, more people will go into medicine, and hence supply will be demand responsive.	If there is resulting pressure on some facilities or specialties, resources will be directed towards extending them.
	4	If, conversely, medical practice is unremunerative, people will leave it, or stop entering it, until the system returns to equilibrium.	Facilities or specialties on which pressure is slack will be slimmed down to release resources for other uses.
Success criteria	1	Consumers will judge the system by their ability to get someone to do what they demand, when, where and how they want it.	Electorate judges the system by the extent to which it improves the health status of the population at large in relation to the resources allocated to it.
	2	Producers will judge the system by how good a living they can make out of it.	Producers judge the system by its ability to enable them to provide the treatments they believe to be cost-effective.

If we look at how actual systems work, as in Table 6.3, we find that both have flaws. We therefore find that in predominantly private systems (such as in the USA) a smaller public system operates alongside the private system to care for those who cannot afford private care, either because they were poor to begin with, or have become poor because of the medical bills generated by persistently poor health. Conversely, in predominantly public systems such as in the UK, a smaller private system operates alongside the public system to care for those who are willing and able to pay for more, or different, or quicker, health care than they are entitled to within the egalitarian public system. So all countries actually have *mixed* systems. The interesting issue is then what ought to determine the relative size of the two sectors and the division of work between them.

If you are a Libertarian, it is important that people who earn more money than other people and wish to spend that money on health care *for themselves* (over and above what they contribute to health care for everybody), should have the right to do so, so that access to health care is seen as part of the society's 'reward system' for 'achievers'. If you are an Egalitarian, however, access to health care according to *need* is every citizen's *right* and there can be no buying of privileges in health care, any more than we can allow the buying of privileges in the criminal justice system. So to encourage the growth of the private sector *vis-à-vis* the NHS is a breach of principle of 'to each according to his need', for it means that more and more people will get access 'according to willingness and ability to pay'.

There can be little doubt that this is what the White Paper proposals intend shall happen in the UK. NHS hospitals can 'opt out' and sell their services both to the NHS *and* to the private sector. They are exhorted to respond to what people *want* (note the change of terminology from what people 'need', which was the term used in the Foreword) and with the extra revenue they earn in this way they will doubtless be able to take advantage of their new powers to set their own pay and conditions, so as to ensure that there are strong financial incentives for everyone in the service to go down the income-earning line. How this combination of powers will differentiate them in essence from American 'for-profit' hospitals is not clear at present but I have no doubt that its purpose is to expand the 'willingness-and-ability-to-pay' sector at the expense of the 'according-to-need' sector, even though the main customers will be still publicly financed patients.

It therefore seems that the assurance that the NHS will continue to operate according to the principles that have guided it for the last 40 years is disingenuous. What seems to be intended is that that part of the current NHS which does *not* opt out will continue to be available according to the existing rules, but all the dynamism and resources will be directed to the opted-out sector which will only be partly dedicated to the pursuit of the old principles and increasingly motivated to attract non-NHS money from private patients. So while it is legalistically true that 'the NHS will continue to be available ...' etc., the NHS will constitute a relatively declining proportion of

Table 6.3: Actual Health Care Systems

Private			*Public*
Demand	1	Doctors act as agents, mediating demand on behalf of consumers.	Doctors act as agents, identifying need on behalf of patients.
	2	Priorities determined by the reimbursement rules of insurance funds.	Priorities determined by the doctor's own professional situation, by his assessment of the patient's condition, and the expected trouble-making proclivities of the patient.
	3	Because private insurance coverage is itself a profit seeking activity, some risk-rating is inevitable, hence coverage is incomplete and uneven, distorting personal willingness and ability to pay.	Freedom from direct financial contributions at the point of service, and absence of risk-rating, enables patients to seek treatment for trivial or inappropriate conditions.
	4	Attempts to change the distribution of income and wealth independently, are resisted as destroying incentives (one of which is the ability to buy better or more medical care if you are rich).	Attempts to correct inequities in the social and economic system by differential compensatory access to health services leads to recourse to health care in circumstances where it is unlikely to be a cost-effective solution to the problem.
Supply	1	What is most profitable to suppliers may not be what is most in the interests of consumers, and since neither consumers nor suppliers may be very clear about what is in the former's interests, this gives suppliers a range of discretion.	Personal professional dedication and public spirited motivation likely to be corroded and degenerate into cynicism if others, who do not share those feelings, are seen to be doing very well for themselves through blatantly self-seeking behaviour.
	2	Priorities determined by the extent to which consumers can be induced to part with their money, and by the costs of satisfying the pattern of 'demand'.	Priorities determined by what gives the greatest professional satisfaction.
	3	Profit motive generates a strong incentive towards market segmentation and price discrimination, and tie-in agreements with other professionals.	Since cost-effectiveness is not accepted as a proper medical responsibility, such pressures merely generate tension between the 'professionals' and the 'managers'.
Adjustment mechanism	1	Professional ethical rules are used to make overt competition difficult.	Because it does not need elaborate cost data for billing purposes, it does not routinely generate much useful information on costs.
	2	Consumers denied information about quality and competence, and, since insured, may collude with doctors (against the insurance carriers) in inflating costs.	Clinicians know little about costs, and have no direct incentive to act on such information as they have, and sometimes even quite perverse incentives (i.e. cutting costs may make life more difficult, or less rewarding for them).
	3	Entry into the profession made difficult and numbers restricted to maintain profitability.	Very little is known about the relative cost-effectiveness of different treatment, and even where it is, doctors are wary of acting on such information until a general professional consensus emerges.

Table 6.3: Continued

Private		*Public*
	4 If demand for services falls, doctors extend range of activities and push out neighbouring disciplines.	The phasing out of facilities which have become redundant is difficult because it often threatens the livelihood of some concentrated specialised group and has identifiable people dependent on it, whereas the beneficiaries are dispersed and can only be identified as 'statistics'.
Success criteria	1 Consumers will judge the system by their ability to get someone to do what they need done without making them 'medically indigent' and/or changing their risk-rating too adversely.	Since the easiest aspect of health status to measure is life expectancy, the discussion is dominated by mortality data and mortality risks to the detriment of treatments concerned with non-life threatening situations.
	2 Producers will judge the system by how good a living they can make out of it.	In the absence of accurate data on cost-effectiveness, producers judge the system by the extent to which it enables them to carry out the treatments which they find the most exciting and satisfying.

the UK health care system as a whole. No-one is going to pay extra to go private unless the private sector is better than the state sector so, as tax revenues decline (partly due to tax concessions for private health insurance) and public expenditure is squeezed, the libertarian urge to 'roll back the frontiers of the state' will surely bite increasingly on the NHS as the contrast is drawn between the thriving private (and quasi-private opted-out) bits of the system and the increasingly left-behind state sector. This will find itself left to cope with the great unglamorous burden of chronic disease, which it is not profitable for the private (or quasi-private) sector to deal with. I sincerely hope that this pessimistic scenario is ill-founded and that the optimists will, in ten years time, be able to pour scorn on my forebodings.

Let me turn now from ideology to efficiency, though unfortunately the two topics are not as distinct as some seem to believe. Being efficient means achieving your objectives at least cost, so to judge whether or not a system is efficient does depend on your objectives and these in turn flow from your ideology. From now on I am going to stay firmly within the existing egalitarian ideology of the NHS, which means that efficiency is seen as being about meeting people's health needs at least cost, *not* about meeting the wants of those with the greatest willingness and ability to pay in the most profitable way.

Need is a slippery concept, which I am going to take to mean 'capacity to benefit', for I cannot see how anyone can really 'need' anything that will not do them any good (Williams, 1978). Doing good in health care means increasing people's life expectancy and/or improving their quality of life by reducing health-related disability and distress. So improving the efficiency of the NHS means generating as much of these benefits as possible, given that resources (human, material and financial) are available for that purpose. Many of the proposals in the White Paper are directed to this end and I approve wholeheartedly of them. I think it a good thing for doctors (both in hospitals and in primary care) to be held responsible for the resources they commit to health care. I think it a good thing that medical audit be extended beyond checking on procedures to include accountability for the use of resources and for the resulting outcomes in terms of patient health. I also think it is a good thing that doctors are accountable for all these things to *managers* as well as to their own professional bodies. I have been arguing so for years, and most of my own personal health service research *and* official advisory activities over the past 15 years have been dedicated to precisely those objectives. I even believe that being efficient is a *moral obligation*, not just a managerial convenience, for *not* to be efficient means imposing avoidable death and unnecessary suffering on people who might have benefited from the resources which are being used wastefully. So I read these chapters of the White Paper with a great glow of satisfaction that the penny seems finally to have dropped.

But then I read that it is envisaged that all of these very costly and disruptive changes are to be introduced simultaneously over a two year period without proper evaluation in the field to test alternative methods of doing them, or to assure ourselves that people have the managerial and accountancy skills to operate them, or even that the information needed is actually there to guide them. When it comes to field trials the holding of budgets by hospital doctors has the longest pedigree of any of the proposals but I doubt whether any of those closely associated with that work would be prepared to argue that it is now at such a level of development that it could be disseminated widely in the NHS (as opposed to being spread selectively where conditions seem favourable). I am myself a strong protagonist of clinical budgeting, so these are not the hesitations of someone looking for excuses not to proceed with these ideas.

To gain some appreciation of the dangers involved in condensing ten years of development work, and careful evaluation of the results, into two years of change by administrative fiat, just consider the main tasks put before the Manager of a District Health Authority by the Review documents, which are to be solved in the two year period between April 1989 and April 1991, despite the fact that it will not be known until half-way through that period what precise legislative framework the manager will be working within. Moreover, in April 1990 the manager is promised a sheaf of 'model contracts' and 'guidance' which will be handed down to him by the NHS Management Executive, who have the unenviable task of solving (in the intervening 12 months) the problems that have defeated everyone else for the past couple of decades—and of solving them in a manner that can be applied (presumably) in the very diverse circumstances in which different Districts find themselves. But no manager can wait for this guidance or these model contracts before starting out on his journey into the unknown, because if any of his hospitals or community services are to become 'self-governing' in April 1991, the case will have to have been made *and* approved at least six months before that date. How otherwise could a Board of Directors be appointed and be in a position to take the key policy decisions, negotiate new contracts, decide on the hiring, firing, and conditions of service of staff, etc. To be acceptable, we are told that a proposal to opt out needs to demonstrate the unit's long-term financial viability, within a three year rolling business plan, which will, of course, need to be based on (a) expected contracts (which will not yet have been formulated or negotiated), and (b) upon annual financial limits set year by year in the wake of the Annual Public Expenditure Review (of which they will be lucky if they know in advance the likely situation in Year 1, and they certainly will not know these limits for Years 2 and 3 until well into Year 1 itself).

The second precondition is to demonstrate the substantive commitment of all those likely to be involved in the new management arrangements, including senior professional staff (for example consultants). They will presumably also be up to their ears in setting up systems of medical audit, which are to include accountability for resources and for outcome. In any time they have to spare over this hectic two year period they will be helping draw up specific contracts of performance for their own specialty, which are to include their weekly work timetable in great detail, and presumably a comprehensive costing of their activities. I do not believe that this can possibly all be done *before* contracts are negotiated and agreed, yet these contracts are needed to assure long-term financial viability and this in turn is to be demonstrated *before* a decision is made whether or not they are fit for 'self-government'. So what will actually happen? District Health Authorities will be expected to buy a pig in a poke and rely on vague assurances that all these things will be sorted out eventually. And 'eventually' may well prove to be quite a long time, if the much vaunted freedoms following upon self-government are really to be exercised. The competition we are likely to witness will be who has the best line in good intentions, not who has the proven ability to deliver the goods as specified.

There are several distinct kinds of contract to choose between, all of which are likely to operate simultaneously for different services. Accurate and timely billing systems are to swing into action. The 'pricing' of services can be on an average or marginal cost basis but must not involve cross-subsidisation. With such a high level of fixed, or common, costs, whose allocation to particular services is ultimately arbitrary, that should keep the accountants, or perhaps even the lawyers, busy wrangling for some time. Then there is the newfound freedom to set pay structures, conditions of service, levels of staffing, etc. It seems however that this freedom is subject to the restriction that 'existing staff will have their statutory continuity of employment (governing redundancy and unfair dismissal and compensation) preserved' and 'staff will retain their existing contracts and all rights arising from them. The only changes will be the substitution of the new employer for the old ...'. This looks like creating another field day for the lawyers. Then there is the system of professional audit to be created and put into operation, involving performance indicators for quality control and methods of testing customer satisfaction. It is not clear who is going to review and act upon this information but, in the atmosphere of crisis management and desperate fire fighting that will dominate the transitional period, this quality assurance is likely to get only perfunctory attention. After all, there are more urgent problems to deal with such as staffing up the management system (and especially the finance branches) to cope with the new burden of work on billing, price setting, costing, debt management, and policy making on performance related financial incentives at all levels in the new budgeting system (new, that is, to all but a handful of authorities). Perhaps it is the management consultants who will make the killing here, selling ready-made systems from the USA or elsewhere. These additional managerial and financial costs could easily absorb the extra one per cent of GNP that the NHS has hitherto been denied.

Throughout this turmoil patients will still be coming in for outpatient appointments, being admitted for inpatient treatment, professional staff will still be working *as practitioners* (when they can be spared from coping with organisational entropy). The needs of the patients are, after all, paramount, so professional staff will not be expected to cope with these additional managerial tasks by diverting their time, energy or skills from direct patient care. They will presumably do it in what has hitherto been their leisure time unless the pressure of clinical work is suddenly to be eased (for example by diverting patients to the private sector).

But the major professional challenge to clinicians (including GPs) is medical audit, which is an area where the British medical profession has been dragging its feet for decades. A few keen, enterprising and energetic individuals have done pioneering work in this field and set an excellent example to their colleagues. But again I doubt whether any of them would be prepared to assert that the developments have yet reached the stage where routine application to all and sundry is feasible. Furthermore, outcome measurement has scarcely proceeded beyond avoidable *deaths*, though in a hospital setting the volume and nature of '*complications*' may also be used as a criterion. But the routine review of outcomes for patients in terms of effects on their general quality of life is at least a decade away and again I speak as someone who is probably the keenest advocate in the UK (if not in the world) of moving as fast as possible in that direction.

Perhaps the justification for this indecent haste is the thought that unless you hold a pistol to people's heads they will not do anything. Until recently there has certainly been a marked lack of any sense of urgency in these matters by the vast bulk of the medical profession. Resistance has centred on two different but related issues. The first is that it is an unacceptable breach of clinical freedom to require doctors to be accountable to *managers* for anything at all. The second is that resource management is the manager's job, not the doctor's job, and that to expect doctors to take into account anything other than the interests of the patient in front of them when conducting their clinical practice is a breach of medical ethics. This is dangerous territory for an economist to enter, but I intend to plunge in nevertheless (see also Williams, 1988b).

Medical ethics consist essentially of 6 injunctions (Ruark *et al.*, 1988).

1. To preserve life
2. To alleviate suffering
3. To do no harm
4. To tell the truth
5. To respect the patient's autonomy
6. To deal justly with patients

The last of these is, as far as I can tell, a relatively recent addition to the list (that is, it has crept in only in the last few decades) and the conflict between it and the others lies at the heart of our present dilemma. It is well known that each of these principles may conflict with one or more of the others, and that in the course of clinical practice every doctor has to exercise his own judgement as to where his duty lies. But the doctor is not at liberty to ignore, still less to reject as irrelevant, any of these principles. As I have already said, refusing to accept responsibility for the efficient use of the resources which are committed by your own clinical decisions is tantamount to rejecting the principle 'do no harm', since using resources wastefully harms the patients who might have benefited from them. Nor is there any escape along the route labelled 'if they are not my patients, I am not responsible for them', since 'dealing justly with patients' is a distributive ethic, not a personal ethic, and it therefore includes *all* patients.

Moreover, those who claim that in their own clinical practice they do not take costs into account and are guided only by what will be best for the health of the patient in front of them at that moment have surely not examined their own behaviour in a very reflective way. At the heart of clinical practice is the doctor/patient relationship. In principle this is a principal-agent relationship in which the patient is the principal and the doctor the agent. If a doctor is acting as the perfect agent of his patient, their respective roles would be that the DOCTOR is there to give the PATIENT all the information the PATIENT needs in order that the PATIENT can make a decision, and the DOCTOR should implement that decision once the PATIENT has made it. If that does not sound quite the way it usually is, try reversing the roles of DOCTOR and PATIENT, so that the relationship now gets described as the PATIENT being there to give the DOCTOR all the information the DOCTOR needs in order that the DOCTOR can make a decision, and the PATIENT should then implement that decision once the DOCTOR has made it. My point here is simply that doctors are *not* perfect agents. They may have to balance the interests of one member of a family against the interests of another. They may have to balance the interests of the patient in front of them against those of future patients by taking time out to do research, or teach the doctors of the future. They also need to take time out for their own family and recreational purposes and so will always be conscious of the need to use their own working time effectively. Their own time is, however, but one of the resources they manage and if it is proper for them to consider the most effective use of *that* resource, it cannot be wrong for them to do so for the others. So I am not impressed by the line of argument which says that it is unethical for a conscientious and caring doctor to consider costs when making clinical decisions. Indeed, I must repeat that to ignore costs is *un*ethical because it means ignoring avoidable death and suffering. People who refuse to count the cost of their actions are not behaving *ethically*, they are behaving *fanatically*, and fanaticism has no place in the practice of medicine.

But what about clinical freedom? We have it on high authority that it is a myth. The President of the Royal College of Physicians, Sir Raymond Hoffenberg, recently wrote:

> 'There is no such thing as clinical freedom, nor has there ever been. Nor for that matter should there be! .... Absolute freedom to make clinical decisions without taking into account the preferences or wishes of the patient could not be countenanced. It is therefore proper that personal, moral, ethical and even legal constraints should be observed. To these must now be added the constraint of limited resources.' (Hoffenberg, 1987)

A slightly different, but equally negative, view was taken by an eminent professor of cardiology:

> 'Clinical freedom is dead, and no-one need regret its passing. Clinical freedom was the right—some seemed to believe the divine right—of doctors to do whatever in their opinion was best for their patients .... If we do not have all the resources to do all that is technically possible then medical care must be limited to what is of proved value ...'.

> 'Clinical freedom died accidentally, crushed between the rising cost of new forms of investigation and treatment, and the financial limits inevitable in an economy that cannot expand indefinitely. Clinical freedom should however have been strangled long ago, for at best it was a cloak for ignorance and at worst an excuse for quackery. Clinical freedom was a myth that prevented true advance. We must welcome its demise, and seize the opportunities now laid out before us.' (Hampton, 1983)

There seems little more to be said on that subject, except perhaps that, defunct or not, clinical freedom remains a very strong myth which has yet to be finally laid to rest. I personally take the view that since the exercise of freedom also carries the duty of responsibility and accountability, what is happening at present is a sustained drive for greater accountability by doctors, of which I approve wholeheartedly. However, the duty of responsibility and accountability applies not only to doctors but also to politicians, which brings us back to the Prime Minister and the White Paper proposals as seen in the context of *democratic* responsibility and accountability.

It is worth noting that the 'consultation' which is being sought on the White Paper is wholly technical. The Minister has indicated that the only views in which he is interested are those which are directed constructively at getting the proposals working. Dissent is then not on the agenda. Counter-proposals are not on the agenda. There is to be minimal consultation with the affected parties, since that will only slow things up. Never mind that the vast majority of the citizenry are worried about the implications of these proposals. The last vestigial links with local democratic representation on Authorities are to be cut and there is to be no local ballot on the opting out of any hospitals. This is much more draconian than the provisions for the opting out of schools and it seems a very curious way of ensuring that 'the patients' needs will be paramount', for we are all past, present or potential future patients (except perhaps those with sufficient wealth or insurance cover to see themselves as not ever needing the NHS). It all seems extraordinarily authoritarian and antidemocratic. We, whose interests are supposedly paramount, are merely invited to salute a hoisted flag. Ours is not to reason why ...!

So let me sum up my views of the present state of the great debate about the future of the NHS.

First, I have grave doubts concerning the genuineness of the stated commitment of the present Government to the ideology of the NHS, since it is completely alien to their own avowed ideology. This must constitute grounds for quite fundamental doubt as to whether the NHS is safe in their hands.

Secondly, on the efficiency issues, although I think many of the proposals in the White Paper and its associated documents have a lot to commend them, they should not be pursued on the broad front *nor* on the time scale envisaged, but in a more selective, deliberative and experimental manner, with careful independent evaluation of their effects. To drive the NHS forward into this largely uncharted territory at this reckless speed is really quite irresponsible.

Thirdly, as regards medical ethics and clinical freedom, these have been the threadbare banners behind which the medical profession has resisted change for far too long. Indeed, I think this medical conservatism is responsible for the building-up of the head of steam which now threatens to destroy the whole edifice. Neither the medical profession nor the politicians have genuinely been putting the patients' needs first, which is not to deny that many of the more far-sighted and clear-minded opinion leaders in the medical profession have been trying to lead their colleagues into this new world for some time. If the White Paper shakes the conservative elements in the medical establishment out of their complacency, much good might yet come of it, but only if we proceed with due caution.

So, unless the time scale of the proposals is changed radically, and the encouragement to expand the private sector is abandoned, and the extra resources put instead into the state sector, I fear that the NHS will be thrown into chaos. But perhaps that is a prospect which everyone does not view with the same dismay as I do.

References

Culyer, A.J., Maynard, A.K. and Williams, A. (1981). Alternative Systems for Health Care Provision: An Essay on Motes and Beams. In Olson, M. (ed.), *A New Approach to the Economics of Health Care*, American Enterprise Institute, Washington DC, 131–150

Department of Health (DoH) (1989). *Working for Patients*, Cm. 555, HMSO, London

Donabedian, A. (1988). Social Responsibility for Personal Health Services: An Examination of Basic Values. *Inquiry*, Vol. 8, No. 2, 3–19

Hampton, J. (1983). The End of Clinical Freedom. *British Medical Journal*, 287, 1237–8

Hoffenberg, R. (1987). *Clinical Freedom*, Nuffield Provinical Hospitals Trust, London

Ruark, J.E., Raffin, T.A. and Stanford University Medical Center Committee on Ethics (1988). Initiating and Withdrawing Life Support: Principles and Practice in Adult Medicine. *New England Journal of Medicine*, 318, 25–30

Williams, A. (1978). Need: An Economic Exegesis. In Culyer, A.J. and Wright, K.G. (eds.), *Economic Aspects of Health Services*, Martin Robertson, London, 32–45

Williams, A. (1988a). *Priority Setting in Public and Private Health Care: A Guide Through the Ideological Jungle*. Discussion Paper 36, Centre for Health Economics, University of York, York

Williams, A. (1988b). Health Economics: The End of Clinical Freedom? *British Medical Journal*, 297, 5th November, 1183–6

CHAPTER 7

RAWP is Dead: Long Live RAWP

Roy Carr-Hill

1. BACKGROUND

One of the few endearing characteristics of the NHS Review *Working for Patients* (1989) is the frequency with which the main document contradicts the working papers. The example considered here is the RAWP formula which has been used since 1977 in allocating resources between Regional Health Authorities (RHAs).

The RAWP formula was developed from proposals of the Resource Allocation Working Party (set up in 1974) for allocating resources between Regions on the basis of *need*. In practice, need is proxied by mortality and allocations to RHAs are based on regional differences in standardised mortality ratios (SMRs). Allocations by Regions to Districts are currently based on similar criteria augmented by an allowance for planned workload and future service development. The original objective of the RAWP formula was to equalise allocations between Regions with similar needs and by 1985 the divergence between actual and target allocations had considerably narrowed although there were still vociferous complaints from the four Thames regions that allocations were not proportioned to their needs. The Department of Health (DoH) therefore instituted a review of the operation and the RAWP formula to consider in more detail an appropriate index of needs.

In the main NHS Review document, RAWP is to be abandoned. The justification for this is that regional allocations are close to targets now that '11 of 14 (RHAs) are within three per cent' (DoH, 1989a, para 4.4). Instead, RHAs will be funded on a capitation basis, weighted to reflect the health and age distribution of the population, including the number of elderly people, and the relative cost of providing services (DoH, 1989a, para 4.8). In contrast, Working Paper 2 explains how allocations are to be based on population weighted for age, (sex) and SMRs (DoH, 1989b) so that the conceptual difference between the new allocation mechanism and the original RAWP formula may be more apparent than real.

In principle, the basis of allocation to District Health Authorites (DHAs) will also be changed: 'Districts will in due course be funded on broadly the same basis as Regions' (DoH, 1989a, para 4.12), that is, on a weighted capitation basis. The proposed changes are due to be implemented by 1992–93 but as many of the Districts are still a long way from an allocation commensurate with their population (Bevan *et al.*, 1989) the Government 'recognises the need for a longer transition period ... because of the greater relative disparities ..' (DoH, 1989b).

Assuming that the process of transition can be smoothed, the question is what will be the impact of the proposed changes. In particular, will the changes:

> 'improve the sensitivity with which the formula measures relative 'need', and accord with the two broad principles enunciated at the beginning of the review process, that:
>   (i) no changes should be made to the formula unless clearly justified;
>   (ii) the formula should remain as stable, robust and as simple and straightforward as possible as perceived "fairness" permits for national purposes.' (DHSS, 1986)

2. ADJUSTING FOR RELATIVE NEED

The main change is to the adjustment for morbidity. In the RAWP formula morbidity is proxied by mortality, and the standardised mortality ratio enters the formula with a weight of unity. Working Paper 2 proposes to adopt the recommendations of the NHS Management Board Report to use standardised mortality ratios with a weighting of 0.5. This coefficient, which looks suspiciously like a muddled political compromise between 'no allowance for SMR' (coefficient 0) and 'proportionality' (coefficent 1), is in fact based on the report from Coopers and Lybrand to the NHS Management Board (Coopers and Lybrand, 1988a). In that report, Coopers and Lybrand had suggested a coefficient of 0.44 but the Management Board selected 0.5 because the figure of 0.44 is 'over precise'. Besides remarking that this expression of the kind of digit preference usually associated with non-numerate respondents when asked their age (the remark that 0.5 is somehow less precise than 0.44) is a worrying commentary on the Report, it is clearly important to understand how Coopers and Lybrand derived their estimate of 0.44.

The background to their analysis is the Interim Report by the NHS Management Review Board which had recommended further research examining 'the whole range of possible factors ... to see which were the best predictors of variations in health service utilisation' (DHSS, 1986). Coopers and Lybrand accordingly produced a stepwise multiple regression analysis of small area data from some Regions with hospital use, presumed to be a proxy for morbidity, as the dependent variable.

The focus on hospital use is curious as a measure of relative need. The Interim Report acknowledges that it is 'necessary to disentangle the effects of historical supply of services' but does not seem to have considered the extensive evidence (Morgan *et al.*, 1987) that variations in professional and patient behaviour affect recourse to hospital (= use) for a given condition (which should be the basis of any measurement of need). More poignantly, the original Resource Allocation Working Party specifically ruled out using hospital-based measures because hospital use is, at least in part, determined by supply.

Carr-Hill (1988) shows how this complicates the problem of modelling demand. The Coopers and Lybrand team attempted to 'control' for the effects of supply by carrying out their analysis at electoral ward level and by introducing a measure of access/availability. However, the most disaggregated level at which data are available does not avoid the 'ecological fallacy', and the adjustment they used based only on distance and available volume ignores all the evidence about variations in professional and patient behaviour. The basic problem is that 'supply' and 'demand' are jointly determined and disentangling this simultaneity requires a more sophisticated approach than those considered by the Coopers and Lybrand team (Carr-Hill and Humphreys, 1989).

Coopers and Lybrand have supplied a more elaborate explanation of the approach they adopted in Annex A (Coopers and Lybrand, 1988b). Their presumption is that there is excess demand throughout the service so that the problem is to model the effect of relative need upon variations in use given variations within the supply regime. Disequilibrium models of this kind have been studied at length in econometrics (Maddala, 1986) but they do not seem to have been considered by Coopers and Lybrand. The 'model' they propose is not therefore based on any standard or theoretically-based modification of the usual simultaneous supply and demand equations but must be considered *sui generis*, as an attempt to predict variations in actual hospital use, and the extent to which this depends upon a presumed proxy for need (SMR under 75) after controlling for supply. Exactly why the coefficients from such a model should be taken to reflect relative need remains obscure.

Attempts at clarification do not help. Following the detailed recommendations of the Interim Report, Coopers and Lybrand carried out an analysis based on small area statistics and postcoded discharge data. When presenting the model at the Health Economics Study Group in December 1988, the reliance on small area analysis was defended as being more likely to reflect the real relation between relative need and resource use given prevailing supply. Superficially this is a very strange argument as it seems to suggest that health workers on the ground have somehow 'got it right' and that the only problem is to adjust for supply. In that case analysis of the relation between need and use is redundant! (Bevan *et al.*, 1989) The key to this paradox lies in their use of the little word 'given': the analyses of Coopers and Lybrand really do presume that supply is *fixed* for each small area so that the health workers are 'getting it right' within a very constrained situation.

Moreover, the use of data on *occupied beds* as the measure of supply adds an element of the surreal to the analysis. Whilst GPs and some patients do spend their time 'shopping around' for an empty waiting list (even without being budget holders), the presumption that the number of occupied beds is fixed conjures up one's worst fantasies of patients hopping into beds just vacated—horizontally?—that morning. This presumption that supply is fixed at the small area level—and for each speciality (Coopers and Lybrand, 1988a, para. 28)—is very unrealistic.

The lack of a proper model and inadequate data make it difficult to place any confidence in the coefficients from simplistic regression analysis of the kind used by the Coopers and Lybrand team, which produced the coefficient of 0.44. But, given that the data on which their analysis was based have not been made available, it is impossible to assess the extent of bias and distortion introduced by their naive and simplistic approach to this analysis.

2.1 The 'correct' relation between need and resources

Separately, these and other analysts have argued that 'the form of the model clearly indicates the need for a constant term' and that 'the inclusion of a constant term attenuates the effect of SMRs' (Butts, 1986; Coopers and Lybrand, 1988a).

The first argument is based upon the general form of a linear regression, $y = a + bx$; when x is 0, y will, in general, be non zero; hence the constant term 'a'. In this context, however, where need is zero, then the derived demand for health care could well be zero. Nevertheless, one might suppose a 'fixed' or 'minimum' level of demand among otherwise perfectly healthy populations because of the vicissitudes of entry to, survival in and exit from this mortal coil. Then demand (or need?) would increase as conditions got worse but the *rate* by which it would increase depends on the relationship between need and demand (measured, in the case of the Coopers and Lybrand report, by use); and, in particular, upon the resources required to provide appropriate (and effective) treatment per unit of need. There is therefore no reason to suppose that, because there is a constant term, the size of the effect of SMRs will be greater than or less than one.

In the absence of substantial evidence on this point, one can only speculate as to exactly how 'need' should be taken into account (whether need is measured by SMRs or by anything else). Changes in the measure of need might overstate the case for more resources (for example, if SMRs are used, because in areas with high SMRs people are dying from conditions not amenable to medical intervention); or changes in the measure of need may understate the case (for example, if SMRs are used, because people become desensitized to high levels of mortality). Moreover, the correct coefficient for policy purposes depends on a view about the balance of these and other factors and confidence in the proxies for need actually used in any empirical work. In the case of the proposed 'abatement' for SMRs, no judgement appears to have been made about these factors.

Moreover, the fact that in all the analyses reported by Coopers and Lybrand the coefficient on SMRs was consistently less than one is not convincing evidence about the appropriate form of the relationship and hardly surprising, given their data and approach to analysis. For their dependent variable is hospital use (usually death and discharge rates, sometimes bed-days) of the population of a small area. This choice of dependent variable effectively measures the financial allocations to the local hospital services, with the population of poorly (well) funded districts using less (more) services. Whilst the analysis by Coopers and Lybrand of course allows for cross-district flows, their access variables depend only upon distances ignoring all the other constraints imposed upon access via local underfunding. Moreover, unlike Regions, underfunded areas will have moved only slowly to their (sometimes fictional) RAWP target—although they may have benefited from Region's movement. Funding (= Resource Use) only partly (less than one) reflects relative need (as measured by SMR).

In the absence of a proper analysis, there is no good case for changing the current, easily comprehensible, one-to-one relationship between variations in SMRs and variations in resources.

3. USING THE DISTRICT ALLOCATION AND GP BUDGETS

The proposal that some practices may opt to be autonomous budget holders introduces a further complexity, for the allocations to practices who become budget holders will be constructed out of an allocation for drugs and for hospital services. The latter is the major component. It will be based on the referral pattern of the practice and on the number of patients on the practice register weighted by age, sex and health of the patients, taking account of local and social factors.

One is entitled to be sceptical that comprehensive data on referral patterns can be made available quickly, and there are evident practical difficulties with general practices which refer to several hospitals. But assuming those can be solved in time (DoH, 1989a, 1989c), two other adjustments are being proposed.

3.1 Adjusting for practice morbidity

First, what kind of health measure will be used for the adjustment? Obviously it will not be SMRs as there are so few deaths among a practice list in any one year; presumably some kind of measure of morbidity. These data are usually collected within the international classification of disease (ICD) framework, for example the national morbidity surveys conducted in 1955/6, 1971/2, and 1981/2. However, the data classified in this form are of little use for assessing the burden of morbidity. Almost the only message of substance is that the rate of consultations for symptoms, signs and ill-defined conditions is increasing (see Table 7.1).

Table 7.1: Patients consulting, episodes of consultation and overall consultation rate—per 1000 patients at risk

Rates	Male			Female		
	1955/6	*1971/2*	*1981/2*	*1955/6*	*1971/2*	*1981/2*
Episodes	–	1540.6	1745.5	–	2109.8	2549.2
Consultation rate	3368.4	2304.2	2710.5	4133.4	3139.1	4021.4
Patients consulting	634.0	620.0	652.2	704.3	701.1	765.8
Symptom, signs and ill-defined conditions	–	109.7	134.4	–	138.8	182.4

Data obtained by the OPCS from about 50 General Practitioners asked to record their 'throughput' in a given period.

In the British context, Blaxter (1984) has suggested that a more useful classification would be between life threatening conditions, functionally incapacitating or painful disease (diseases requiring specialist referral), urgent disease, requiring long-term supervision, symptoms not clearly diagnosed, conditions which could be self-treated and self-limiting conditions. Blaxter showed how the classification made epidemiological sense and that the classification system was relatively easy to use. It might, however, appear a little homespun and 'lacking statistical validity'.

The main, statistically pukka, contender from the US is some version of the diagnostic-related groups. For example, Weiner (1989) proposed a system of classification into Ambulatory Care Groups (ACGs) where the major criteria of classification, for example acute/chronic, self-treatable or not, are rather similar to those proposed by Blaxter. In Weiner's case, the groups were derived by using a modification of the Automatic Interaction Detector software which was discredited as a group finding device nearly 20 years ago (Cramer, 1971). Despite this discouraging backcloth, Weiner claims that his analysis shows how a substantial proportion of the variation in resource use over a year (whether measured by costs of ambulatory care, numbers of visits, or total charges) can be accounted for by a regression equation including dummy variables for these ACGs. The equations do not seem to work so well prospectively.

There are problems with a morbidity index based on reported consultations. First, as with hospital use, there is interaction between supply and demand; indeed, the literature on supplier-induced demand tends to focus on primary care professionals. Secondly, as the emphasis of primary care is meant to be more preventative, this is difficult to capture in a morbidity index. The only effective methods of assessing the need for primary care among a practice population is to screen the patients regularly. Will the management fee include an allowance for screening for the health of every patient on the GP list every year?

3.2 Adjusting for deprivation

The proposed allowance for local and social factors which will presumably involve adjustment of weighted capitation by an index of deprivation is likely to cause similar fun and games. For the difficulties of constructing an index of deprivation are well-known. The choice of measure or measures should be theoretically based and empirically valid; that is, indicators should be based on a clear definition of 'need' and variations in those indicators should reflect variations in need. For example, a high bed-occupancy ratio can reflect over-zealous doctors as much as effective use of resources; a low ratio may be due to a lack of supervising doctors as much as low levels of morbidity. The pitfalls in interpreting such statistics for policy purposes are well-known, but very similar ambiguities occur with socio-economic data.

It might be argued that the demand for a theoretical justification of the indicators chosen is a counsel of perfection. But without any justification, we cannot know what precisely is being measured, how it relates to 'need' and, most importantly, how the allocation formula should be modified.

A wide variety of indices of social deprivation have been proposed in the literature. Some are 'general purpose', some are specific to health. The usual procedure has been to construct an index on the basis of Census data. In this context of allocation to general practices, the most likely choice of index is the GP underprivileged area score (Jarman, 1983; Irving and Rice, 1984) which is, like other indicators, based on the 1981 Census.

(i) *Limited choice of variables.* For a variety of reasons, the Census is restricted in the kind of data it elicits from the population. The obvious restriction, which affected the 1981 Census was the ethnic minority question which asks about country or origin rather than ethnic group membership (Booth, 1986). As shown elsewhere this produces a distorted picture of the distribution of ethnic minorities between regions of the country as compared to any other survey (Carr-Hill *et al.*, 1987). But there are similar, though less severe, problems with interpreting other variables: for example, the proportion who have changed address within a year includes yuppies as well as vagrants; even the unemployment variable has no contemporary referent because of frequent changes in definition and method of counting. Even more limiting, in the context of constructing an index of deprivation, is the absence of a direct question about income or wealth.

(ii)*Circumstances may have changed since 1981.* None of them can be updated in a similar form as they depend on very specific kinds of data which are only collected at Census. This is acknowledged, yet remains important. It will become an increasing embarrassment over the next five years until corresponding analysis of the 1991 Census data is available. Moreover, if the formula remains the same, there will be a sudden and mostly unpredictable shift in the pattern of allocations.

Moreover, the GP underprivileged area score is a bit of a methodological mystery. It is based on arbitrary transformations for a selection of the Census variables combined according to weights from a sample of GPs. The selection of factors GPs were asked to weight were selected by a totally unrepresentative sample of London GPs, so the Index has a built-in London, south east and urban bias. Unsurprisingly, there is no factor to represent the problems of, for example, sparse populations.

Of the social factors for which Census data were available, Jarman originally chose ten: Under Fives, Unemployment, Poor Housing, Ethnic Groups, Lone Parent Families, Elderly Alone, Overcrowding, Lower Social Classes, Mobility, Fewer Married Families. In subsequent applications, the 'poor housing' and 'fewer married families' variables have been dropped, hence the UPA8 (eight-item Under Privileged Area score). Whilst the latter variable was dropped for apparently technical reasons—it 'proved difficult to define accurately from Census data'—the explanation for the exclusion of the former is more interesting. Jarman (1984) reports, it was 'because of the responses received by members of the committee [the underprivileged areas subcommittee of the General Medical Services Committee of the BMA] when the results *from their own areas* were considered' (p.1590, my italics). Essentially, the results did not fit their preconception.

The transformation, which involves taking the inverse of the sine of the square root of each variable, is mystical. The idea is to make the distributions of each of the component variables symmetrical; and indeed it probably does. But the 'real world' is not symmetrical. There might be an argument for transforming the combined score (rather than a component variable) if it were claimed that the thing the index is meant to represent —workload pressure on GP—is symmetrical, but that also seems unlikely. It makes the interpretation of the index very difficult.

The scores were obtained from responses to a questionnaire sent to a one in ten sample of all general practitioners in England (N = 2584) about the importance of economic and social factors. Of these, 1802 questionnaires were used in the final analysis, giving a 'response rate' of 70 per cent. These weights were used to construct an index and scores have been devised for all 9821 wards in England and Wales (Irving and Rice, 1984).

The method of combining variables involves an unknown element of double counting. This is both because of the weights and the overlap between the variables. Assuming, for example, that there is some common element to localities with more lone parents, more unskilled, more unemployed, and more overcrowded, the weighting system means that this 'common element' will be counted thirteen times (3.01 + 3.74 + 3.34 + 2.88 = 12.97). It is not sufficient for Jarman (1984) to point to the relatively low intercorrelations between crucial pairs of variables (as between ethnic minorities and the unemployed) and so argue that, in fact, there will be not much double counting; because his procedure used the inverse of the sine of the square root of the variables, the transformed variables are likely to be more highly correlated because they are all forced towards a particular kind of distribution. Indeed, the whole procedure appears to be a bunch of arithmetical tricks applied to Census data for no obvious reason (Tukey, 1977).

4. CONCLUSIONS

The choice of criteria for allocating resources makes a considerable difference to the final distribution of resources and statistical wizardry will tend to obfuscate rather than illuminate the nature of those initial choices. The debate over RAWP in the UK is exemplary. The complex statistical analysis carried out by Coopers and Lybrand for the review of RAWP did not address the fundamental questions of how to measure (relative) need and the intrinsic simultaneous inter-relationships between need for and provision of health care.

The problems are compounded when considering the appropriate allocation to general practice budget holders, for there are many idiosyncracies with the index likely to be used to reflect local and social factors. Even assuming that the statistical issues could be resolved, one can anticipate several difficulties with using any formula. First, there is the problem that the patients from a practice may be drawn from several Districts. Whilst this could be handled by assigning deprivation scores to each individual, the systematic application of the procedure requires extensive computing power which is not available (Carr-Hill *et al.*, 1987). Secondly, there is the problem that, in order to argue for their allocations, practices will have to screen their patients in order to assess their average health.

Most importantly, where a practice opts to have its own budget, a District Health Authority will be in the position of dealing with two different allocation procedures: those governing their own allocation relative to other

DHAs depending on age, sex and SMRs only; and those governing the allocations they make to practices which opt for their own budgets which depend on age, sex, health of the patients and on local and social factors.

There will, presumably, be some resolution. One possibility will be for the DoH to give up and simply hand out resources on a capitation basis—if one can any longer believe census data after the introduction of the Poll Tax. Perhaps the most likely outcome is a return to a consistent RAWP—under another name. If this happens, could we suggest the acronym TRUE—a Thatcherite Revised Utopian Estimate.

References

Bevan, G., Holland, W. and Mays, N., (1989). NHS Resources Allocation after the 1989 White Paper: A Critique of the Research for the RAWP Review. Mimeo, Department of Community Medicine, St. Thomas' Hospital, London

Booth, H. (1986). Identifying Ethnic Origin. In *Britain's Black Population*, 2nd edition, Gower, Farnborough

Blaxter, M. (1984). Equity and Consultation Rates in General Practice. *British Medical Journal*, 288, 1963–1967

Butts, M. (1986). Questioning Basic Assumptions. *The Health Services Journal*, 19 June, 826–827

Carr-Hill, R.A. (1988). *Indexing Deprivation and Modelling Demand*, Discussion Paper 41, Centre for Health Economics, University of York

Carr-Hill, R.A., Kirby, P., Fordham, R. and Houghton, K. (1987). *Locality Health Planning: Constructing a Data Base*, Discussion Paper 34, Centre for Health Economics, University of York

Carr-Hill, R.A. and Humphreys, K. (1989). *Analysing the Factors Affecting Health*, mimeo, Centre for Health Economics, University of York

Coopers and Lybrand (1988a). *Integrated Analysis for the Review of RAWP*, London, 1988

Coopers and Lybrand (1988b). Annex A, *A Note on Access*, Personal Communication

Cramer, F.M. (1971). Review of Sonquist, J., Multivariate Model Building. *Psychometrika*, 36, 440–442

Department of Health (DoH) (1989a). *Working for Patients*, Cm. 555, HMSO, London

Department of Health (DoH) (1989b). *Funding and Contracts for Health Services*, Working Paper 2, HMSO, London

Department of Health (DoH) (1989c). *Practice Budgets for General Medical Practitioners*, Working Paper 3, HMSO, London

Department of Health and Social Security (DHSS) (1986). *Review of the Resource Allocation Working Party Formula*, Final Report by the NHS Management Board, para. 1.3, 1988, HMSO, London

Irving, D. and Rice, P. (1984). *Information for Health Series Planning from the 1981 Census*, 84/11, Kings Fund, London

Jarman, B. (1983). Identification of Underpriviledged areas. *British Medical Journal*, 286, 705–709

Jarman, B. (1984). Underpriviledged areas: validation and distribution of scores. *British Medical Journal*, 289, 1587–1592

Maddala, G.S. (1986). Disequilibrium Models. In Griliches, Z.V.I. and Intriligator, M.D. (eds.), *Handbook of Econometrics*, Vol III, Ch 28, North Holland Publishing Company, Amsterdam

CHAPTER 8

The Challenge of Community Care Reform

K. G. Wright

1. INTRODUCTION

Other chapters in this book examine the National Health Service Review White Paper published in January 1989 (DoH, 1989a). This chapter is concerned with the White Paper on Community Care, *Caring for People* (DoH, 1989b), published in November 1989 and complementary to the NHS Review. The aim is to examine different systems of budgeting allocation which would move the provision of social care in the direction of improving consumer choice. In particular, the discussion is focused on moving the existing system of social care from its present supply or provider-led domination to one which is demand or consumer-led.

The system is supply-led because budgets are allocated via departmental chiefs to service managers, who then control the amount of assistance given to users. This contrasts with a demand-led system in which service managers would receive their budgets not by direct allocation but by receipts from people who use the service. Of course, the present system is not so insensitive that it takes no account of consumer preference. Moreover, it is unlikely that any new system will be founded on consumer sovereignty. The current challenge in the provision of social care is to develop procedures which respond to consumer choice but not necessarily to purchasing power.

The White Paper distinguishes between community care and social care. 'Community Care means providing the right level of intervention and support to enable people to achieve maximum independence and control over their own lives' (para. 2.2, p.9). 'Social Care and practical assistance with daily living are key components of good quality community care' (para. 2.4, p.9). The services which will improve the quality of life of people with care needs include:

- help with personal and domestic tasks
- disablement equipment and housing adaptations
- transport
- budgeting
- good quality housing
- day care
- respite care
- leisure facilities
- employment and educational opportunities

Using these definitions it seems that social care covers many aspects of the lives of people who receive it. It also covers people with a wide variety of physical and mental disabilities, from all ages and both sexes as well as a variety of family and household circumstances. The main objectives of social care policies might be summarised as helping people with chronic disabilities to:

a. pursue education, training and employment opportunities;
b. enjoy their leisure time;
c. live in a comfortable and safe domestic environment which ensures privacy, dignity and choice over daily living routines;
d. gain access to general community facilities including factories, shops, offices, public transport, recreational and cultural facilities;
e. integrate into and participate in their local communities;
f. maintain or improve their independence in activities of daily living.

Given this breadth of coverage, it is not appropriate to consider a single market for social care. People will wish to participate in several different markets, some of which are quite general such as employment markets or the use of recreational services. Others such as the provision of medical and nursing care can be very specialised. One major general aim of social care, however, would be to ensure that there are no special barriers to disabled people's participation. At present, many domestic, general and occupational environments are not designed to make life easy for disabled people. It is not possible for some physically disabled people to find employment because of difficulties in access to the work place, or the absence of suitable transport or even the difficulties of getting out of their own houses. People's independence in the activities of daily living is threatened by the failure to replace baths with showers, by lack of provision of toilets on the same level as main living-rooms and by the failure to provide cooking equipment or kitchen furniture at an appropriate height for a person confined to a wheelchair. None of these problems is new; there is a great deal of evidence to show how different environments hinder mobility and threaten personal mobility and independence (Blaxter, 1976). One reason for the continuation of this regrettable state of affairs is that the consumers or those acting on their behalf have not been able to exercise choice or influence in the way in which houses are built, environments are developed and how offices, shops, factories, theatres and many other civic amenities are designed, staffed and operated.

2. PROBLEMS OF SUPPLY-LED SOCIAL CARE

Many of the problems of the present system of social care have been set out by the Audit Commission (1986). The thrust of the Commission's criticisms was that the existing financial arrangements and organisation were responsible for the very slow progress being made to replace institutional by community care, especially the closure of hospitals for people with a mental illness or a mental handicap. In particular, the report highlighted the poor achievement of targets for the provision of residential home places for people with a mental illness as set out in DHSS guidelines (DHSS, 1975) and of places in day care for people with a mental handicap. One major cause suggested for this slow progress was the lack of a co-ordinated policy for financing community care.

From a financial viewpoint the existing methods of organising and financing social care are not conducive to efficiency and the achievement of policy objectives. From a consumer's point of view they are not conducive to providing the quality of life that is preferred, even with the existing levels of expenditure. Apart from the general problems of excess demand for social care services, current provision is either inaccessible or inappropriate for many disabled people or their carers.

The confusing array of services provided by NHS authorities, local authority social services, education and housing departments, deters rather than encourages consumer participation. Although the additional help from voluntary societies is always welcome, it provides yet another door through which users must trek to obtain help. In addition, the systems of social security allowances and housing benefit provide further sources of help— but also of confusion. Small wonder that people do not seek the help and allowances to which they are entitled.

These problems are exacerbated by two other factors. First, the services are not provided in a manner which is sensitive to individual circumstances and second, the type and amount of service provided is susceptible to wide local variations.

The insensitivity of services to individual circumstances is a major consequence of social care being producer- rather than consumer-led. Examples of this abound in the literature on social care. The prime example of course is the failure to replace institutional by community care. Some people may argue that this is not really so bad, not because institutional care is good, but that facilities in the community are inadequate. However, how would consumers react to this argument? In effect they are being denied choice since they have to remain in the institutions. By contrast, residential accommodation which is responsive to individual preferences in terms of a domestic scale living environment coupled with satisfactory standards for personal privacy, choice over household routines and the preservation of dignity, would be meeting the declared objectives of social policy and would be closer to consumers' preferences. It is unfortunate that the debate about hospital versus community care is carried out in terms of providing more places here and less places there rather than about how to provide a range of facilities appropriately staffed where necessary to meet the wide variety of needs of people who would benefit from them.

There are many other examples of the way in which services are not geared to meet individual circumstances. The lack of domiciliary services in the evening or at the weekend, the provision of meals-on-wheels, the whole problem of producing readily accessible day services, the inappropriate use of day hospitals by people who do not need medical or nursing care because of the lack of suitable alternatives are well documented in the literature on social care (Donaldson *et al.*, 1985). These problems are well known to service providers but they are often prevented from helping people to an appropriate level and mix of services by the existing system of finance and organisation. Thus, it may well be easier for consultants in geriatric medicine to bring people into a day hospital because they control the access to that service rather than to prescribe intensive domiciliary care or other forms of day care because access is controlled by people in other organisations who may wish to provide appropriate care but do not always have the resources to deliver it.

The national picture of social care is a very varied one, especially in the provision of domiciliary care and day services. In some areas of the country domiciliary services are available on every day of the week: there are 'twilight', 'tucking-up', 'getting up' as well as regular meals and home help services. Even within one local authority area the availability of services such as day centres can vary enormously. Different perceptions are held of this variety. The most critical see it, as the Audit Commission did (1986), as a major worry since needs are not likely to vary between areas as much as services do. In addition, it appears that authorities which are low in provision on one set of services do not compensate their residents by being high on others (Gray *et al.*, 1988). A less critical stance is that this variety is the consequence of local democracy and reflects decisions about priorities of local authority expenditure. The most favourable perception of this variety would suggest that it reflects the pioneering efforts that local managers have pursued to meet the challenge of innovation in social care. However, potential users living in an area of relatively low provision of domiciliary care or day services would probably regard themselves as being very deprived.

It is difficult to know how far the existing finance and organisation of social care suffers from a misallocation of rather than a shortfall in resources. The debate about the growth of private residential care typifies this doubt. It is now widely known that the growth in the use of social security to finance people entering residential care has caused an astronomical rise in this aspect of income support. The expenditure on this item has increased from £17 million in 1979 to £459 million in 1986, at 1986 prices (DHSS, 1987). Critics would argue that the money could have been used to improve community care services to prevent people entering residential care. However, the evidence produced so far, on a small sample of locations and related specifically to elderly people, would not uphold this criticism. Bradshaw and Gibbs (1988) found that social work assessments of elderly people entering private residential care suggested that only a minority (17 per cent) could have been kept at home using intensive domiciliary care. In this research project the social workers were making subjective judgements about alternative courses of action without having the benefit of working intensively with the elderly person and setting up an appropriate system of domiciliary care. In the Kent Community Care Scheme (Challis and Davies, 1986), where social workers acted as case managers and had budgetary control over the delivery of domiciliary and other relevant services, very frail elderly people were successfully maintained at home at costs below those of residential care. The lesson from this is that a case manager with an appropriate budget providing the flexibility in prescribing and delivering services to meet individual circumstances can produce very efficient community care.

The use of a budget to meet individual needs also occurs when people leaving long-stay hospital care take with them an annual capitation allowance or 'dowry' which can be used to finance their future care. However, case management is not a common feature of these schemes and the capitation allowance is frequently devoted to the provision of residential care, rather than used as a budget to develop a tailor-made system of social care. Since these allowances are based on the average cost of hospital care, they are not always adequate to finance the care of people who need full-time surveillance or social care. In this respect there is an unambiguous shortfall of resources. The failure to produce bridging finance to help agencies to provide domestic scale residential environments for people in need of continuing social care is a major reason for the slow achievement of the objectives set out in the 1981 Green Paper (DHSS, 1981).

3. CONSUMER CHOICE AND SOCIAL CARE

The economics of consumer choice is generally concerned with the way in which consumers choose to spend their limited incomes on a range of goods and services in such a way as to maximise their utility. The analogy in markets for social care services would be to explore ways in which consumers dispensed their 'social care budget' on a set of social care goods and services. This raises three important topics for discussion:

i) what set of goods and services could be included in the catch-all phrase 'social care'?
ii) who are the consumers and how far can they make their own choices?
iii) how is the 'social care budget' determined?

Although these topics are listed and discussed separately below, they are clearly interlinked.

In a consumer-based model, many services would be charged out at prices fixed for all users. NHS services would still be at zero price at point of consumption, but local authority day and domiciliary services would not be zero-priced and consumers would have the cash to choose between the different agencies, public and private, which provided them with those services which met their requirements most satisfactorily. In addition, some services which are presently not paid for, such as help from relatives and friends, might substitute for more formal services. These could also attract a payment. Such a scheme may appear abhorrent to those who regard paying for such help as introducing the spirit of commercialism into friendship and personal relations that would perhaps encourage people to do things for others for the wrong motive. Nevertheless, some payment is now made through the social security system in the form of invalid care allowance and there is a growing literature on the costs, both financial and psychological, which carers bear suggesting that payment in cash or kind would be helpful to compensate them for all their efforts (Parker, 1985).

4. THE BUDGET CONSTRAINT

There are many questions which need to be tackled in the determination of a budget for consumers of social care services. For example:

– Is the budget to be graded according to levels of disability and if so in what steps and by whose assessments?
– Should the budget be means-tested?
– Should allowances be made for family circumstances?

One current parallel payment is the attendance allowance which is a disability-related, non-means-tested cash benefit which can be used to buy goods and services which meet the needs of the disabled person. The allowance is in effect a sum which can be used to top up existing levels of service provision: it is not intended to substitute for all service provision. An allowance which was aimed at providing for all services would need to be considerably greater than the attendance allowance for very disabled people in need of a great deal of care and attention. The disability premia payable as part of income support under the social security legislation provide an example of a means-tested disability payment. A third type of care budget, but only in partial use and not dispensable by the consumer, is the 'dowry' allowance which is designed to pay for the care of people leaving long-stay hospitals. This allowance is not related to disability level but to the average cost of care in the hospital. The great majority of 'dowries' appear to go towards residential care in the community. Fourthly, there is the arrangement set up in the Kent Community Care project (Challis and Davies, 1986) whereby a budget is used to buy in services for very frail elderly people. In this case, the budget is related to the cost of residential care for old people and is related to disability in so far as the allowance is restricted to frail elderly people who would almost certainly be admitted to residential care without intensive domiciliary care.

The lessons learned from these budgets suggest that they provide opportunities for disabled people and their helpers to obtain services in a flexible way from private, voluntary, statutory and informal care sectors which supplement the existing services (Challis and Davies, 1986; Renshaw *et al.*, 1988). They are aimed mostly at people who have severe disabilities. There is very little experience so far to draw on from people who are less severely disabled, or from the use of a budget to cover all the services received. Thus, many of the questions posed earlier remain unanswered. The main problems revolve around the purpose of allowances to disabled people. Are they designed to compensate for disability *per se* or are they designed to compensate for the higher costs of living for disabled people or, as in the last two examples, are they designed to provide incentives to the efficient allocation of resources? If the allowance is to compensate for disability *per se*, then extended attendance or mobility allowances would appear to be the models to follow; if they are to cover extra costs, the means-tested disability premia would appear to be more appropriate. Incentives to substitute one form of care for another suggest the use of cost-related payments.

5. THE CONSUMER AS PURCHASER

Two main doubts are always cast on the practicality of consumer sovereignty in social care. First, there are worries that people do not know what services are available or how well they are likely to serve the consumers' purposes. Such doubts may well be conditioned by whether the social care services use procedures such as certain therapeutic or casework procedures which are beyond the understanding of laymen. However, for those services which are broadly concerned with domestic chores, socialisation opportunities or personal care routines, there is every chance that the lay people will have sufficient information or experience to choose for themselves. People having special learning, behavioural or orientation problems may not be able to exercise choice over many goods and services. In such cases a relative, frien or volunteer could act as agent. (It is important to distinguish this allocati of a budget to an individual or a chosen agent from the case management approach discussed below.)

Secondly, it is not known whether people will knowingly use a budget 'inappropriately' by substituting consumption of possibly harmful goods or services, for social care services, even if, as individuals, they may consider such consumption to be perfectly satisfactory. Although it may be easy to identify consumption patterns which are grossly unsatisfactory there are many shades of opinion about what can be termed 'harmful' even for those people who feel that paternalistic methods of monitoring consumption may be appropriate. There is very little empirical evidence that can be used to evaluate the merits of giving disabled people opportunities to make their own choices about the help they wish to receive. One small-scale study in London showed a quite marked difference of opinion amongst disabled people themselves in that out of 596 people questioned, 227 (38 per cent) considered that they did not get the services they needed and 172 (76 per cent) of these would have preferred extra help in the form of cash rather than services. In comparison, 334 respondents (56 per cent) were quite satisfied with the services they received (Patrick and Scrivens, 1989, p.136).

6.   THE CASE MANAGEMENT APPROACH

It is not clear from Sir Roy Griffiths' *Community Care: Agenda for Action* (1988) whether the notion that budgets for social care be paid directly to consumers was not considered or was considered and rejected. The process of management set out in the Agenda and accepted by the White Paper on Community Care, *Caring for People* (1989b), closely follows what Bleddyn Davies has termed the 'core tasks' of case management (Davies and Challis, 1986), viz:

    a. case finding and screening;
    b. needs assessment;
    c. case management including care planning, arranging for services, monitoring and reassessment;
    d. programme review;
    e. filling the gaps in service availability.

Case management can be carried out in a variety of ways by different personnel. It may be individual-based (key worker) or team-based (involving general or specialised staff). There are formal approaches as developed in the Kent Community Care Scheme (Challis and Davies, 1986) or informal schemes based on mixed discipline community terms or planned programmes for individual care, training or rehabilitation. Each approach has its own advantages and disadvantages as shown in the recent pilot projects or the care in the community initiative (Renshaw *et al.*, 1988, p.110).

Compared to the existing system of community care, the case management approach has the general merit of simplifying access to community care for people confronted with a bewildering maze of cash benefits and service provision as described in the Audit Commission's Report (1986). If case management is armed with budgetary command over the purchase of services, it has the advantage of giving the case manager the means to ensure that an appropriate service mix is delivered to meet the individual's requirements. Compared to the idea of giving consumers budgets, it avoids the worry that money may be spent inappropriately.

However, many of the issues raised by consumerism still apply to the case management approach, including how the budget constraint is to be determined and the variety of services which have to be purchased. In addition, some people would argue that the case management approach is unnecessarily paternalistic and that choices of some services are best made or guided by people who have experience of the relevant disability.

The development of the case management approach can be seen as a move towards consumer-led choice in social care. Although this does not go as far as paying care allowances directly to users, it is a major improvement on the existing system. The details as to how budgets are to be held, the 'pricing' system for services, the nature and size of the budget constraint and the professional behaviour of case-management need to be resolved.

7. BUDGETING ARRANGEMENTS AND CASE MANAGEMENT

The Audit Commission's Report on Community Care (1986),having clearly set out the tangled web of financial arrangements which are used to fund community and social care, made a number of recommendations:

i) 'A rationalisation of funding policies must be undertaken from the centre so that the present policy conflicts are resolved and the block grant disincentives to the build-up of local authority community care services removed.

ii) Adequate short-term funding must be provided to avoid the long-term waste of two inadequate services struggling along in parallel indefinitely.

iii) Social security policies must be co-ordinated with community care policies, and present conflicts and 'perverse incentives' encouraging residential rather than community care removed.

iv) A more rational organisational structure must be established; local responsibility, authority and accountability for delivering a balanced community-based care service for different client groups need to be more clearly defined.

v) The organisational structures of the different agencies need to be aligned and greater managerial authority delegated to the local level.

vi) Staffing arrangements must ensure provision of an appropriate supply of properly trained community-based staff.

vii) Provision for cost-effective voluntary organisations must be sufficient to prevent them being starved of funds for reasons unrelated to their potential contribution to the support of clients and those caring for them in the community.' (Audit Commission, 1986, pp. 3–4).

After his study of community care, Sir Roy Griffiths' Agenda (1988,p.1–2) presented some very similar but in many aspects more specific, recommendations including making local authorities responsible for:

a. assessing the need for residential care and where appropriate meeting the costs of care for people who cannot pay themselves;
b. funding community care projects currently supported through Joint Finance;
c. spending the money currently allocated to the community care grant elements of the Social Fund.

To carry out these responsibilities the following financial arrangements were also recommended.

d. Resources should be transferred between central and local government to match defined responsibilities.
e. Social services authorities should be supported by general and targeted specific grants providing a significant proportion of the total cost of the programme.

The main difference between the recommendations in Sir Roy's Agenda and the Audit Commission Report was in the treatment of NHS funds devoted to community care services. The Audit Commission suggested that local authorities might hold all the funds for community care and 'buy in' the required NHS services. Sir Roy recommended that NHS authorities should retain the funds used on community care services but the cost involved should be separately identified, and ring-fenced.

Most of these recommendation on funding were not accepted in the White Paper on Community Care (DoH , 1989b). Health authorities will continue to fund mainstream community health services from within their budgets, and this spending will not be ring-fenced. Specific grants will be used only in the case of people with a mental illness. The fate of Joint Finance arrangements remains undecided. The recommendation to allocate the funds for caring for people in residential and nursing home care was accepted. Thus, although the incentive to place people in residential and nursing home care without a full consideration of alternative methods of meeting their needs was removed, many of the early criticisms of the Audit Commission on the funding of community care are still relevant. A multiplicity of budgets will remain in community care—NHS budgets, care in the community funds, joint finance (possibly) and all the individual budgets of different departments in local authorities. Uncertainty about planning totals will continue. The perpetual struggle to identify the resources intended for community care and to protect them from the other sectors of the NHS or departments in local authorities will also continue.

The discussions on the advantages and disadvantages of specific grants have raged for many years. According to the White Paper on Community Care (1989b) the balance still lies with the disadvantages of specific grants and the advantages of block grants. In particular the Rate Support Grant encourages local responsibility for expenditure and fosters efficiency by ensuring that community care needs are best met by careful consideration of local circumstances. The rejection of the ring-fencing of NHS funds was based on the need to maintain feasibility in budgeting arrangements to meet the changing circumstances of community health care.

These decisions have profound implications for case management and budgetary arrangements in the reorganisation of community care. The White Paper offers some answers to the question posed in the previous sector on budgets. The case managers' budgets will be set by their local authorities and will be dispensed on residential, day and domiciliary care services. These services may be provided by local authorities, voluntary agencies or private firms. The so-called mixed economy approach is likely to be most in evidence over this range of services.

For related, complementary community health and housing services, case managers will be reliant on collaborative arrangements with NHS authorities, local authority housing departments and housing associations. They will not have purchasing power to ensure the delivery of the appropriate mix of services and the White Paper emphasises the need for case managers to include other professions in assessment and care planning systems to obtain the necessary collaboration. The inherent danger is that goodwill will not overcome budget constraints in the NHS or housing agencies. If it is not possible to deliver the required services, the problems of bed-blocking, inappropriate use of day hospitals and shortage of suitable, adapted housing will continue.

However, the main question deliberately left unanswered by the White Paper is how budget limits will be set for case managers. Although community care plans must include details of budgetary arrangements put into place, their actual form and operation are left to local determination. It is stated that these limits could be set for groups or individuals. There is no guidance, however, on whether limits should be related to criteria such as disability levels or to economic factors such as levels of expenditure on existing services or proportional costs of alternative forms of care as currently practised in the Kent Community Care Scheme (Challis and Davies, 1986). The exception to this is the specific grant payable for people with mental illness which will be paid only if suitable care plans are agreed for the individuals concerned.

One pragmatic approach to client-group budgeting would be to use a simple per capita sum based, for example, on the average expenditure per client in the existing system. Case managers would receive this budgeting allowance for all people in their existing case-load. Such a method is straight forward, like care in the community payments which are related to the average cost of hospital care, and would be useful as a starting point but would be rough justice to case managers whose case-loads were dominated by people with 'above average need'. Two refinements could follow. One would be to attempt to equalise 'needs' in case-loads; the second would be to develop weighting systems to reflect 'needs'. Both of these methods require the development of methods for measuring 'needs' which would address factors such as mobility, self-care, behaviour, family circumstances and, possibly, incomes.

A different approach would be to take case managers' estimates of expenditure for clients and then develop the total budget by aggregating across all clients and case managers. These estimates of total expenditure would then be compared with the actual affordable expenditure and, if the former exceeds the latter, case managers' allocations would be reduced accordingly. The major problem would be the incentive to over-estimate expenditure requirements and case-audit may have to be implemented.

8. CONCLUSION

The White Paper on Community Care has placed great emphasis on case management as a way of improving social care in Britain. However, the problem for community care in the co-ordination of social care with all other aspects of life for people with long-term disabilities is that the onus must once again rest on that well-worn plea for collaboration between agencies and between agencies and users. The recent history of collaboration has not been a spectacular success, mainly because of the different financial constraints and mechanisms used to fund community care. The White Paper has suggested leaving most of their financial systems as they are. Thus, there may be mixed-economy approach to residential, day and domiciliary care but its success depends as much on the working of related health, housing, employment, cultural and transport systems as does on its own endeavours.

References

Audit Commission for Local Authorities in England and Wales (1986). *Making a Reality of Community Care*, HMSO, London
Bradshaw, J. and Gibbs, I. (1988). *Public Support for Private Residential Care*, Gower Publishing Company, Aldershot
Blaxter, M. (1976). *The Meaning of Disability*, Heinemann, London

Challis, D. and Davies, B. (1986). *Case Management in Community Care,* Gower Publishing Company, Aldershot

Davies, B. and Challis, D. (1986). *Matching Resources to Needs in Community Care,* Gower Publishing Company, Aldershot

Department of Health (DoH) (1989a). *Working for Patients,* Cm. 555, HMSO, London

Department of Health (DoH) (1989b). *Caring for People,* Cm. 849, HMSO, London

Department of Health and Social Security (DHSS) (1975). *Better Services for the Mentally Ill,* Command 6233, HMSO, London

Department of Health and Social Security (DHSS) (1981). *Care in the Community: A Consultative Document on Moving Resources for Care in England,* HMSO, London

Department of Health and Social Security (DHSS) (1987). *Public Support for Residential Care,* Report of a Joint Central and Local Government Working Party, DHSS, London

Donaldson, C., Wright, K. and Maynard, A. (1985). *Utilisation and Performance of Day Hospitals for the Elderly in South Yorkshire,* Trent RHA, Sheffield

Gray, A., Whelan, A. and Normand, C. (1988). *Care in the Community: A Study of Services and Costs in Six Districts,* Centre for Health Economics, University of York, York

Griffiths, Sir Roy (1988). *Community Care. Agenda for Action,* HMSO, London

Parker, G. (1985). *With Due Care and Attention,* Family Policy Studies Centre, London

Patrick, D. and Scrivens, E. (1989). Allocating resources to meet needs. In Patrick, D. and Peack, H. (eds.), *Disablement in the Community,* Oxford University Press, Oxford

Renshaw, J., Hampson, R., Thomason, C., Darton, R., Judge, K. and Knapp, M. (1988). *Care in the Community: The First Steps,* Gower Publishing Company, Aldershot

CHAPTER 9

Evaluating the Reform of the NHS

John Brazier, John Hutton, Richard Jeavons

1. INTRODUCTION

Much speculation has taken place over exactly how the proposed changes to the NHS, advocated in the White Paper *Working for Patients* (DoH, 1989), will be implemented. This chapter steps back from the detailed debate to take a strategic look at the White Paper proposals in the context of basic objectives and the range of available methods of financing and organising health services. These are described in Section 2 and used in Section 3 to classify the schemes advocated by various interest groups prior to the publication of the White Paper. Section 4 discusses the criteria by which the success or failure of reform proposals might be judged. In Section 5 these criteria are used to assess three of the major changes proposed in the White Paper.

2. CONTEXT AND BACKGROUND

In the context of the NHS review, there are a number of combinations of methods for financing and organising the provision of health care in the United Kingdom. These options are summarised in Table 9.1 below and provide the framework in which actual proposals for reform of NHS may be classified.

All systems are pluralistic to some degree, so the debate is less about exchanging one monolithic system for another, than about changing the relative balance of financing and provision methods. For example, the NHS is primarily funded from general taxation, but also has elements of co-payment for dental services and prescriptions, and the use of vouchers for opticians' services. A private health sector financed by insurance and direct out-of-pocket payment also exists in the UK. Similar diversity is to be found in the provision of services, particularly in non-acute care.

2.1 Methods of finance

Uncertainty over future needs for health care and the cost and effectiveness of different treatments, leads individuals to prefer some form of insurance against the cost of health services, either through guaranteed free provision or re-imbursement of costs incurred. Direct out-of-pocket payment for health care is not the dominant method of finance in any proposed system and has therefore been excluded from the categorisation. However, this method is present to some degree in all the proposals under review and may have a key role in specific services. The four main methods of financing are taxation, social insurance, private insurance, and service entitlement fees paid directly by the consumer. (For a more detailed discussion see Culyer *et al.*, 1988 c and d).

Taxation
Health care finance can be raised through general taxation or through specific taxes, earmarked to provide for health services. The taxes can be raised centrally, as in the UK, or locally as in some Scandinavian countries. Budgets are allocated by the Government to health service providers and care is provided free at the point of use for consumers. Contribution to funding is not directly linked to use of services for any individual.

Social insurance
Social insurance exists in a variety of forms in many countries (McLachlan and Maynard, 1982). It can be administered by a regional government, national government or a quango, and enrolment may be compulsory or provide for opting-out by those with private insurance. The premium is often deducted directly from employees' incomes and collected from employers in the form of a payroll tax. If funds collected in this way are used to provide health services free at the point of use then there is little difference between social insurance and taxation—in effect the only difference is the tax-base. However, if the provision is organised so that consumers must pay for services and claim reimbursement, then the implications are rather different.

Private insurance
Insurance companies charge a premium in return for a guarantee to cover an individual (or family) for the costs of treatment in the event of illness. Premiums may be averaged across a large group, for example a firm's workforce, or experience-rated, that is, actuarially based on the estimated risk of each person requiring treatment in the future. There is, therefore, the possibility of some link between utilisation of services and payments by individuals through variations of premiums. The extent of insurance cover is related to premium levels so individuals can choose the level of cover they wish, provided they can afford it. The poor and the elderly are usually

offered subsidies in some form to bring their level of cover up to minimum acceptable standards.

Figure 9.1: A Classification of proposed schemes for the UK Health Care System

Organisation of Health Service Provision	Dominant Method of Finance			
	Public Finance		Private Finance	
	A. Taxation	B. Social Insurance	C. Private Insurance	D. Service Entitlement Fee
1. NHS with internal change				
2. Prospective Payment System	Flexed budgets – NAHA (1988)			
3. Provider Markets	Internal Markets – Enthoven (1985a) Provider Markets – Culyer (1988)			
4. Provider Markets with consumer choice	HMUs – Pirie and Butler (1988) MHCOs – Goldsmith and Willets (1988)	Whitney (1988) Brittan (1988)	Green (1988)	

Service entitlement fee

This method of private finance is usually associated with Health Maintenance Organisations (HMOs). It involves the consumer voluntarily enrolling with an organisation and paying a fixed annual fee, like a premium. In return the providers accept the risks of covering their health care needs.

This in effect cuts out the third party between consumer and provider and combines finance with provision within a single organisation. For a pre-determined fee the provider guarantees a certain level of service. Thus the consumer is offered services free at the point of use, as in a tax financed system, but chooses his provider and pays an annual sum not directly related to the cost of services actually used.

2.2 Methods of organising provision

Classifying methods of organising the provision of health services is more complicated than categorising financing systems because of the plurality of systems, referred to above, and the mass of minor variations which occur. (These aspects are discussed in Culyer and Brazier, 1988a; Culyer *et al.*, 1988b). Methods of organising the provision of health care can be distinguished by reference to the following characteristics:

- whether purchasing agencies are separate from the providers of health care;
- how purchasing agents receive their finance (for example fixed budgets, per capita payments or fee for services);
- who provides services and whether they are public or private sector; and
- how providers are paid (for example fixed salary, per capita fee or fee for service).

Using these pointers, four broad methods of organising the provision of health care, which are relevant to the UK debate, may be distilled from the myriad possibilities.

The NHS before the White Paper
For comparative purposes the NHS before the White Paper will be used. The essential features are: a hospital sector with the purchasing and provision of services carried out by District Health Authorities (DHAs) with fixed budgets determined by capitation and activity levels; and a primary care sector, administered by Family Practitioner Committees (FPCs) with services provided by self-employed general practitioners, dentists, opticians and pharmacists. Any proposal for significant alterations in these basic features may be regarded as a separate proposal for reform.

The NHS is not, of course, a static and unchanging system. For example, its last major re-organisation as the direct result of the Griffiths Management Inquiry is still being felt in the NHS. Any comparison should take account of ongoing changes initiated within the NHS.

Prospective payment for item of service
Prospective payment per item of service (PPS) relates payment to the type of case treated, with a fee schedule for all cases determined in advance. The fee is related to the average cost of actual service provided. The difference between PPS and traditional fee for service systems is that the payment in PPS is based on a complete episode of care for the patient, not an aggregation

of fees for individual medical services. The system has been developed and applied in the USA using diagnosis related groups (DRGs) to classify cases for the calculation of the payments schedule.

Provider markets
Provider markets involve the separation of responsibility for ensuring that patients receive care from the responsibility for the direct provision of that care. A purchasing agent with statutory responsibility for ensuring that care is available to those resident within the area, will provide it by a combination of contracting with other agencies and direct provision. For example, under this system a health authority might use its budget to buy services in from other health authorities, private hospitals, general practitioners, private nursing homes and local authority social service departments. A version of this approach restricted to contracts between the NHS authorities is often referred to as an NHS 'internal market'.

Provider markets with consumer choice
This is a development of the provider market approach which allows more freedom to the individual to select his purchasing agent. The purchasing agent then contracts to supply the full health care requirements of consumers, and must buy in from outside any specialist services which cannot be provided directly. Where local competition exists there is greater pressure on purchasing agents to keep consumers satisfied with their services. This type of organisation can be funded from general taxation (in a voucher system) or by a direct out-of-pocket payment of the annual fee by consumers.

2.3 Proposals put to Government

In a previous paper (Brazier *et al.*, 1989) eight proposals were appraised, which had been submitted for consideration by the NHS Review. The eight proposals which were described in the previous paper, have been placed within the classification system (Figure 9.1). All eight had been published and received some critical attention during the NHS debate in 1988 and, as a set, represented a broad range of opinion on potential reform.

The classification of proposals in Figure 9.1 clearly illustrates how proposals were concentrated on the reform of provision with only limited discussion about changing the dominant method of financing. Most of the proposals adhered to the NHS principles of access to services on the basis of clinical need, and funding from general taxation. Green (1988), Whitney (1988) and Brittan (1988) all proposed an enhanced role for private insurance (as well as provision) to make it easier for those able to pay to obtain more health services and increase total expenditure. Their schemes encouraged the development of a two-tier system—a basic level of state financed services available to all, and further services available to those willing to pay through private insurance or directly out-of-pocket. Green and Brittan would allow those with private insurance to opt out completely from funding the state-supported 'safety net' service. The Whitney proposal would maintain the general tax funding of the state supported service, but would encourage 'topping-up' from consumers' own resources.

There was broad agreement across the proposals that there should be a greater use of competition between suppliers to improve efficiency though the precise organisational form varied. The proposals differed primarily on the purchasing agent and whether they should compete for custom. Enthoven (1985a) and Culyer (1988) saw the role of purchasing agent being best fulfilled by Districts, or newly formed local health boards, holding a capitation-based budget to spend on their residents within their geographic boundaries. Pirie and Butler (1988) and Goldsmith and Willetts (1988), regarded consumer choice of purchasing as an important additional mechanism for promoting quality care, as well as being important for its own sake. It was noticeable that no proposal advocated an increased role for planning as a means to improve efficiency.

3. THE WHITE PAPER PROPOSALS

The NHS Review White Paper brought forward a range of proposals, some of which have been elaborated upon in a series of nine working papers. Only three of these proposals represent, in the terms set out in Section 1, substantive reforms of the method of financing and organising the provision of health care in the UK.

3.1 Self-governing hospitals

The proposal that any hospital can become a self-governing, NHS Hospital Trust involves redefining the relationship between all hospitals and Districts on the basis of being respectively providers and purchasers of certain health care services. The actual separation of the role of providing health care from its financing, achieved through hospitals having Trust status and contracting with Districts and GP budget holders, is to be mirrored in a quasi separation of these functions across the whole NHS through the use of contracts between Districts and their directly managed units. Within the classification set out in Table 9.1, this proposal involves a change in the method of organising health care provision towards a provider market model. This is not an internal market as described by Enthoven (1985a) since the core of the proposal is not to establish trading of services between Districts. Their main responsibility will be to act as purchasing agent on behalf of their respective resident populations, contracting with hospitals as providers of services to secure appropriate care. In theory hospitals will compete with each other, whether they are self-governing or remain under direct control of Districts, to provide services to purchasing agents, be they Districts, GPs holding budgets for some services or, indeed, other hospitals seeking to 'share' the provision of some services.

A number of other proposals contained within the White Paper and its Working Papers can be seen as necessary to support this basic change towards the separation of purchasing from provision of services in the hospital sector. To allow them to behave more competitively in the new provider market, hospital trusts will have greater freedom and control over the use of both their assets and revenue, including the ability to set their own terms and conditions for the recruitment of staff (Working Paper 1). Districts, as purchasing agents, will be given control over all the resources available for their resident population. This will be achieved by replacing the Resource Allocation Working Party formula (RAWP) with a resident population capitation. Cross boundary flow adjustments will be replaced by contracts and direct payments for the services involved. In general, the new relationship between Districts and hospitals, created by the separation of purchase and provision, will be defined in detail by contracts specifying the quantity and quality of service to be provided for a given cost (Working Paper 2).

3.2 Practice budgets for GPs

The principle, established in the hospital sector, of separating the purchase and provision of services will be reinforced by giving GP practices with at least 11,000 registered patients the option of holding budgets to cover the costs of purchasing a range of services on their behalf (Working Paper 3). In this way the potential exists for a larger number of smaller purchasing agents to be created and competition between providers for their business promoted. In terms of the classification set out in Table 9.1, this again moves the organisation of health care provision towards provider markets though none of the proposals summarised in the table envisaged GPs acting as purchasing agents. As with the hospital sector, the new relationship between GPs as purchasing agents and providers of services will need to be defined by detailed contracts.

3.3 Tax exemption for the elderly

The third proposal, which registers as a substantive shift in the method of financing health care in the UK, is income tax relief on premiums for private medical insurance for those aged 60 and over (DoH, 1989a, page 69). This change did not specifically form any part of the proposals put forward by Green, Whitney and Brittan, though they all envisaged an enhanced role for private insurance in the UK health care system. In terms of Table 9.1, this change will not shift the dominant method of financing health care in the UK, which will continue to be general taxation, but as a statement of intent it is clearly a move in that direction.

3.4 Other proposals

Three White Paper proposals (self-governing hospitals, practice budgets for GPs and tax exemption for the elderly) are substantive reforms of the method of organising and financing health care in the UK. The remaining proposals in the White Paper may be viewed as either necessary to support those substantive reforms or as independent of both them and the reform of organisation and finance. Indicative prescribing budgets, capital charges, medical audit, consultants' contracts and changes to Family Practitioner Committees (Working Papers 4–8) are all reforms which have been mooted for some time and could have been introduced strictly within the confines of the NHS before the White Paper.

4. EVALUATION CRITERIA

To determine whether the proposed changes will lead to improvements over the current NHS, it is necessary to specify the objectives of the system. Advocates of the changes claim concern with improving efficiency and equity, and increasing the scope for consumer choice. However, closer examination reveals that there are many different interpretations of the term 'efficiency' and different conceptions of what an 'equitable' system is. Furthermore, even when there is agreement on the definition of objectives there may be disagreement over the relative importance of each. The pre-requisite of a comparison of the proposals for reform is a set of criteria, by which each can be appraised, which explicitly recognises these differences, as well as the more obvious differences in institutional arrangements.

4.1 Efficiency

In general terms most people accept that efficiency relates to how well inputs are used to produce desired outputs. In the case of health service provision there are three levels at which the efficiency of a system can be measured.

Technical efficiency
An activity is technically efficient if the maximum possible output is being obtained from a given quantity of inputs, or a given output target is being achieved with the minimum use of resources. The cost of the inputs and the value of the output are not directly relevant to technical efficiency which is concerned with the physical relationships between inputs and outputs.

Cost-effectiveness
The second level of efficiency adds the cost dimension to technical efficiency by requiring that target outputs are achieved in each activity by the least cost method. For many health problems there are a number of effective treatments which differ according to their probability of success, their net effect on the health status of patients and their cost. A cost-effective treatment is one

which maximises the beneficial impact on the patient for a given level of cost, or minimises the cost of obtaining a given level of benefit. The cheapest treatment may not be the most cost-effective because the more expensive options may also be much more effective. Cost-effectiveness comparisons require the technically efficient method of delivery of each treatment to be identified first.

The key issue is the way in which effectiveness is measured. One approach is to assume that individual patients do not have the technical knowledge to judge the relative merits of different treatments and therefore require an agent, usually a doctor, to advise them on what choice to make. The expert advice should be based on an assessment of the likely impact of various treatments on the patient's health. In this way the relative benefit of different treatments for the same patients can be compared, and also the relative benefits from attempting to treat different patient groups (Williams, 1985).

An alternative approach is to assume that the patient is the best judge of the benefit of different treatments and that the benefit enjoyed will be indicated by patients' willingness to pay for different services. Research to identify the health benefits of different procedures is rendered unnecessary, and cost-effectiveness is judged by the profitability of service provision to the providers. These different approaches have been described as 'extra-welfarist' and 'welfarist' respectively by Culyer (1989).

Social efficiency

Cost-effectiveness analysis assists choice between predetermined alternative uses of resources in health care but gives no indication of what overall level of health care expenditure is worthwhile. To decide this requires information on all other possible uses of the resources involved and a social judgement as to whether the correct balance has been struck between health services and, for example, education, leisure, transport or housing. Social efficiency (also known as global, allocative or high level efficiency) is achieved when the benefit to people from further expenditure on health services is no greater than that from alternative uses of resources. This raises an important question as to whether the benefits from health care should be valued by an agency on behalf of consumers or by individuals themselves in the market place.

In a tax-financed system such as the present NHS, a political decision is made on the appropriate size of the health care budget. For example, as new techniques and procedures are developed, decisions must be taken as to whether they are to be made available to all patients under the NHS. In systems involving private finance new procedures will be introduced and will result in an expansion of the system if patients are willing to pay for them without reducing demand for other health services. (This is more likely to happen in a system financed through insurance rather than direct patient payment). Advocates of private finance assume social efficiency to be automatically achieved in these circumstances as consumers are free to obtain the level of services they desire.

4.2 Equity

The notion of equity in the provision of health services has many ideological interpretations. The aspect of equity most often discussed is that concerning access to services; for example, the principle behind the NHS is that individuals should have equal access to services solely on the basis of clinical need (that is, irrespective of willingness or ability to pay). Equality of *access* does not guarantee equality of use; or of benefit from services, or ultimately of health status; all of which have been put forward as alternative bases for defining equity in consumption of health services. Equality of access is generally considered in geographical terms, but the willingness of different social groups to make use of services, ostensibly equally accessible, will also vary. Hence the need to consider utilisation as well as physical accessibility.

An alternative definition of equality of access is that individuals who themselves perceive a need for health services should have access to the system. This would be reflected in a system which generated equal treatment to those willing to pay an equal amount.

As important as equity in the distribution of benefits is equity in the distribution of the burden of financing the health sector. One view of equity is that contribution to the cost of the system should be related to the individual's ability to pay, rather than the amount of services consumed. In this approach those disadvantaged by ill health are not given an additional financial handicap. An alternative approach is to regard equal payment for equal consumption of services as equitable. Those worried about the potential cost of fees and charges for treatment should cover the risk with health insurance. Clearly the method of distributing costs will affect the distribution of benefits as it will influence consumers' readiness to make use of services.

4.3 Consumer choice

The third objective is less tangible but is nevertheless a significant objective of many proposals for systems of health care provision and finance. Individuals may value choice for its own sake, regardless of whether these choices give them other benefits such as improved treatment or reduced costs. This objective therefore relates to individual freedom as an *end* in itself and should not be confused with the advocacy of more consumer choice as a *means* of achieving greater efficiency.

4.4 Conflicting objectives and ideologies

Where multiple objectives are being pursued there is always the possibility of conflict between them. In theory, the efficiency objectives are complementary. The principles which determine the best overall level of health care expenditure are also the principles which determine the best level of provision for each of its components. In practice, the drive to achieve cost effectiveness may also be stimulated by constraining the overall level of resources. Conversely, a system which is primarily concerned with ensuring that the total level of resources is sufficient to meet society's demands is likely to find the achievement of technical efficiency or cost-effectiveness more difficult at the hospital or clinic level.

A more commonly cited conflict is that between efficiency and equality of access. The most obvious dimension of this conflict is geographical but it also occurs between social classes and income groups. If economies of scale exist in the provision of services then some degree of centralisation is indicated to make efficient use of resources. If this takes place then communities will have different types and levels of service immediately available to them and will face different travel and time costs to reach the centralised service. The distance from appropriate facilities may also affect the health benefit ultimately achieved from the treatment.

On the other hand, there can be complementarity between equity and efficiency. If resources are devoted to those services giving the greatest improvement in health status to patients then there need be no conflict with the objective of giving access on the basis of clinical need. If the latter is defined in terms of potential to benefit from treatment, then pursuit of equity or efficiency should lead to provision of the same level and mix of services to similar populations.

Similarly, the relationship between efficiency and consumer choice is open to differing interpretations. Centralisation of services to achieve economies of scale will reduce consumer choice by cutting down the number of hospitals offering a given treatment. Freedom of choice of treatment for consumers, in a system where access is determined by willingness to pay, may lead to demands for services which are less effective in producing improvements in health status. This can be because treatment is not given to those who could benefit most (because they are unwilling to pay) or less cost-effective treatments are given because they have other characteristics attractive to consumers. For example, patients without the technical knowledge to judge the relative merits of the clinical services provided by different hospitals may take account of factors they can judge, such as the quality of hospital environment and the 'hotel' services offered.

There is also a conflict between freedom of choice and the financing of health services. The type of service in tax-financed systems is generally determined by the professional groups responsible for its provision. The quality of work is judged by the providers' professional peers. Such systems allow finance to be raised from those most able to pay (through progressive taxation) and provide equal opportunity of access to services to all income groups without charge at the time of use. Although paying for the service through taxation, the patient is not in a position to act like a consumer since any individual patient s satisfaction with the service has little influence on the behaviour or income of the providers. Such a situation generally prevails in the NHS and those people who wish to have greater control over the timing and nature of their treatment can choose to pay for private services (but cannot opt out of their tax contribution to the NHS). Several proposals have been made to strengthen the position of the patient as consumer, without undermining the fundamental equality of access principle of the NHS. Those schemes advocating more direct charges, tax relief on insurance premiums, or 'basic' public health services with better facilities open to those willing to pay, are not consistent with that equity principle as increased freedom of choice in a market situation gives greater benefits to those with more money to spend.

The relative weight given to each objective, and the interpretation placed on its definition will be governed by ideological perspectives. To avoid argument at cross-purposes the different ideological perspectives behind reform proposals must be made explicit. Two broad schools of thought can be identified (Williams, 1988). The mainstream public sector school lays emphasis on equality of access on the basis of clinical need; finance through progressive taxation; benefits defined in terms of improvement in health status; and the use of cost-effectiveness analysis to identify the appropriate allocation of resources within the health sector. The overall size of the health sector should also be determined by rational analysis of the contribution of health care to improving health status, as opposed to the health benefits of, for instance, improved road safety or better housing. An underlying assumption is that individuals are not well informed about the likely effects of different treatments and therefore consumer choice has little role to play in resource allocation.

The 'individualistic' approach emphasises the need to link payment with consumption of services, regarding equity as being achieved if consumers pay for what they consume—redistribution of income is not regarded as a function of the health sector. Consumer preferences are the guiding principle of resource allocation, and therefore objective measures of health benefits are regarded as unnecessary. This approach is based on the idea that individuals are responsible for their own health and that direct payment for health services will provide a clear incentive for the adoption of more healthy life styles. Many proposals for reform mix aspects of the two broad approaches, making it necessary to identify whether the relative weighting of objectives is being changed from that of the current NHS, or whether reforms are being proposed to achieve existing objectives more effectively.

4.5 A checklist of questions

With these difficulties in mind, a checklist of key questions (see Figure 9.2) is suggested as a means of establishing the differences between proposals for reform of the NHS, and examining their relative merits in the light of empirical evidence. For each of the first four criteria the questions address four main areas:

1. The definition of objectives in order to establish the ideological position of what the health sector should be doing and how its success should be judged.
2. How the proposed change should work in terms of the (predominantly economic) theory underlying it.
3. Whether the proposed change is likely to work in the light of results of published evaluations of similar schemes elsewhere.
4. What might be required to overcome perceived difficulties with the proposed change.

Figure 9.2: Key Questions for the Evaluation of Proposals

Technical Efficiency
This is assumed to have a common definition regardless of ideological viewpoint.
1. What mechanisms exist for minimising the cost of each activity carried out?
2. What evidence exists that these mechanisms work?
3. What is the implication of these mechanisms for the cost of managing the system?
4. What adjustments to the scheme might improve its performance?

Cost-effectiveness
1. How is cost-effectiveness defined in the proposal:
   a) by reference to an objective measure of gain in health status; or
   b) by reference to consumer satisfaction with services as indicated by willingness to pay?
2. What are the proposed mechanisms for achieving cost-effectiveness?
3. What evidence exists that these mechanisms work?
4. What adjustments might be made to the scheme to improve its performance?

Social Efficiency
1. How is the socially desirable overall size of the health sector defined in the system:
   a) by reference to the relative valuation by the community of measured gains in health status, derived from all forms of health care and promotion, and benefits derived from other forms of public and private expenditure; or
   b) by reference to the relative valuation by individuals of the benefits derived from health services and the benefits from the purchase of other goods and services?
2. What are the proposed mechanisms for achieving the appropriate overall size for the health sector?
3. What evidence is there that these mechanisms will work?
4. What adjustment might be made to the scheme to improve its performance?

Equity
1. What aspects of equity in the finance and provision of health care concern the authors of this proposal?
2. What mechanisms are proposed to achieve such equity?
3. What evidence exists that these mechanisms will promote equity?

Consumer Choice
What effective opportunities will the proposal offer consumers to choose:
1. their method of payment for health services;
2. their level of expenditure on health services;
3. their providers of health services (e.g. doctors, hospitals); or
4. the timing of their treatment?

The questions about consumer choice seek to establish, in more detail, the potential influence of the proposal in this area.

5. REVIEW OF PROPOSALS

Section 2 selected the three principal reforms of health care delivery and finance proposed in the White Paper: self-governing hospitals, GP budget holders, and tax exemption on health insurance for the elderly. Here we evaluate these proposals by attempting to answer the checklist of questions on Figure 9.2.

5.1 Self-governing hospitals

The separation of the role of providing health care from its finance would be achieved by the creation of self-governing hospitals. This form of provider market creates a mechanism for minimising the cost of activity (and hence promoting technical efficiency) by encouraging competition amongst NHS hospitals and the private sector, to win contracts. Districts or GP budget holders, as purchasing agents, can exploit variations between hospitals in the cost of each activity to increase the quantity of health care for their population. In the longer term there will therefore be an incentive for suppliers to cut the costs of their activities by reducing waste and where possible, take advantage of lower labour costs.

In practice, the extent of competition may be limited outside the main metropolitan areas. Indeed, Districts and GPs with budgets could be exploited by hospitals with a local monopoly in certain services. The Government has recognised the importance of regulating the health care industry. One method is through the Secretary of State's right to intervene directly to prevent cross-subsidisation, excessive prices and other market abuses. A less interventionist method is to reduce the barriers to entry into the market and encourage more competition by improving hospitals' access to capital for service developments. Self-governing hospitals are to have the privilege of being able to borrow either from Government or the private capital markets. These borrowing privileges are to be restricted by a financing limit. This may lead to a conflict between the micro-economic aim of promoting competition and the macro-economic policies of the Treasury.

Each year hospitals will negotiate contracts for all the services they provide. The agreement of hospital doctors is essential if a hospital is to meet its contractual obligations, since it is they who principally determine the number and type of patients treated, the resources used and quality of care. UK experiments with budgeting and resource management have encountered considerable difficulties in achieving agreements (Wickings *et al.*, 1985; DHSS, 1986b). The dialogue between managers and clinicians may be improved by the new job descriptions and reformed merit award system but will also depend on having credible information on costs, activities and outcomes.

There is no evidence on whether provider market competition in hospital services promotes technical efficiency. Evidence on the immediate potential for one-off gains from trade can be obtained from static comparisons of resource use between hospitals. For example, Department of Health Performance Indicators show large variations in use of beds and other resources between NHS hospitals, even after adjusting for differences in type of workload (DHSS, 1986a). Comparisons between sectors have found private providers of non-acute care to be cheaper (Knapp, 1986; Knapp and Missiakoulis, 1985; Judge *et al.*, 1986). In none of these comparisons has quality been adequately controlled for, so drawing conclusions regarding efficiency is fraught with difficulties.

The only experience with genuine competition in the NHS has been with contracting out ancillary services. This has been estimated to save between 10 to 20 per cent of costs (Key, 1988; Domberger *et al.*, 1987). Domberger and colleagues also examined the number of 'contract failures', that is sackings or serious breaches of agreement, as a proxy for quality. They found that the absolute number of failures had increased in the first year of contracting-out but argued that this may be a consequence of initial teething problems. The problem of measuring the impact of competition on the quality of ancillary services remains unresolved. Measuring quality in the provision of clinical services is an even more daunting prospect.

The only other experience of funding acute hospital activity prospectively is from the US Medicare Programme, which finances inpatient hospital care for those aged over sixty-five. This system is different from the proposed provider market, since quantity is not specified in local contracts and hospitals compete only on quality and not price (which is nationally determined). The similarities are in the incentive to reduce cost per inpatient case (as classified by diagnosis related groups). Evidence from this prospective payment system suggests that costs of inpatient cases have been reduced (Guterman and Dobson, 1986) but this may have been achieved by shifting costs to other areas (Carroll and Erwin, 1987), by reclassifying cases into higher paying patient groups, known as 'DRG Creep' (Ginsberg and Carter, 1986; Hsia *et al.*, 1988), or by cutting the quality of care provided, about which there is little evidence (Fitzgerald *et al.*, 1988).

A major weakness with this proposal is a lack of incentive to serve patients well. Quality would need to be specified in contracts and successful tenderers would have to provide effective quality assurance mechanisms for cost reductions not to be at the expense of patient outcome and well-being. The proposal therefore requires considerable enhancements of the hospital data collection systems on cost, activity and outcome. Good quality information will be important for making and monitoring contracts, for hospitals to ensure their prices cover costs and for hospital doctors auditing their work. The White Paper recognises that there will be costs attached to this information technology and the setting and monitoring of contracts but does not provide an estimate of either implementation costs or revenue consequences. It is assumed these costs will be met out of efficiency savings.

In the White Paper (DoH, 1989a), the definition of cost-effectiveness is by reference to some objective measure of gains in health status, although consumer satisfaction with services is to be given greater importance. A mechanism for promoting cost-effectiveness is in the contract specification of the activities to be purchased by Districts and GPs which maximise health status. Regions may provide guidance but unless Districts are rewarded on the basis of their success in promoting health status there is no guarantee they will take decisions which promote cost effectiveness.

This proposal does not address the highest level of social efficiency, that is the optimal overall size of the health sector, since the provider market operates within a predetermined cash-limited budget. The Government has reaffirmed its support for the principle of access to health care being determined by need and not willingness to pay. This reform could promote geographic equity if resources were allocated to Districts and GPs on the basis of capitation. It would be easier than the existing system since only money and not physical provision would need to be moved. The extent to which this mechanism will succeed depends on overcoming political barriers associated with the protection of vested interests in the status quo.

Social group equity may be adversely affected if patients have to travel large distances to receive care as a result of contracts. Districts and GPs would, in effect, be transferring some of the costs of care to the patients. Both the financial costs and time costs would discriminate against lower income groups (Le Grand, 1982). To overcome any disincentive effects, either Districts, or GPs or Local Authorities would have to compensate lower social groups for both direct financial and time costs (for example, lost income) by issuing for instance 'travel vouchers'.

Enthoven (1985b) recognised in his proposed 'internal market model' that a major flaw is the lack of consumer choice. Despite numerous references to patient choice in the White Paper, this proposal does not extend their freedom and may constrain it. The Government is intending to make it easier for individuals to change their GP but the choice of hospital, though ostensibly to remain with the GPs, is likely to be restricted by their District's contractual agreements.

5.2 GP budgets

The incentive for GPs to enter the scheme is the prospect of being able to plough back any savings into their practice. How effective the proposal is in attracting the interest of GPs remains to be seen. The White Paper claims that GPs will have an incentive to minimise costs so as to increase the surplus and improve patient care. It also claims that cost reduction will not be at the expense of quality since GPs will need to attract patients onto their list to maximise personal remuneration, as well as increase the total income of their practice. The White Paper has reaffirmed the intention of the preceding Primary Care White Paper, *Promoting Better Health* (DHSS, 1987), to increase the capitation element of GP's income and hence the incentive to attract more patients.

The resolution of these conflicting incentives between minimising costs and attracting patients depends partly on the ability of consumers to judge quality of care. This ability is likely to be severely restricted by the dearth of evidence on the costs and outcome of most medical procedures. Where there is information, then GPs are likely to have an advantage over consumers. As in any health system, professional trust is necessary to avoid abuse.

The overall impact on efficiency of these counteracting pressures is ultimately an empirical question. The only NHS experience with budgets for clinicians is from the clinical and management budgeting experiments in hospitals, but to date there has not been an operational clinical budget system (Wickings *et al.*, 1985; DHSS, 1986b).

Practices of GPs with budgets are similar in concept to the HMOs referred to in Section 1. The most quoted study of these organisations was undertaken by the Rand Corporation. It found that the HMOs studied had 28 per cent lower total costs than alternative insurance cover, with no apparent adverse effects on outcomes for the majority of members, the exceptions being low income individuals who were unhealthy when they first enrolled with the HMO (Manning *et al.*, 1984). This evidence is contradicted by a more recent study which found a significantly higher mortality in populations with a greater proportion of HMO enrollees (Shortell and Hughes, 1988). In addition, US evidence is difficult to translate into the UK context. In practice HMOs are quite different from the proposed GP budget holders in the range of procedures they cover, organisation and culture. The same cost per annum reductions could not be expected in the UK, since they were mainly achieved by lowering admissions into hospital and rates are already much lower here than the USA.

As with self-governing hospitals, GP budget holding will considerably increase the information and administrative costs of group practices. Practices are going to engage in a variety of activities unrelated to direct patient care, including negotiating and monitoring hospital contracts, auditing prescribing and referral patterns and producing more sophisticated annual accounts. The Government has accepted that additional costs may arise and proposes an extra practice allowance to cover them though the amount has not yet been agreed.

This proposal has no direct implications for the total size of the health care budget (that is, social efficiency), but has potentially far-reaching implications for the distribution of primary care resources. GP practice budgets are to be set on the basis of a compromise between current service use and capitation adjusted for health characteristics. If in the long run budgets move towards the latter basis, this will improve the geographical distribution, and Family

Practitioner Service expenditure (and that element of Hospital and Community Health Services covered by GP Budgets) will more closely match health needs.

It is claimed in Working Paper 3 on practice budgets that there will be no financial incentive for GPs to select comparatively healthy individuals of a given age. Yet adjusting payments for variations in patients' health cannot be sufficiently sensitive to take account of all individual differences. There will always be a range of individual health state profiles from which to select, whichever patient category system is used.

One solution is to prevent GPs from being able to refuse patients. In the USA, it has been argued that HMOs have overcome this restriction by using more subtle ways of selecting or attracting healthier patients by location, advertising, and public image. The existence of such 'cream skimming', however, remains a subject of considerable debate and conflicting evidence (Eggers, 1980; Luft, 1981 and 1987; Berki and Ashcroft, 1980; Blumberg, 1980).

A major objective of introducing this proposal is seen to be an increase in consumer choice. Extending the choice of purchasing agent for selected hospital procedures gives consumers more control over where they go for treatment. Clearly, the existence of such choice depends on consumers having access to one or more practice of GPs with a budget.

5.3 Tax exemption for the elderly

The proposal to allow income tax relief on private medical insurance premiums for the over 60's reduces their real price and might be expected to result in an increase in private spending on health care. It therefore has implications for the overall level of health care spending.

On purely efficiency grounds this change may not lead to an improvement in welfare as by subsiding private health care insurance it distorts market prices and may lead to over-consumption. The argument that the subsidy is a cheaper way for the Government to increase expenditure on health care is not supported by a recent forecast of the effects of this proposal. Propper (1989) estimated the likely impact of tax relief for the elderly on health insurance purchase. Her findings indicated that, unless there are changes in the types of policies offered, the impact on new sales is likely to be limited. The short run revenue implications for health sector expenditure are likely to be small compared to the total and would be less than the loss of revenue to the Treasury.

Tax relief will benefit only those elderly people with taxable income or whose families have sufficient income to pay on their behalf. The direction of the impact on the distribution of health care is away from the equal access principle and towards willingness to pay, even if the change is likely to be quite small. This consequence runs counter to the apparent equity objective of UK health policy.

The proposal does not directly increase the set of choices open to consumers, though indirectly it may encourage the private sector to develop a new range of policies. Its immediate effect will be to extend the affordability of private health insurance to lower income groups.

6. CONCLUSIONS

While previous NHS reform proposals tended to emphasise changes in organisation rather than financing, examination of the White Paper proposals reveals an even greater concentration on organisational change. No part of the proposals will influence the overall size of the health sector without explicit intervention by the Government. The attempt to encourage the uptake of private insurance by the elderly is dependent on government subsidy, and only if the necessary resources to finance this come from Treasury, rather then DoH budgets, could it lead to greater spending on health care.

The main organisational changes such as self-governing hospital trusts and GP budget holding are intended to harness the mechanisms of greater choice and competition in order to stimulate greater technical efficiency and cost-effectiveness. Evidence that they will succeed in doing this is hard to find and there are major worries over the quality of care which might be provided in a competitive contract system. Routine data on resource use are far from satisfactory and equivalent data on the effectiveness of care are virtually non-existent.

Faced with these difficulties, advocates of the reforms have emphasised the benefits of greater consumer choice in its own right. However, it is not clear how much scope for individual choice will be left if Health Authorities and GPs are required to make fixed term contracts for specific services from particular providers. Freedom to chose a GP remains with the patient but the information for comparison of GP performance in an objective way is not available yet within the service. Many choices will still be made on the basis of subjective factors and if the general standard of service can be made consistent then choice becomes less important.

On the equity issue, the White Paper proposals do not appear to challenge the principle of access to care on the basis of clinical need. The emphasis on the role of patient as consumer is, however, unlikely to encourage greater access by disadvantaged groups who are less willing or able to deal with professional services and bureaucracies. In the uncertainty likely to be created during the implementation of the changes, those with greater financial and human capital resources are more likely to obtain the service they need. The proposal to subsidise private health insurance for the first time is the one clear break with the currently accepted equity principle. However insignificant the effect of this proposal may be expected to be, the fact that public money (in the form of tax relief) will be used to encourage access to private care represents an important precedent.

References

Berki, S.E. and Ashcroft, M.L.F. (1980). HMO Enrollment: Who Gains What and Why? A Review of the Literature. *Milbank Memorial Fund Quarterly*, 58, 588–632

Blumberg, M.S. (1980). Health Status and Health Care by Type of Private Health Coverage. *Milbank Memorial Fund Quarterly*, 58, 633–655

Brazier, J., Hutton, J. and Jeavons, R. (1988). *Reforming the UK Health Care System*, Discussion Paper 47, Centre for Health Economics/York Health Economics Consortium, University of York

Brittan, L. (1988). *A New Deal for Health Care*, Conservative Political Centre, London

Carroll, N.V. and Erwin, W.G. (1987). Patient Shifting as a Response to Medicare Prospective Payment. *Medical Care*, 25, 1161–1167

Culyer, A.J. (1988). *The Radical Reforms the NHS Needs—and Doesn't*, Evidence to House of Commons Committee on the Social Services, mimeo, University of York,

Culyer, A.J. (1989). The Normative Economics of Health Care Finance and Provision. *Oxford Review of Economic Policy*, 5, 34–58

Culyer, A.J. and Brazier, J.E. (1988a). *Alternatives for Organising Health Services in the UK*, IHSM, London

Culyer, A.J., Brazier, J.E. and O'Donnell, O. (1988b). *Organising Health Service Provision: Drawing on Experience*, IHSM, London

Culyer, A.J., Donaldson, C. and Gerard, K. (1988c). *Alternatives for Funding Health Services in the UK*, IHSM, London

Culyer, A.J., Donaldson, C. and Gerard, K. (1988d). *Financial Aspects of Health Services: Drawing on Experience*, IHSM, London

Department of Health (DoH) (1989a). *Working for Patients*, Cm. 555, HMSO, London

Department of Health (DoH) (1989b). *Self-governing Hospitals*, Working Paper 1, HMSO, London

Department of Health (DoH) (1989c). *Funding and Contracts for Hospital Services*, Working Paper 2, HMSO, London

Department of Health (DoH) (1989d). *Practice Budgets for General Medical Practitioners*, Working Paper 3, HMSO, London

Department of Health (DoH) (1989e). *Indicative Prescribing Budgets for General Medical Practitioners*, Working Paper 4, HMSO, London

Department of Health (DoH) (1989f). *Capital Charges*, Working Paper 5, HMSO, London

Department of Health (DoH) (1989g). *Medical Audit*, Working Paper 6, HMSO, London

Department of Health (DoH) (1989h). *NHS Consultants: Appointments, Contracts and Distinction Awards*, Working Paper 7, HMSO, London

Department of Health (DoH) (1989i). *Implications for Family Practitioner Committees*, Working Paper 8, HMSO, London

Department of Health and Social Security (DHSS) (1976). *Report of Resource Allocation Working Party (RAWP)*, DHSS, London

Department of Health and Social Security (DHSS) (1986b). *Resource Management in Health Authorities*, DHSS, London, unpublished

Department of Health and Social Security (DHSS) (1987). *Promoting Better Health*, Cm. 249, HMSO, London

Domberger, S., Meadowcroft, S. and Thompson, D. (1986). Competitive Tendering and Efficiency: the case of refuse collection. *Fiscal Studies*, 7, 4, 69–87

Eggers, P.W. (1980). Risk Differential Between Medicare Beneficiaries Enrolled and not Enrolled in an HMO. *Health Care Financing Review*, 1(3), 91–99

Enthoven, A.C. (1985a). *Reflections on the Management of the National Health Service: An American Looks at Incentives to Efficiency in Health Services Management in the UK*, Nuffield Provincial Hospitals Trust, London

Fitzgerald, J.F., Moore, P.S. and Dittus, R.S. (1988). The care of elderly patients with hip fracture: changes since implementation of the prospective payment system. *New England Journal of Medicine*, 1392–97, Nov 24

Ginsbury, P.B. and Carter, G.M. (1986). Medical Case-Mix Index Increase. *Health Care Financing Review*, 7, 4, 51–66

Goldsmith, M. and Willetts, D. (1988). *Managed Health Care: A New System for a Better Health Service*. Health Review No 1, Policy Challenge, Centre for Policy Studies, London

Green, D. (1988). *Everyone's a Private Patient*, Hobart Paperback 27, IEA, London

Guterman, S. and Dobson, A. (1986). Impact of the Medicare Prospective Payment System for Hospitals. *Health Care Financing Review*, 7, 3, 97–114

Hsia, D.C., Krushat, W.M. *et al.* (1988). Accuracy of diagnostic coding for medicare patients under the prospective payment system. *New England Journal of Medicine*, 318(6), 352–355

Judge, K., Knapp, M. and Smith, J. (1986). The Comparative Costs of Public and Private Residential Homes for the Elderly. In Judge, K. and Sinclair, I. (eds.), *Residential Care for Elderly People*, HMSO, London

Key, T. (1988). Contracting Out Ancillary Services. In Maxwell, R. (ed.), *Reshaping the NHS*, Policy Journals, Hermitage, London

Knapp, M. (1986). The Relative Cost-Efficiency of Public Voluntary and Private Providers of Residential Child Care. In Culyer, A.J. and Jonsson, B. (eds.), *Public and Private Health Services*, Basil Blackwell, London

Knapp, M. and Missiakouliss, S. (1982). Inter-sectoral Cost Comparison: Day Care for the Elderly. *Journal of Social Policy*, 11, 335–354

Le Grand, J. (1982). *The Strategy of Equality*, Allen and Unwin, London

Luft, H.S. (1981). *Health Maintenance Organisations: Dimensions of Performance*, John Wiley and Sons, New York

Luft, H.S. (1987). How do health maintenance organisations achieve their "savings"? rhetoric and evidence. *New England Journal of Medicine*, 298, 1336–43

Manning, W.G., Leibowitz, A., Goldberg, G.A., Rogers, W.H. and Newhouse, J.P. (1984). A controlled trial and effect of a prepaid group practice on use of services. *New England Journal of Medicine*, 310, 1501–1505

McLachlan, G. and Maynard, A. (eds.) (1982). *The Public/Private Mix of Health*, Nuffield Provincial Hospitals Trust, London

National Association of Health Authorities (1988). *Funding the NHS: Which Way Forward?*, A NAHA Consultation Paper, London

Pirie, M. and Butler, E. (1988). *The Health of Nations: Solutions to the Problem of Finance in the Health Care Sector*, Adam Smith Institute, London

Propper, C. (1989). *Working for Patients: The Implications of the NHS White Paper for the Private Sector*, Occasional Paper 6, Centre for Health Economics/York Health Economics Consortium, University of York

Shortell, S.M. and Hughes, E.F. (1988) The effects of regulation, competition and ownership on mortality rates among hospital inpatients. *New England Journal of Medicine*, 318, 17, 1100–1107

Whitney, R. (1988). *National Health Crisis: A Modern Solution*, Shepheard-Walwyn, London

Wickings, I. Childs, T., Coles, S. and Wheatcroft, C. (1985). *Experiments Using PACTS in Southend and Oldham Health Authorities, A Final Report of the DHSS of the PACTS Project at Southend Health Authority and Oldham*, 1979–85, CASPE Research, King Edwards Hospital Fund, London

Williams, A. (1985). Economics of coronary bypass surgery. *British Medical Journal*, 291, 326–329

Williams, A. (1988). *Priority Setting in Public and Private Health Care*, Discussion Paper 36, Centre for Health Economics/York Health Economics Consortium, University of York

CHAPTER 10

Research Implications of the NHS Review

Alan Williams

The NHS Review White Paper *Working for Patients* (1989) has been widely criticized for pressing ahead in reckless haste to implement proposals whose feasibility is questionable and whose likely outcomes are not known with any reasonable degree of certainty. Moreover, in many respects the White Paper lacks crucial detail, a deficiency which has not been significantly ameliorated by the supporting working papers published at the time, nor, for that matter, by those that have followed.

It seems more than likely, therefore, that the NHS is about to become the victim of yet another round of change which does not deserve even to be called 'experimentation', since an 'experiment' suggests systematic controlled variation accompanied by careful measurement and evaluation of results. It appears at present that the thinking capacity of the principal actors is going to be fully occupied with increasingly desperate attempts to meet impossible deadlines for sheer *implementation*. Even with the subsequent lowering of ambitions (for example on information systems which were supposed to be in place before embarking on this adventurous voyage into the unknown) and some notable backtracking (for example on the basis of the valuation of fixed capital assets), all this frenetic activity is still likely to leave those within the system who are capable of sustained thought too exhausted to employ it on anything more distant than the problems they are likely to face in the next six months.

Trying desperately to extract from this unseemly haste some crumbs of comfort for the future, one might observe that it places a great responsibility on the health services research community to engage in the thinking about the medium term (that is, the next five years) which is otherwise likely to go by default. Whether that thinking will, in the event, prove fruitful will, of course, depend on whether shouldering this responsibility enables the health services research community to attract (largely from Government) the resources necessary to do the work which the Government itself should have commissioned *in advance*. It might be objected that it is no use investing in locks for the stable door now that the horse has bolted, but I suspect that this particular horse is not going to get very far before returning to the stable for further fodder and schooling. I doubt whether even the staunchest supporters of the present proposals imagine that the new era to be ushered in by the promised legislation is going to 'solve' any problems or 'settle' any issues. What it is going to do is test the survival power of the system, and (*if properly monitored and evaluated*) indicate whether the proposed general line of advance might enable us to make more progress (at reasonable cost) than we have made in the past 20 years. It is virtually certain that a further comprehensive review will be required in five or ten years time when the dust has settled, and it is for *that* review that we in the health services research community need to prepare now.

Health services research is a multi-disciplinary activity, and each discipline will have its own characteristic focus of interest and special skills. Here I have concentrated on the issues that are likely to be of particular interest to health economists and where they may have something to offer. It is not intended to be a 'staking out' of territory which we health economists would claim to be our *exclusive* domain but an invitation to each of the other disciplines to provide a similar agenda. We could then see where our interests overlap and our respective skills could be used in a complementary rather than in a competitive manner, for if my judgement is accurate, there is more than enough work to keep all of us occupied productively for far more time than we are actually going to have at our disposal!

The manner in which I came to the list of priorities given below was as follows. I first of all went through the White Paper and the initial batch of Working Papers, paragraph by paragraph, and noted the questions each of them raised in my mind. I then classified these very disparate points according to a schematic picture of the structure of the discipline of health economics which we in York have found useful (with slight variations) on several previous occasions (Williams, 1987; Culyer, 1987). This schema is reproduced as Figure 10.1, and for a fuller explanation of its content and implications see one of the references just cited.

The full list of points, classified according to this schema, is appended as an Annexe to this chapter. But the interesting thing to note immediately is that the White Paper raises very few issues relevant to Boxes A, B and C (that is, about the determinants of health, its value, and how these matters influence the demand for health care). The action concentrates primarily in Boxes D and H (the supply of health care and planning, budgeting and monitoring mechanisms), with a moderate amount of attention also paid to matters concerning E, F and G (the working of markets, and evaluation at both micro and macro level).

A list of topics of this kind is bound to be a bit idiosyncratic, and to juxtapose big issues of principle alongside smaller matters of detail in a rather haphazard way. I and some of my colleagues therefore separately identified the matters which we thought to be of the most significance, and on which we thought it most important to concentrate the energies and talents of economists.

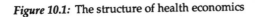

Figure 10.1: The structure of health economics

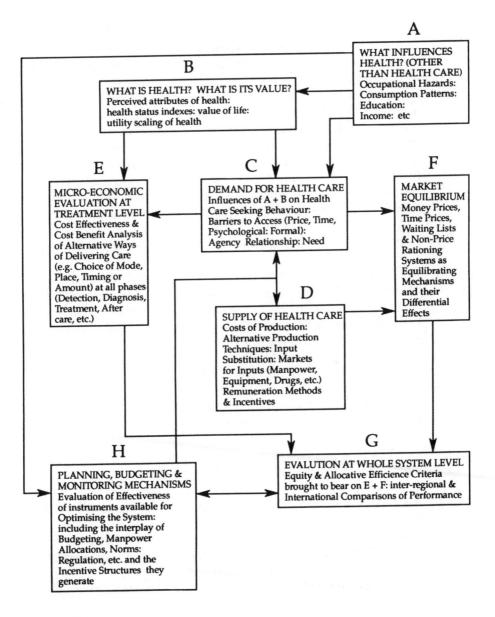

The result of this exercise was general agreement that the three most important sets of issues on which work should be done all fell within Box D and were these:

1. (Working Paper 3/4.1 ff)   What is known about the different components in GP's costs, what determines them, what incentives are required, and what 'standard' composition is optimal? How will the behaviour of GP's vary during the transition period ... and is some systematic experimentation and evaluation possible?
2. (Working Paper 3/1.2) How is it envisaged that GP practice budgets will be 'structured to ensure that GP's have no financial incentives to refuse to treat any categories of patients or accept them onto their lists'? How might the upper limit on the costs for treatment falling on a GP's budget be determined, and with what expected effects? Does US experience with 'co-payment' schemes shed any light on the expected effects?
3. (White Paper 3.1 ff) To what model of hospital behaviour (and market context) do the proposed self-governing hospitals most closely approximate? What predictions about their behaviour seem to follow from the experiences reported in the literature? What data would be needed to test these hypotheses? What baseline data are needed immediately to make such testing possible? How should it be done?

These three sets of issues were only marginally ahead of the following two:

4. *Box D.* (White Paper 3.6 ff) At what level of detail, in terms of price, quantity, quality and nature of service, can contracts be specified? In the event of failure, and the loss of patients and revenue, what happens to the under-utilised resources? How much slack will the system need for competition to be a realistic phenomenon? What will be the costs of this 'reserve capacity'? How will they be met? What are the implications for the overall level of NHS funding?
5. *Box E.* (White Paper 1.4) Which of the 'ever-widening range of treatments made possible by advances in medical technology' are actually worth injecting more and more money into?

I will not rehearse in equal detail the six other questions which occupied the next 'tranche' in order of importance, but in summary they were:

6. *Box D.* White Paper 5.12 ff: about consultants contracts; White Paper 7.3: about GP's contracts;
7. *Box E.* White Paper 4.2: about cost-effectiveness of whole 'services';
8. *Box F.* White Paper 3.8: about whether competition reduces costs;
9. *Box G.* White Paper 6.4: about GP practice budgets;
10. *Box F.* White Paper 5.3 ff: about consultants' contracts.

They are set out in full in the attached schedule of questions in the Annexe.

My colleagues also raised some *additional* matters which they felt were not covered adequately in my original shopping list, and they were:

a. The consequences of the proposed RAWP changes. Possible links between GP budget holders and RAWP. The links between the distribution of health and the funds allocated for health care. Equity issues more broadly.

b. In the capital budgeting field:
    1. the nature of the allocation process of capital funds from Regions to districts and units, and its interaction with charging mechanisms, cash limits, and cost control, particularly in the context of the growth in self-governing hospitals;
    2. the incorporation of capital costs into resource management, competitive tendering and pricing formulae for contracts with self-governing and non-opted-out hospitals, including issues of cost allocation;
    3. the economics of the process of estate rationalisation and capacity utilisation and planning in the context of the Review proposals;
    4. the incentive and behavioural implications of the proposed system of capital charges and of possible variations in the system.

c. In the field of performance measurement:
    1. the role of performance assessment and monitoring after the White Paper for self-governing and other hospitals;
    2. the inclusion of performance criteria in contracts and prices between DHAs and units;
    3. the available techniques and information relevant to performance monitoring, auditing and contracting.

In each of these cases there is a need for different kinds of research activity. Most *urgent* of all is the collection of baseline data so that 'before and after' monitoring and evaluation are possible. It is well known that collecting such data retrospectively is a poor second-best, and it may already be too late to collect such data *prospectively* without them being contaminated by people's knowledge of the kinds of uses to which the data are likely to be put. Thus even the simplest of monitoring activities may prove to be impossible.

A second potential source of data for evaluative purposes is that which relies on 'cross-sectional' (rather than before-and-after) comparisons. It is an unfortunate attribute of change in the NHS that it typically follows a sharp crack of the whip by whoever happens to be the Ringmaster at the time, whereupon all and sundry are expected to jump through the hoop. An exception to this has been the clinical-budgeting/resource-management initiatives, but even they have been evaluated only skimpily, and the next move has been made before the lessons of the previous ones have been properly assimilated. In this situation we have little option but to turn to foreign experience as a source of comparative data, despite all the interpretative difficulties that are involved in imagining how a particular measure would work in a different institutional and cultural context. But in the Country of the Blind the One-eyed Man is King!

There may still be time, however, to set up some simulation experiments, over, for instance, variations in contract terms and scope, or over budgeting arrangements, getting the main actors to role-play in a controlled situation which mimics as far as possible what the new situation might be. Indeed, some such 'experiments' have already been set up by some Regions. This might provide some clues as to likely behavioural responses under different regimes, whose complexity is too great to permit forecasting of outcomes by purely analytical means. But again, this needs to proceed quickly and extensively if it is to inform those designing the system in detail.

At the end of the day there is really no substitute for systematic experimentation and evaluation, but I fear that we shall be forced into evaluation based on the observation of a mass of uncontrolled variables. This is likely to be confounded by strong selectivity effects (for example, with GP budgets and self-governing hospitals) which will make it difficult to find suitable comparators. But even this kind of work needs careful planning and funding *now* if the resources (human and material) are to be in place before the innovations get started.

The UFC has recently conducted an evaluation exercise on the universities which it estimated cost about one per cent of the resources at stake. In the case of the NHS that same fraction would imply setting aside some £250 million to evaluate the outcome of the White Paper. Is anyone thinking in those terms, and, if not, why not?

APPENDIX

RESEARCH ISSUES ARISING FROM THE NHS REVIEW

Note In what follows, the citation codes used have the following meaning:

W = White Paper
P = Working paper, immediately followed by its number.

The final numbers, e.g. 1.4 or 4.10 are the relevant paragraph numbers.

A: WHAT INFLUENCES HEALTH (OTHER THAN HEALTH CARE)?

W1.1   To what extent are longer life expectancy, fewer still births and lower rates of perinatal and infant mortality due to the NHS as opposed to socio-economic factors?

B: WHAT IS HEALTH? WHAT IS ITS VALUE?

W1.1   What evidence is there that age-standardised quality of life is improving (as a result of health care)?

C: DEMAND FOR HEALTH CARE

W1.2   To what extent is the NHS open to all regardless of income (when standardised for 'need')

W1.4   What is the precise nature of the 'rising demand'? What are its determinants? Is it supply induced or technology led?

D: SUPPLY OF HEALTH CARE

W1.8   What have been the trends in job satisfaction and rewards for different groups of NHS staff as a result of past reorganisations, and how are they being affected by these latest proposals? How will we know which staff have 'successfully responded to local needs and preferences' and which have not, so that we can test the differences in their rewards and job satisfaction?

W1.13   How should 'optional extras and amenities' be priced, to what extent do they enhance or detract from the clinical effectiveness of care, and what are the equity issues involved as perceived by both patients and staff.

W2.18   What is the evidence from other public services concerning the relative effects on the overall level of pay, relativities, grading structures and industrial relations, of 'plant level' bargaining versus national bargaining (assuming that the employees' associations remain national?)? What are the relative merits of individual and group-related performance 'bonuses'? What are the implications for inter-disciplinary relationships within the health care team at the level of contact with patients? Will the funding levels reflect any consequent differences in pay?

W2.24   What will be the impact of the proposed capital charging and funding system upon capital-labour ratios in the delivery of health care? What are the implications for optimising replacement/ maintenance routines? Will equipment be treated symmetrically with structures, and what effects will follow for space 'requirements' and other such elements in building notes, etc? Will new capital investment still be 'rationed', or will the required service charge be used as an equilibrating mechanism? What are the implications for option appraisal in the future?

W3.1 ff To what model of hospital behaviour (and market context) do the proposed self-governing hospitals most closely approximate? What predictions about their behaviour seem to follow from the experiences reported in the literature? What data would be needed to test these hypotheses? What base-line data are needed immediately to make such testing possible? How should it be done?

W3.6 ff At what level of detail, in terms of price, quantity, quality and nature of service, can contracts be specified? In the event of failure, and the loss of patients and revenue, what happens to the underutilised resources? Where will the patients go if there is no slack in the system? How much slack will the system need for competition to be a realistic phenomenon? What will be the costs of this 'reserve capacity'? How will they be met? What are their implications for the overall level of NHS funding?

W4.15 Can competition for the supply of core services really be made effective outside the large metropolitan centres? What happens to the staff and facilities if a hospital 'loses' its contract, and which other hospital is likely to have sufficient capacity to take on a 'double' load? Does an annual contract inhibit long-term service development?

W4.18 + At what precise stage will emergency treatments be cross-charged
P2/2, to the area of resident *ex post facto*? What part of the costs of the
18 basic level of provision will be covered in a District's own accounts, and what part can be charged out? Will the tariff be a national one, or reflect local costs? Will special provision be made in advance for this capacity in specially vulnerable areas?

W4.29 Through what mechanisms will supplementary funding for training and research be channelled? What is known about which differential costs are attributable to these functions? What performance indicators will be used on quantity/quality of training and research to establish accountability? Will training/research activity be subject to specific contracts too?

W5.12 ff What will be the effect on workload and quality of outcome of the different sorts of consultant contract which are likely to emerge? Are the effects of movement to a greater fee-for-service element predictable from other countries' experiences? How should this be monitored and evaluated? Will contractual arrangements differ markedly between specialties (especially between those with a large acute/emergency element such as orthopaedics, and those with very little of this kind of work, such as dermatology)? Is an annual contract too short to accommodate long-term service development needs? Would three year rolling contracts be available here too? Should not distinction awards be coterminous with contracts? Should not variations be tried out and systematically evaluated for their respective effects on contract performance?

W6.11 ff On what basis will hospital services be charged to GPs? What incentive structure is envisaged (e.g. as between what GPs might do for themselves or buy in)?

W7.3 What will be the impact on GP behaviour of consolidating separate fees into the capitation rate, and setting targeted incentive payments, etc?

W7.15 ff Who will monitor and evaluate the indicative drug budgets? Will there be some systematic variation in rewards/sanctions? Will it apply equally to all practices (including those with own practice budgets?)? What systematic comparisons will be possible?

P2/2.14 Who will monitor and evaluate the differential impact of the different forms of contract in different places?

P2/2.16 Can 'common approaches to the principles of cost allocation' be developed without a common view as to what incentive effects are desired, what behavioural reactions are likely to follow, and what circumstances they will be used in? Will not self-governing hospitals be free to go their own way?

P2/3.2 Is there a role for simulation studies of various possible ways in
+ 3.3 which DHA/FPC contracts for supplying services to GPs (whether with own budgets or not) might lead the various parties to react regarding referral decisions within and outside contracts, and in the light of various reward/penalty systems?

P2/4.2 ff What cost allocation mechanisms/incentives will be generated by different ways of arranging the separate funding of training and research activities?

P24.14 ff By what criteria could services be selected for top-sliced central (or Regional) funding, *as opposed* to charging out to District of residence? How are fixed and variable costs to be distinguished where mixed funding is envisaged? What incentives are generated by different possible arrangements?

P3/1.2   How is it envisaged that GP practice budgets will be 'so structured to ensure that GP's have no financial incentives to refuse to treat any categories of patients or accept them onto their lists?' How might the upper limit on the costs for treatment falling on GP's budget be determined, and with what expected effects? Does US experience with 'co-payment' schemes shed any light on the expected effects?

P3/   What is known about the different components in GP's costs, what
4.1 ff   determines them, what incentives are required, and what 'standard' composition is optimal? How will the behaviour of GP's vary during the transition period ... and is some systematic experimentation and evaluation possible?

P3/   In the context of GP's as small businessmen, how can (why should)
4.10 ff 'budget flexibility' be so arranged as to limit the spending of surpluses to practice improvements as opposed to personal profit?

E: MICRO-ECONOMIC EVALUATION AT TREATMENT LEVEL

W1.1   For what conditions have the 'dramatic increases in the number of people treated in hospitals' occurred, and what evidence is there that those additional hospital treatments are cost-effective?

W1.1   Has 'commonplace' transplant surgery led to an increase in success rates *and/or* reduced cost-effectiveness as less suitable patients are treated? Is the effective limit the availability of transplantable organs or suitable recipients? Which margin could be the best one to push outwards?

W1.4   Which of the 'ever-widening range of treatments made possible by advances in medical technology' are actually worth injecting more money into?

W1.13   What are the costs and benefits of different means of making patients and their relatives better informed?

W1.13   What is the cost-effectiveness of reducing delay in getting the results of diagnostic tests, etc., to various maximum times, and is there a trade-off between speed and reliability?

W2.13   What is the scope for skill-substitution within nursing, betweenthe nurses and doctors, between nurses and the remedial professions, with clerical and secretarial assistants, etc., and what would be the implications for training, professional qualifications, and pay scales?

W4.2   What studies exist of the cost-effectiveness of whole 'services'? Can these be built up from cost-effectiveness studies of individual treatments? If not, what global measures of effectiveness (in terms of patient outcome) could be used at whole service level, and related systematically to costs?

W9.2   What evidence is there on the relative cost-effectiveness of the NHS and the private sector at the level of comparable treatment of comparable patients?

W9.10   Where have the greatest gains from competitive tendering come from? What accounts for them? What have been the greatest failures? What accounts for them? What different issues arise with competitive tendering for patient care, as opposed to support services? What types of contract, pricing structures, performance criteria seem appropriate? Has there been (will there be) careful monitoring and evaluation of different contractual arrangements and the incentives they generate, and the consequential changes in behaviour?

W9.13   As for W9.10, but with respect to 'joint ventures' instead of 'competitive tendering'.

F: MARKET EQUILIBRIUM

W1.12   What has been the specific impact of the £64 million spent on reducing waiting lists and waiting times? Which responses seem to have been the most cost-effective, and why?

W1.13   What differences to average waiting times do appointment systems actually make? Do they actually result in longer waits (but at home) because of the impossibility of seeing a GP *without* first getting an appointment?

W3.9   What principles will underlie the notion of an 'unreasonably high' price, and what are their implications for funding? Is price to be used as an equilibrating mechanism where demand exceeds supply (high marginal costs? charging what the traffic will bear?) or where there is excess capacity (low marginal costs attracting business which might be charged more later). Where there are substantial common (i.e. unallocable) costs, will multipart tariffs be necessary? Is the purpose of pricing allocative efficiency, or financial viability? Where they clash, which predominates? Will prices be influenced by horizontal equity as well as all the preceding considerations?

W3.8   What evidence is there from other countries that competition between hospitals reduces costs? What is the most likely form of non-price competition to develop if price-'norms' develop (either from the government side or from collusive behaviour by managers/professionals)?

G: EVALUATION AT WHOLE SYSTEM LEVEL

W1.2   What are the trends in financing the NHS (e.g. general taxation vs. other sources) and to what extent is this likely to change with more trading activities and the offering of services to private patients?

W1.3   What evidence is there that labour productivity has grown in the NHS over the last ten years? Has the volume of work done, or health improvements gained, varied proportionately to the growth in the numbers of doctors or dentists?

W1.4   What evidence is there that the quality of care and the response to emergencies remain among the best in the world? What factors account for any international differences?

W1.6   What are the causes of the wide variations in treatment costs, waiting times, GP's drug prescribing habits and referral rates, and what mechanisms are there for determining what is *optimal* and for moving the system in that direction?

W1.8   District by district, what access do patients have to different services, in what respects will accessibility change *de facto*, and will it become more, or less, equally distributed across different locations (e.g. London vs NW Scotland)?

W1.18   To what extent does private treatment 'take the pressure off the Service', i.e. would the NHS actually have treated those patients, if not, why not, and could it have done so if it had had the resources that were diverted to the private sector instead? Again, is there an equity/efficiency trade-off here?

W1.19   What is the likely effect on the relative use of NHS and private facilities of the new tax relief on health insurance for the elderly, and will private provision be more efficient?

W2.8   What is the *relative* cost-effectiveness of those services which in
and 2.9 some regions are a Regional responsibility, in others a District responsibility, and in still others contracted out?

W4.4   What will be the distributive effects of the revised distribution formula? What index will be used to reflect geographical cost differences? Is the extra three per cent to the Thames Regions *additional* to this cost adjustment *and* on top of the funds earned by treating patients from other Regions? If so, on what basis? Is relative poverty to be taken into account?

W6.4   What will be the effects of GP practice budgets on referral rates and patterns, waiting lists, prescribing habits, patient travel time/costs compared with *prior* patterns or with comparable practices without budgets? How will this be monitored and evaluated? Who is now collecting the baseline data?

W6.5   What will be the effects on internal practice organisation (including investment in staff and equipment) of the new arrangements (including those outlined above)?

H: PLANNING, BUDGETING AND MONITORING MECHANISMS

W1.5   What have been the results, in terms of better health and/or lower costs, of the introduction of general management in 1984?

W1.7   What evidence is there that leaving 'local staff to respond to local needs' leads to better outcomes and/or lower costs than whatever the alternative is [national (or regional) policies aimed at national (or regional) needs?]? Is there an efficiency/equity trade-off here?

W2.2   To what extent has the national framework of objectives and priorities as promulgated during the last decade actually led to a shift in resources and an improvement in performance at local level in the desired direction? What are the reasons for good/bad/no response? To what extent will things be substantively different in future? What objectives and priorities relating to health does the Government have and how clearly quantified are they? How do they relate to the WHO target of *Health for All by the Year 2000*?

What monitoring has occurred in the past with respect to these targets, and what will be relied on in future?

W2.3,   How will the level of detail involved in the review processes and
W2.4   between Government and Management Board/Executive;
and   Management Board/Executive and Region; Region and District;
W2.7   and District and Unit, differ from the content of the present review process? How will the required information be generated and by whom, and what will it cost? What will be the differences in the content of the review process between an 'opted-out' hospital and an NHS hospital?

W2.14   What systematic evidence is available to judge the cost-effectiveness of the Resource Management Initiative? What factors explain differential achievement? What are the implications of experience to date for the likely costs and benefits of extending the system, *either* in a carefully discriminating way *or* via a 'big bang' approach? In what precise ways have (how many) patients actually benefited (and to what extent?)?

W2.15   What kind of medical audit is already possible within an RMI framework? What will be the extra costs and extra possibilities generated by the proposed upgrading of the activity data? What have been the effects on clinical practice so far? In what ways have patients benefited?

W2.30   What resources will the Audit Commission need to cover its wider remit, and what will be the relationship between its 'value for money' studies and the monitoring referred to (in W2.3, W2.4 and W2.7) above, and to medical audit (since the latter is to include resource use, and Audit Commission will include 'professional audit' in its remit)? Whose responsibility will it be to generate the data on which all this feeds? What will be the nature of that data? What will it cost to provide, collate, and analyse? What will be the volume and quality of the extra staff involved?

W3.13   What are the likely incentive effects of the proposed relationship between the capital and revenue accounts of hospitals? Can private capital be substituted freely for public capital if the terms for raising private capital are more favourable? What are the implications for ownership and control? Will an equity element be allowed, or will it all be fixed-interest debt? Will individual hospitals be free to choose their own depreciation rates and provisions? Is it envisaged that inequalities in historical endowments will gradually be equalised?

W4.25   What will the published hospital performance indicators cover? Will they be disaggregated by specialty (or by consultants), and include quality variables such as complication rates, death rates, and length of stay by condition? Will the detailed tariffs and contractual arrangements also be publicly known? What incentive structure does this generate for consultants and GPs, and what will be the effects of different data on their respective behaviour and the treatments which patients get? What can be learned from the DRG system in the USA about all this?

W5.3 ff   If medical audit is to include quality of care, use of resources, *and* outcome for patients, for what elements are hospital consultants responsible to whom? What will be the respective roles of the Unit Manager, the contracting District, the Audit Commission, the local professional network, the Royal Colleges, etc? What will be the nature of the rewards/sanctions? Will they be formally linked to Distinction Awards? What effects will audit have on the selection of case-mix? What cost-effectiveness norms will be used, and how will they be generated (see section E)? What will be the likely costs of setting up and running an accurate and timely system of data gathering and processing?

W6.14   What sanctions will be used against overspending GPs with practice budgets? Bankruptcy? How will taking away their independent budget help the NHS (or the patients)? Will they have to repay the 'start-up' grant? Will they be subject to the same capital budgeting regime as hospitals? If not, what?

W7.10   What will be the role of accountability for resource use and outcomes in medical audit of GPs, and to whom will G's be accountable for what? What rewards/sanctions are envisaged? On what information system will it feed, and who will set it up and pay for it? Will it be the same for GPs with *and* without practice budgets?

W10.21   How will the DRG-related tariff for Scotland, for cross-charging patient transfers between districts, relate to English tariffs? Will SHARE move in line with RAWP? If different systems persist, is there scope here for cross-sectional comparisons of consequences?

References

Culyer, A.J. (1987). *Health Economics: The Topic and the Discipline.* In Horne, J.M. (ed.), Proceedings of the 3rd Canadian Conference on Health Economics, 1986, University of Manitoba, 1–18

Department of Health (DoH) (1989). *Working for Patients,* Cm. 555, HMSO, London

Williams, A. (1987). Health economics: the cheerful face of the dismal science. In Williams, A. (ed.) *Health and Economics,* Macmillan, London

Index